PERSONAL LEADERSHIP IN
HIGH-CHALLENGE ENV...

THRIVE

When Trouble Visits

Being Your Best in Tough Times

The Power of Purpose, Passion and Presence

MARK SULLIVAN

Cover design created by William D. Sullivan, image ©Shutterstock, Inc.
Back Cover photograph courtesy John P. Sullivan.

www.kendallhunt.com
Send all inquiries to:
4050 Westmark Drive
Dubuque, IA 52004-1840

Copyright © 2019 by Mark Sullivan

ISBN 978-1-5249-5573-1

Published in the United States of America

It is the darkness of the night that allows the stars to shine — or, to see them fall from the sky to crash and burn. Hence, it is in our trouble, the heat and darkness that it brings, that can become our greatest gift, our biggest burden, or both.

Dedication

Dedicated to my recently deceased 95-year-old mother, Florence Sullivan, who never gave up;
To my speech therapist who showed me a way to the land of the talking;
and to my wife, Mary Rose, who makes life and love an immutable force
for bringing joy and excellence into everyday moments.

Also,
To our youth, the next generation of leaders, and to the rest of us trying to make better-best in tough times!

A Special Thank You

A heart-felt thank you for the signature support of the 50 plus contributors

(Each of the Contributor's interview has been curated in short form, as an
abridged story; and can be found on the book website)

Government:

- **Congresswoman Joyce Beatty**, US Representative for Ohio's 3rd congressional district since 2013
- **Governor Steven Beshear**, 61st Governor of Kentucky from 2007-2015
- **Mr. Glenn Carle**, CIA Deputy National Intelligence Officer – strategic terrorism; Reported to US President for intelligence assessments
- **Speaker Jo Ann Davidson**, Speaker of OH House of Representatives 1995-2000; Chair of OH Casino Control Commission
- **Governor Mike DeWine**, Former Ohio AG, U.S. Senator and Lt. Governor; serving currently as the 70th OH Governor
- **Governor Michael Dukakis**, 65th and 67th MA Governor and nominated by the Democratic Party for president in the 1988 election
- **Mr. David Gergen**, Advisor to four U.S. Presidents (i.e. Nixon, Ford, Reagan, Clinton), and CNN senior political analyst
- **Dr. Elaine Kamarck**, Former Clinton White House senior staff and senior policy advisor to Al Gore. Senior Fellow at Brookings Institute
- **Mr. Rolf Mowatt-Larssen**, Former Chief Directorate of CIA European Ops; Deputy Associate Director of CIA for Military Support
- **Mr. James Lawler**, Former Member of CIA's Senior Intelligence Service; Chief of Nuclear Takedown Team; Known as the 'Soul Catcher'
- **Honorable Mary Beth Long**, Former Assistant Secretary of Defense and Chair of NATO's nuclear policy HLG/High Level Group
- **Astronaut Story Musgrave**, A physician and NASA astronaut credited as being the only one to have flown on all five space shuttles
- **Ms. Valerie Plame**, Former covert CIA operative that headed a variety of strategic secret missions in the Middle East
- **Mr. Michael Reagan**, an American political commentator, former radio talk show host, and author. He is the son of former U.S. President Ronald Reagan and his first wife, actress Jane Wyman.
- **Astronaut Al Worden**, USAF Test pilot, NASA astronaut and command module pilot of Apollo 15 Lunar Mission

Business:

- **Ms. Jane Grote Abell**, Chairwomen – *Donatos Pizza*: featured in Emmy-winning TV reality series, "Undercover Boss"
- **Ms. Jeni Britton Bauer**, Founder, CEO of Jeni's Splendid Ice Cream, a fast-growing, coast-to-coast purveyor of premium ice cream
- **Mr. Bill Diffenderffer**, CEO of Eastern Airlines – System One and Founder, CEO SkyBus, a once major high growth airline charter
- **Mr. Jordan Hansell**, President of Rockbridge Capital Partners, and formerly President of NetJets Airlines

- **Mr. Steven Lindseth**, Sr. Advisor (Aspen) - *Triple Tree Capital Partners*: Founder of many technology firms; and venture capitalist
- **Mr. Cameron Mitchell**, Founder, CEO – *Cameron Mitchell Restaurants (CMR)*, 32 resaurants, 13 different concepts, within 12 states
- **Mr. Joshua Siegal**, Principal – 66 Design Studios, Global on-demand design and fulfill-ment services
- **Mr. Steven Salopek**, Head of Small Cap Strategies at VOYA Investment Mgmt (Formerly ING Investment Mgmt on Wall Street)
- **Mr. Weston Smith**, Whistleblower CFO, Fortune 500 company reporting multi-$B fraud to FBI.
- **Mr. Yaromir Steiner**, Founder and CEO, Steiner + Associates: a major retail development and leasing company, over $1.7B projects
- **Ms. Emilia Kovacevic Vogue-Tipping**, Founder and CEO, Hummingbird Real Estate Group, Inc. and 360 Tech Labs, Inc.
- **Mr. Les Wexner**, Founder and CEO of L Brands (i.e. Parent company of Victoria's Secret, Pink, and Bath & Body Works)
- **Mr. Jeff Wilkins**, Founder of Compuserve, first major online service provider and often referred as the "Father of Email."

Health and Science:

- **Dr. Delos (Toby) Cosgrove**, President and CEO (Ret.) of the Cleveland Clinic
- **Mr. Peter Geier**, CEO and COO (Ret.) of *The Ohio State University Wexner Medical Health System* (Deceased)
- **Dr. Jonathan Heavey**, Emergency Services Physician - *Cleveland Clinic*: Iraq War Combat Physician
- **Dr. Jo-Anne Lema**, Founder, CEO - *AFL/After Fifty Living*, NC-based, popular 'boomer' life-style social media business
- **Dr. Ryan Nash, MD**, Clinical Director and Chair, *The Ohio State University Center for Bioethics*.
- **Ms. Helene Neville**, Cancer survivor turn marathoner that ran through all 50 states, coast-to-coast, for Cancer-curing research funds.
- **Ms. Barbara Lopez**, Former Health & Life Science Battelle President; Current CEO of DC-based, *DIA/Drug Information Association*
- **Dr. Ehud Mendel**, Clinical Director and Chair – Neurological Surgery; and OSU Professor, Internal Medicine - ER
- **Ms. Lindsey Moeller**, Founder, Concur, a natural life-style, organic health and wellness product company
- **Dr. Raphael Pollock**, Director, The Ohio State University Comprehensive Cancer Center
- **Ms. Jansi Straveler**, Nurse, *Ohio Health HomeCare and Hospice*

Sports, Media and Entertainment:

- **Miss Emma Baranski**, Team USA three-time gold medalist, synchronized swimming, in the *Pan-American Games*
- **Ms. Karen Hough**, CEO of *ImprovEdge* - a *National Silver Stevie Award* Recipient; and former stage, theatre and TV actress

- **Mr. Dolph Lundgren**, Featured in over 40 Hollywood movie roles including Rocky 4's Ivan Drago as the Soviet boxing star
- **Mr. Tom Meagher**, US Olympic Trials Starter; Director, Boston Marathon Finish Line
- **Mr. Jim Morris**, Featured in the movie, "The Rookie," played by Dennis Quaid, about a true-life story of a 36 yr. old walk-on MLB player
- **Mr. Vince Papale**, from the true-life sports drama and movie of a walk-on NFL player played by Mark Wahlberg, "The Invincibles"
- **Mr. Irlan Silva**, Brazilian ballet dancer and Soloist for the *Boston Ballet. From a Sao Palo urban ghetto to stardom*

Education:

- **Miss Sara Abou**, Syrian refugee: from non-English speaking immigrant to America to nationally acclaimed poet in three years
- **Dr. Joseph Alutto**, two-term interim President of The Ohio State University and former OSU Fisher College of Business Dean
- **Dr. Roger Blackwell**, American marketing expert, and global executive education lecturer; SEC challenge on trading practices
- **Dr. Scott Cowen**, 14th President of Tulane University; named by Time Magazine as one of America's Ten Best College Presidents
- **Dr. Michael Drake**, 15th President of The Ohio State University, physician and Distinguished Professor of Ophthalmology
- **Mr. David Freel, JD**, Ethicist and attorney; OSU Business School Professor, Ohio Insurance Commission Executive
- **Mr. Batmandah Mangalam**, OSU business honors student raised in Mongolia, a land of multiple cultures and extreme conditions
- **Mr. Jim Tressel**, 10th President of Youngstown State University and 22nd Head Coach of the OSU Football Team.

Faith & Community:

- **Miss Isatu Barry**, African native, women's health care advocate and activist
- **Ms. Ann Bischoff**, CEO of Star House, a nationally recognized model of serving homeless youth between 14-24 years of age
- **Ms. Cheryl Cromwell**, Mashpee Wampanoag Tribal Council Leader– Overseer of Health, Human Services and Education to US Govt.
- **Mr. Shin Dong-hyuk**, Only defector from a North Koreanean prison camp to have existed on torture and starvation for 24 years
- **Mr. Rick Hahn**, Owner of Columbus-based, *Nancy's Diner*, Featured three times on Food Network's *"Diner's, Driven-In's and Dives"*
- **Ms. Mary Jo Hudson, JD**, Partner-Squire, Patton Boggs; Former OH State Insurance Commissioner; and LGBT regionally acclaimed spokesperson
- **Mr. Chris Kowalski**, Restaurant owner of popularly acclaimed *Jack's Diner* in Columbus
- **Mr. Ben Lesser**, One of the very few to have survived the Buchenwald Death Train and to be liberated from the WWII Nazi Prison Camp Dachau, in 1945
- **Mr. Jorge Mandoza Iturralde**, Owner of Boston's North-end four star *Vinoteca di Monica* Restaurant

- **Dr. Molly McGinn**, Founder, Tree-House, a nationally recognized Arizona-based, collegiate residential addiction recovery institution
- **Reverend Dr. Otis Moss Jr.**, Southern Baptist Minister, and Civil Rights activist, partner/friend with both MLK Jr. and MLK Sr.
- **Mr. William Raff**, 9/11 Survivor and Senior Vice President, The Fuji Bank, Ltd., 2 World Trade Center, 82nd floor.

Military & Law Enforcement:

- **Lt. Colonel Charles Buchanan**, Army Ranger with combat command responsibilities in Afghanistan
- **Sargent Adam Carr**, Former Army Special Forces Green Barret (Airborne); Executive Director, Warrior Village-Save A Warrior
- **Capt. Medina Boyd**, Soviet-raised, now retired US military clinical psychologist in psy-ops
- **Master Sargent Daniel Dixon**, Green Barret Sniper with multiple combat tours
- **Mr. John Foley**, Former FBI Ast. Special Agent in Charge: Field Commander; Investigative Lead in the 2013 Boston Marathon Explosions
- **Major Francis Leahy**, Former MA State Police, Executive Officer: Intelligence and Investigative Services with gangs and the underworld
- **General Stanley McChrystal**, Retired Four Star General: Commander of Joint Special Operations Command (JSOC)
- **General Ellen Pawlikowski**, Retired Four Star General: Base Commder, Wright Patterson Air Force Base
- **Lt. Colonel Alfred Shehab**, WWII combat officer at the Battle of the Bulge – Hitler's month-long final offensive on the western front
- **Major Michael Thesing**, Marine Naval Aviator, Military Professor, Marine Officer Candidate School Faculty and Pilot Instructor
- **FBI Assistant Director James Trainor**, Retired senior executive and FBI special agent reporting to Director James Comey

Also, I am appreciative of the many hours of devoted time, effort and expertise from my book team made up of graduate and undergraduate students from The Ohio State University Fisher College of Business and the Schools of Medicine and Journalism. They include the following:

Courtesy of The Ohio State University Max M. Fisher College of Business

First Row (left-to-right): Nicholas LoPrinzi (Student Coordinator), Elsa Warren (Curator), Mark Sullivan (Author), Adrienne Myton (Transcriber)

Second Row (left-to-right): Rachel Bules (Curator), Justyn Bostic (Profiler/Coder), Tyler Remis (Profiler), Will Sullivan (Curator), Alicia Blake (Profiler/Coder), Ashley Nelson (Curator), Anna Huttner (Curator), Maria Riley (Profiler/Coder), Madeline Gelis (Curator)

Also, a note of gratitude to my editor, Susan E. Warner, a talented professional who brings insight and wisdom to any writing project. Her many years as a writer at The Pew Charitable Trusts, The Philadelphia Inquirer and The Wharton School of University of Pennsylvania, was self-evident in her key contributions in bringing this book project to the next level. I have deep appreciation for her thoughtful work in shaping and curating the narrative. A delight to work with, Susan is an editor's editor.

Table of Contents

Introduction XV
   ■ Satisfaction. Winning. Joy. Success xv
   ■ My story: Giving Voice to A Better Future xv
   ■ The Journey Begins xvi
   ■ How the Story Grew xviii
   ■ A Word About the Contributors: Who Are They? xix
   ■ How Did I Come About Meeting the Contributors? xx
   ■ Book Website xx
   ■ The TOP 10 THRIVE TIPS WHEN TROUBLE VISITS xxiii
   ■ TOP 10 THRIVE SUMMATION: Agility as Master-key xxvii
   ■ Final Note xxvii

Chapter 1   PURPOSE: What Matters 1
   Featuring 1
   Ms. Helene Neville: Cancer survivor turn marathoner that ran through all 50 states, from one Cancer-hospital to the next to raise funds and support patients
   Reverend, Dr. Otis Moss, Jr.: Southern Baptist Minister, and Civil Rights activist, partner/friend with both MLK Jr. and MLK Sr.; Marched at Selma, AL and beyond
   Purpose on The Run: Helene Neville 2
   Making the Most of Purpose: What Say You? 4
   Having Faith in Your Purpose: Otis Moss, Jr. 5
   Purpose That Brings Light and Lift to Darkness: Courage, Care, Competence, Community and Curiosity 6

Chapter 2   PASSION 13
   Featuring 13
   Mr. Irlan Silva, Brazilian ballet dancer and soloist for the Boston Ballet Company. From a Sao Palo urban ghetto to stardom
   Ms. Jeni Britton Bauer, Founder and CEO of Jeni's Splendid Ice Cream, a fast-growing, coast-tocoast purveyor of premium ice cream
   PASSION: Leveraging Fire and Heat 13
   Irlan Silva Interview: The Power of Passion 17
   Passion – A Close Cousin of Purpose 19
   British Mariner Sir Earnest Shackelton: Purpose-Driven, Passion-Fueled 20
   Jeni Britton Bauer Interview: Passion in many flavors 21
   Passion in Perspective 22

Chapter 3 PRESENCE: Engaging, Under-the-Skin Impact 29

Featuring 29
Dolph Lundgren: Starred in over 40 Hollywood movie roles including Rocky 4's Ivan Drago
Valerie Plame: Former covert CIA ops officer who focused on nuclear proliferation issues.
What is presence? Why does it matter? 29
Leveraging a Gestalt View: A Platform for Presence 30
Dolph Lundgren Interview: Presence through vulnerability 33
Valerie Plame Interview: Presence in the midst of betrayal 36
Perspective: Growing Awareness to Be More Present 37
PRESENCE AWARENESS INDEX 39

Chapter 4 FIVE PERSONAL LEADERSHIP STYLES: Transformational Stages of Capacity 43
Making the Best of Where We Are At; and Exploring a Line of Sight For Growth and Opportunity

Featuring 43
Mr. Jim Tressel: 10th President of Youngstown State University and 22nd Head Coach of
 The Ohio State University Football Team
Mr. Cameron Mitchell: Founder and CEO – *Cameron Mitchell Restaurants* (CMR), 32 restaurants
 under 13 different concepts, within 12 states. The company also oversees the Rusty Bucket
 Restaurant and Tavern, which operates in 23 locations in six different states
The Story of United Airlines Flight #232: Tragedy and Triumph In the
 Sky and On the Ground 44
Tragedy Defining Character and Capacity in Different Ways: Flight #232 46
Personal Leadership: Stages of Capacity Based On Experience 49
Personal Leadership: Knowing and Valuing Embedded in Five
 THRIVING Transformational Stages of Capacity 51
Putting It All Together: Knowing and Life-Valuing Orientation 54
Knowing and Valuing Themes That Lead to Success and Satisfaction 56
Jim Tressel Interview 57
Cameron Mitchell Interview 60

Chapter 5 PERSONAL LEADERSHIP STYLES: An Overview 65

Featuring 65
General Stanley McChrystal: Retired Four Star General: Commander of Joint Special
 Operations Command (JSOC)
Governor Steven Beshear: 61st two-term Governor of Kentucky (2007–2015)
Personal Leadership Style: PROTECTOR 67
Personal Leadership Style: PROBLEM SOLVER 69
Personal Leadership Style: CREATIVE STRATEGIST 71
Personal Leadership Style: Thriving as a GLOBALIST 73
Personal Leadership Style: GLOBALIST 76
Summary 80
General Stanley McChrystal Interview 83
Governor Steven Beshear Interview 85

Chapter 6 PERSONAL LEADERSHIP STYLES: The PROTECTOR 89
*PLS Characteristics: Speed, Decisive, Resourceful, Attentive to Interests, Creates Loyalty,
Family and Clan Cultures, Examples of Working Against the Odds-Making Things Happen*

Featuring 90
Shin Dong-hyuk, North Korean Prison Camp Defector
Weston Smith, HealthSouth CFO Whistleblower

Shin Dong-hyuk Interview 93
Weston Smith Interview 96

Chapter 7   PERSONAL LEADERSHIP STYLES: The Problem Solver 101
*Focus on Getting Things Done; Achieving Unit, Community and Collaboration in
a High-change Environment*

Featuring 101
John Foley: FBI Street Field Commander of the Boston Marathon bombing
Bart Decker: First 9/11 Special Forces Horse Soldier Team in Afghanistan
Mr. John Foley Interview 104
Bart Decker Interview.. 108

Chapter 8   PERSONAL LEADERSHIP STYLES: The Optimizer 113
Focused, Magnetic, Responsive, Excellence, Attentive to Details, Accelerated Performance

Featuring 113
Harold Donahue: Congressman (1947-1974), House Judiciary Committee during
    Congressional Watergate hearings
Mr. Ben Lesser: One of the very few to have survived the Buchenwald-Dachau Death Train
    and to be liberated from the WWII Nazi Prison Camp Dachau, in 1945
Enter the World of Government and Public Service... 117
Ben Lesser Interview.. 119

Chapter 9   PERSONAL LEADERSHIP STYLES: The Creative Strategist 125
Curious, Insightful, Systemic Thinker, Disciplined, Keenly Aware, Inclusive, Imaginative

Featuring 125
Dr. Story Musgrave, A physician and astronaut credited as being the only one to have
    flown on all five space shuttles
Dr. Raphael Pollock, Director, The Ohio State University Comprehensive Cancer Center
Dr. Story Musgrave Interview.. 131
Dr. Raphael Pollack Interview... 134

Chapter 10   PERSONAL LEADERSHIP STYLES: The Globalist 139
*Visionary, Inspiring, Open to the Unknown, Community-Minded, Multi-Faceted Wealth
and Wisdom*

Featuring 140
Mr. David Gergen: Advisor to four U.S. Presidents (i.e. Nixon, Ford, Reagan, Clinton),
    Harvard Kennedy School Professor of Public Service and CNN Senior Political Analyst
Mr. Les Wexner: Founder and CEO of L Brands (i.e. Victoria's Secret, Pink, Bath &
    Body Works)
Globalists in History 140
Contemporary Globalists 144
Dr. David Gergen Interview... 145
Leslie Wexner Interview 148

Chapter 11   The Promise of Life-Long Potential – The Evolving Self 153
The challenge and Opportunity of Transformation

Examples of Expanding Capacity – Featuring... 153
Ms. Jane Grote Abell: Chairwomen – *Donatos Pizza*: 150 locations in 9 states; featured in
    Emmy-winning TV reality series, "Undercover Boss."

Dr. Delos (Toby) Cosgrove: Retired President and CEO of the Cleveland Clinic, the no. 1 hospital for cardiology and heart surgery 23 years in a row, as ranked by *U.S. News.*

One More Time: What is Personal Leadership? 154
Personal Leadership Styles: A Way of Knowing and Valuing 157
Style Envy 158
Linking Awareness and Action to Our Personal Leadership Styles 160
The Different Ways THRIVING As Capacity Enablers Shows Up 161
A Perspective on Learning and Development 164
Ms. Jane Grote Abell Interview 165
Dr. Delos (Toby) Cosgrove Interview 169

Chapter 12   The Summary — A Few Thoughts About Us, the Situation, and Our Future 173
Looking Back — Looking Forward: Packing for the Journey

Examples of Transformational Journeymen — Featuring 174
Dr. Scott Cowen: 14th President of Tulane University; named by Time Magazine as one of America's Ten Best College Presidents
Dr. Molly McGinn: Founder, Tree-House, a nationally recognized Arizonabased, collegiate residential addiction recovery institution

Agility in Our Personal Life 174
Challenging the Better You For a Better Future 176
COACHING IN HIGH-DEMAND ENVIRONMENTS 178
Triple Loop Learning: Linking and Leveraging Capacity for Impact 178
Remembering the Context: Recognizing the Severity of the Demand 180
The Future 183
Final Stories: On A Life Worth Living — Embracing the Heat of the Fire Close-Up 183
Dr. Scott Cowen Interview 184
Dr. Molly McGinn Interview 189
A Few Final Thoughts 192

Contributors Appendix: Profile 197

Bibliography 205

Index 209

Introduction

Satisfaction. Winning. Joy. Success.

Most of us appreciate it when we experience special moments. Yet, life is complex. Just when you think you have the answers, *trouble* comes along.

Maybe not now, or tomorrow, but it has a way of coming when we're not looking. It does not wait for an invitation. Just like success; rejection, loss, disappointment, and pain come in many forms.

Other times, we know trouble is something that emerges from very early on in our life. Surprisingly, for better of for worse, the imprint it has on our soul and spirit can take on a life of its own. This is what got me interested in the business of trouble.

My story: Giving Voice to A Better Future

At the age of two I had an unrelenting need for adventure that drew me to sneak into my mother's kitchen pantry, a forbidden area of the house. It was a magical place with many shiny and sharp tools, knives, bowls and serving trays. One day, I found the skeleton key in a glass jar and opened the pantry door. I was nervous and excited. Surprisingly, no one was around. Beyond the open door I found much to take in. At the very top of the floor-to-ceiling shelves were some amazingly bright and shiny, yellow objects that were calling out to me.

With no time to spare, I pulled out the heavy wooden oak bureau drawers adjacent to the shelves. As I climbed on to the top drawer, I attempted to balance my little body, as I stretched to reach out to the very tippy-top shelf. Then, for a moment, I had one of those shiny sharp objects in my hand. A pencil! As I lunged for it, I lost my balance and screamed. I fell five feet from the top drawer, crashing to the floor with the pencil lodged in my throat. The oldest of my three sisters found her usually very active, younger brother on the pantry floor quite still, listless and turning purple.

The emergency room doctors told my distraught parents that with the fall, combined with a pencil in my upper trachea, had blocking oxygen to the speech centers of my brain. They somberly suggested that I may not be able to talk again. If you are lucky, they told my parents, they might be able to understand me, but most people would not.

That moment and the many more to follow was the beginning of a journey from trouble, and many years later to triumph, with everything in between.

The Journey Begins

In kindergarten and the early grade school years, children in the playground would taunt me with names such as "mumbles Mark" and "retard." Teachers were afraid to call on me given my unusual speech intonations that could punctuate the classroom with awkward moments of shock, silence and embarrassment — by me, and by extension, them. In first grade, I would walk home alone with school work full of red marks all over my paper work. I didn't know what it meant, but I guessed it was not good. So, I hid most of my work in bushes behind our garage until I could burn it in the outdoor fireplace on weekends. There were moments, many moments, when I was not proud of being me. I wanted to speak out in the worst of way, to be heard, to be me – a loved and capable me, whatever that meant. Yet I was scared to death in doing so. I was confused, lonely, fearful, angry, and eager for a better way.

Two truly bright and exceptional individuals came to the aid of that scared little boy. One, was a strong-willed, independent, loving, determined, Irish-American woman, raised in the Depression on almost nothing. She was a WWII nurse that later contracted polio while helping others with the same; ending up wheel-chair bound. With months of no progress while lying in the quarantined, open-air polio hospital bed, she incredulously checked herself out of the state institution and singularly willed herself back to health and mobility. She exemplified a never-say-die spirit that defined how passion, purpose and presence could make the aspirational real; the tragic not so much; and the future better than the painful present could fortell. This woman was my mother, Florence Sullivan.

The second was a tough, German-American speech therapist, Miss Haus. She never married, but many knew her as married to a mission of bringing the voiceless into the speaking world. Miss Haus was known for rigorous, disciplined, non-stop coaching for the speechless, the incurables in the 1950s, who no one else could help. For more than 48 years she had changed the lives of many hundreds of boys and girls all across New England. I was one of them.

As a boy, one of the ways I could find enjoyment was to climb our big century-old trees in our yard. I would climb as high as I could. One day, when I was high aloft in the big elm tree leaning next to the kitchen, I inadvertently overheard my mother yelling at my father. Somehow, she said, we need to teach this boy to talk. Even if it kills us. He's going to talk. Both wailed and wept, and I had trouble climbing down the tree. I felt I was broken in need of repair. Was I worth it?

I did not know it, but my mother had been looking all over New England to find the best speech therapist. She learned it would be Miss Haus, in Worcester, Massachusetts, or no one. With me in tow, she arrived un-invited to Miss Haus's office late one summer afternoon. We found the office full of boxes as Miss Haus was packing. My mother immediately explained what was needed; to which Miss Haus explained she was retiring, packing and literally going home for the last time. My mother said she could not do that as she had one more boy to save. Miss Haus forcefully stated she was retired and to find someone else. So, it began: two strong-willed, independent women, both loud and determined, not accepting what the other had to say.

During this scary verbal volley, I stood shaken in the back corner of the room. Somehow, the therapist in Miss Haus caused her to stop for a moment, turn around and look at me. To this day I remember she stooped down and looked at me, eyeball to eye ball. "What do you want Marky?" she asked. "Make it go away. Make it all go away," I replied. She knew exactly what I meant. She had spent almost five decades helping the emotionally abandoned, timid and lost.

She turned back to my mother and said she was still retired, but to deliver me to her living room every Monday, Wednesday and Friday at 9 a.m. for cookies, milk and speech therapy for six months. She told my mother she would have to work with me the other six days a week. Seven years later, the six months was completed. I could talk. Thousands of hours of practicing with marbles and marshmallows rolling in my mouth, and countless other exercises, day and night, had paid off.

But I didn't feel done. I moved from speech therapy to speech craft. I competed in every speech contest I could get into from grade school to high school. I hungered for the trophies and the attention. I didn't know how much I was trying to fill a gaping hole in my soul with affirmation and acceptance. To be accepted as lovable and capable. The speech tournament trophies meant I might be valued by someone other than my family and Miss Haus. I came from a loving family but was bruised so badly I needed more.

In my senior year of high school, I was competing in my last speech tournament, a national one hosted by Readers Digest magazine. I had already won the All-City, County, District and State tournament. Now I had qualified for the finals. The night before my last speech I was staying in a hotel. The front desk delivered a Western Union telegram to my room. It was from Miss Haus, now actually retired and living in a nursing home. The city newspapers had run an article about me: Local boy makes good in national competition, with the background detailing my speech accident. Someone had read the story to Miss Haus. She wrote me:

> "Mark, I have heard of your recent success. You have done well – but probably could have done better! (This was her very discerning and demanding ways coming through even now! I couldn't help but chuckle). Regardless, Mark, I want you to know that by your efforts, you have singularly validated the life of a very old lady who in her dying days knows she can now go to rest recognizing my gift to you and others made a difference. You have given far more to me, than I to you. Now, it's your turn, your time to step up and share what you have with those in need, as you have God's gift waiting to be multiplied. So tomorrow, do your best, but know that what matters is what you do after tomorrow, with competence and confidence[1]."

The next day, I didn't win. But I felt I did. For the night before, I held Miss Haus's Western Union message in my hand and shook and cried uncontrollably for a long time. I didn't realize at that moment, it was the beginning of a purge at my deepest and most inner-core of many years of toxic, painful moments. No surprise, Miss Haus's final gift to me was a challenge to be my biggest, boldest, best self, not simply for a contest, but for life.

Several decades later, the pained, voiceless halting school boy had grown up into something almost unimaginable. He was now an Eagle Scout, a Harvard alumnus, a Ph.D graduate, father of three successful growing young men, husband to an incredibly kind, smart, loving wife, a business executive, C-level officer and an organizational psychologist. Something had happened. Was life perfect? No. But the tectonic plates that had shaped my interior life and outer world had moved in both an evolutionary and revolutionary manner.

---

1   The quote is based on memory and could vary slightly in word count but certainly not in message or intent as recalled by the author.

How the Story Grew

Since the earliest of those scary days, I started to think about what happens when trouble visits others. Does effort, intellect, emotion and willpower address what is needed under duress, or is there more to the story?

Why is it that some of the smart and strong succumb and the weak and worn may thrive? Is it simply luck or happenstance? Why is it we can have an amazing capacity to perform at a high functioning level at one point, and later find ourselves struggling?

How do we thrive when resistance and its accompanying force for destruction and control push us back to a safer, known, but less functional place? Or worse, to a space of not knowing, one filled with confusion, fear or frustration. How do we create a thriving ecosystem that nurtures capability, competence and confidence in the eye of the storm?

Interestingly, self-help books, leadership tomes, training workshops, and motivational speakers don't always provide the insight and informed action to guide our way through the many forms that trouble presents itself? Think dieting, change workshops, addiction counseling, performance coaching, etc. Why, when we know or see the answer, it is not good enough. For example, how can health care workers overeat, drink or smoke when they know better? Additionally, why can early success set us up for later disappointment? Clearly, self-help books with all their prescriptions for the masses have not always held sway in any sustainable fashion. Why is that willpower and resilience, as important as they are, do not inoculate us from the full force of trouble's trajectory?

Many of the above questions have led me to look at the heroes and demons in our lives; to research, social history and to the great leaders of our times. I looked at my own life and wondered what it would be like without the kind of tough, but loving, care and support I received at the right time. I wondered what my life would have been if I gave in to a host of competing impulses pleading for safety, comfort and sameness. Could I find redemption for the moments where I actually did give in? Could I appreciate the moments when out of desperation, or faith, I trusted the better angels in myself and others when I saw no light at the end of the tunnel?

Finally, I wondered what I would be like if I never had such an accident, or if I had a consequential one later in life with a different set of resources, or lack thereof. The promise of potential and performance with the spiritual salve of solace and safety may often seem attractive yet elusive. It becomes far less abstract when challenge gets the best of us. As good as we are; as deserving as we are.

Many of the contributors to this book brought legs and lift to the reality of what trouble is and how best to navigate to a fruitful way beyond. Was there any one way to do so across the interviews? The simple answer is no. Yet themes emerged both with this extraordinary group of contributors and among the larger group of Ohio State University students with their own stories and discussion highlights from both the undergraduate (18 majors) and graduate (MBA and Executive MBA) ranks[2].

---

2 During the first of two phases of research, qualitative themes were extracted from one-on-one interviews with over 50 contributing participants (i.e. Sample #1 of #2); and other broader themes were extracted through "Legacy Capstone Papers" from MBA students in my *Crucial Conversations* course and essays from the authors' *Foundations of Management* course. Qualitative thematic analysis and varied statistical correlations will be deployed during the phase two of the research. Findings will be reported in version 2.0 of *THRIVE: When Trouble Visits!*

As they shared their stories it became apparent that trouble, a time of significant challenge, was not simply a momentary inconvenience or twist in one's daily rituals. Rather, it was based on an emerging criteria as described below:

- **When stakes are high**
  - ➤ *When it matters most; when the answer is consequential to who you are or what you will be; or what needs to get done.*
- **When demand is great and capability is limited**
  - ➤ *When the knowing-doing gap prevails; and the need to deliver has more risk, and less competence and confidence.*
- **When the future is unpredictable**
  - ➤ *When there is a high degree of uncertainty, recognized or not, that influences, distorts or constrains an ability to plan and predict options and actions today and beyond.*

A Word About the Contributors: Who Are They?

The 50 plus book interviewees are an amazing collection of notable individuals leading successful lives, all with stories of how they addressed some of their greatest challenges. They were simply asked three questions:

1. What people or experiences influenced the person you are today?
2. Describe a significant life challenge and how you addressed it in the beginning, middle and end. What did you learn that you re-purpose in other challenges or share with others that makes a difference?
3. What do you recommend to our youth the next generation of leaders and to the rest of us trying to make better-best in tough times?

Each were told it was roughly an hour-long discussion. These were incredibly busy people. It included a billionaire, two Astronauts, a Four-Star general, a leader in the Civil Rights movement, an American- Indian leader, presidential advisors, neurosurgeons, media broadcasters, CEO's, Hollywood movie stars, university presidents, world class performing artists, elite athletes, and so on.

Yet, in many cases, the one-hour turned into something far longer and deeper than what was perhaps advertised. As they talked, there was something deep within them, the wisdom of lived experience, that created space to explore and synthesize the peaks and valleys of key moments that mattered in their own struggles and achievements.

For me, it was humbling, inspiring and sacred as tender moments of knowing, not-knowing and new-knowing was shared with candor. They offered a gift of self for no other reason than to help others toward a better life. I am indebted to their gift and walked away both uplifted and burdened by the responsibility of sharing their conversation in a way that would honor their intent.

How Did I Come About Meeting the Contributors?

I traveled and talked to people all around the country. Additionally, some of the stories reflected journeys of refugees and immigrants from faraway lands, and others from across the hall-way of my Campus Office at The Ohio State University.

It started with Les Wexner. Most know him as an incredibly accomplished business genius that turned a $5,000. loan from his aunt into a multi-billion-dollar global business empire. I met him after an OSU event where he was the featured speaker. He graciously agreed to contribute to this book project and post-interview, was exceedingly helpful in connecting me with other interviewees.

Other times, I would be at a variety of events from NASA, the Boston Ballet, an American Indian Nation Pow Wow, a political rally, a corporate or government consult and find someone whose presence was inspiring or illustrative of thriving in difficult circumstances. Soon I would be hearing a story they had that was almost surreal, yet riveting.

For example, I met 51-year-old Jorge Mandoza Iturralde on a Cape Cod, West Dennis beach readying himself for Kite-Boarding. This is not a sport for the faint of heart. Given the need for strong winds, one is usually at an ocean beach with surf, straddled between a mini (surf) board, five lines on a harness that connects you to a sail, some 100 feet above. Done correctly, you take off like a rocket gyrating or spinning out to sea!

As I helped Jorge ready himself pre-launch, I found through normal chit-chat, he was something more than the owner of one of Boston's most favorite Italian restaurants on the *North End*. He was a political refugee that had barely escaped a South American dictator whose government had threatened to kill him and his whole family. This was no ordinary family, as they had a 400-year noble lineage to the founding Spanish explorer of his country and his ancestral sponsor, the Castilian King. Jorge, and family left everything behind for freedom in this country.

His story of going from great wealth and notoriety to poverty, pennilessness in a drug-infested, American neighborhood ghetto; to bootsrapping himself to survive; to building and running one of America's great restaurants, was both humbling and instructive to say the least.

This was an example of living life in the raw; the high-highs, low-lows and everything in-between. Through it all he reflected a certain level and type of maturity, temperance, spirit, competence, and willpower that helped to engage in the moments to months of enduring trouble. This formed the emerging template for the story ahead. (Mandoza's curated interview can be found with over 50 other interviews in the book web-site.)

Book Website

The following developmental tools and frameworks are illustrative of the actionable efforts presented to assist in further enriching effectiveness in each of the five leadership styles. They are explained in greater detail in the book website in-order to link and apply deeper insights with action for impact and value.

A composite of thrive themes: purpose, passion and presence support each of the five differing personal leadership styles in embracing challenges of many kinds. Together, the themes and styles may align and expand potential and capacity for meaning, value and impact. The above framework illustrates an integrative developmental strategy with suggested capacity enablers from the three THRIVE themes to consider initial efforts to further facilitate ways to thrive in high demand environments. For example, a *protector* may want to work on a care strategy that reviews how to build strength and focus towards a set of concrete purposeful near term actions. A *globalist* in a demanding environment may want to revisit what actions and efforts may further nurture the broader community or how the community could help oneself in moving forward. The framework

THRIVE Themes & Capacity Enablers	Protector	Problem Solver	Optimizer	Creative Strategist	Globalist
THRIVE Theme: **PURPOSE** (CAPACITY ENABLERS) Competence Curiosity Care Courage Community	Developmental Strategy *Lead With:* ✐ **Care** ✐ **Courage**	Developmental Strategy *Lead With:* ✐ **Competence** ✐ **Community**	Developmental Strategy *Lead With:* ✐ **Care** ✐ **Competence**	Developmental Strategy *Lead With:* ✐ **Curiosity** ✐ **Community**	Developmental Strategy *Lead With:* ✐ **Community** ✐ **Courage**
THRIVE Theme: **PASSION** (CAPACITY ENABLERS) Enjoyment Excellence Effort	Developmental Strategy *Lead With:* ✐ **Enjoyment** ✐ **Effort**	Developmental Strategy *Lead With:* ✐ **Effort** ✐ **Excellence**	Developmental Strategy *Lead With:* ✐ **Excellence** ✐ **Effort**	Developmental Strategy *Lead With:* ✐ **Enjoyment** ✐ **Excellence**	Developmental Strategy *Lead With:* ✐ **Excellence** ✐ **Effort**
THRIVE Theme: **PRESENCE** (CAPACITY ENABLERS) Agile Awareness Authenticity Affirmation	Developmental Strategy *Lead With:* ✐ **Affirmation** ✐ **Awareness**	Developmental Strategy *Lead With:* ✐ **Affirmation** ✐ **Awareness**	Developmental Strategy *Lead With:* ✐ **Awareness** ✐ **Agile**	Developmental Strategy *Lead With:* ✐ **Agile** ✐ **Authenticity**	Developmental Strategy *Lead With:* ✐ **Authenticity** ✐ **Agile**

Figure i.3: Book Website Sample Framework

(Note: The themes and capacity enablers are described in greater detail in select chapters.)

is essentially a capacity map that assists oneself in leveraging their personal leadership style with capacity enablers that resonate with one's style.

Calibrating what to do more or less within a personal leadership style (PLS) is further reflected in PLS Roles. These roles describe what to leverage, what to do more of and in some cases what to consider doing less of. They are only suggestive in nature with more details providing how best to consider suggestions within specific PLS high demand environments. The overarching framework of the roles are illustrated in figure i.4. The 14 Capacity Enablers in figure i.3 are embedded in the PLS Roles. More details in how to use the PLS Roles can be found in the web-site.

Contributing to the dynamic operating model as illustrated in figure i.5. are different thrive components: thrive themes (i.e. Purpose, Passion and Presence), personal leadership styles (i.e. *protector, problem solver, optimizer, creative strategist and globalist*), and capacity facilitator (Agility). Further, the THRIVE operating model, in figure i.5, is an interdependent framework illustrating ways theses components interact with each other using a computer metaphor: hardware operating system (i.e. personal leadership styles); applications (i.e. thrive themes); and the interface layer or GUI (i.e. agility).

Finally, as described in the book website, there is a section highlighting the *"Top 10 THRIVE Tips For When Trouble Visits!"* This section further provides tools that notable book contributors and I have recognized as being helpful to thriving in challenging moments. Each of the ten tips will have examples and actions of what works and what doesn't for many folks in high demand environments.

ROLE NAVIGATOR

Legend	Do More Of	Do Less Of	Do More Of the Same	XP Experiment	Leverage Your Strengths	Aspirational: Target For Later Success

Personal Leadership Style ROLES

PLS Personal Leadership Style	CRITIC Assert More Opinions	INNER ANGEL Take Stock of Your & Other's Gifts, Strengths; Affirm & Appreciate Both	IMPROVISER Attempt What Is New; Flex, Adapt, Stretch with Self, Others and Things	BROKER Give and Take With Different Mix of People; Network, Pro-Actively Engage; Solicit Feedback and Advice	Executor Hands-On; In-The Mud; "Just Do It" in Both a Spontaneous and Planful Way	WATCH TOWER Reflect, Perspective-Taking; Observe For New Insights, Meaning
Protector	Do Less Of	Do More Of	Experiment	Experiment	Leverage Your Strengths	Aspirational
Problem Solver	Do More Of	Experiment	Experiment	Do More Of	Leverage Your Strengths	Aspirational
Optimizer	Do More Of	Do More Of	Leverage Your Strengths	Experiment	Do More Of the Same	Do More Of
Creative Strategist	Do More Of the Same	Do More Of the Same	Do Less Of	Do More Of the Same	Do More Of	Leverage Your Strengths
Globalist	Do More Of the Same	Do More Of the Same	Do Less Of	Do More Of the Same	Do More Of	Leverage Your Strengths

Figure i.4: Book Website Sample

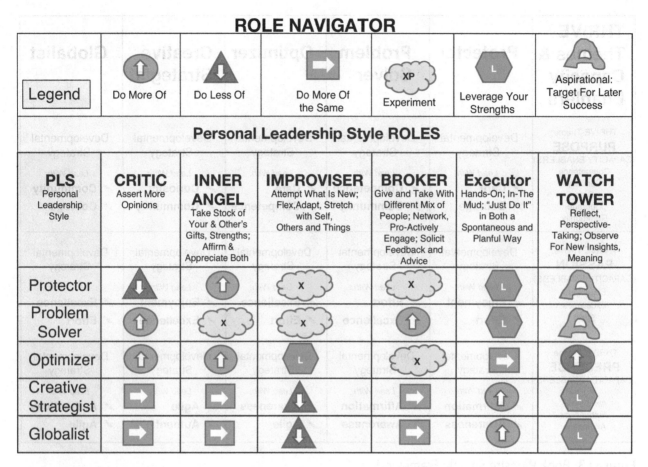

THRIVE FLY WHEEL OPERATING MODEL IN HIGH DEMAND EVIRONMENTS

Externally-Focused Functions like Apps/ Applications

Capacity Facilitator Is the Interface Layer Between the Internal (inside) and External (outside) Environment

Internally-Focused Functions like the Operating System

Thrive Purpose Passion Presence APPLICATIONS

Agility

Five Personal Leadership Transformations

#1 Protector | #2 Problem Solver | #3 Optimizer | #2 Creative Strategist | #5 Globalist

OPERATING SYSTEM

Figure i.5: Book Website Sample

The TOP 10 THRIVE TIPS WHEN TROUBLE VISITS

1. Recognize things are not normal

Accepting and even naming at least in part some of what is happening is critical to a better way forward. In the fog of it all it is easy to distort reality; to put things off; or to attempt to convince yourself things are not as bad as they are – or could be. This normalizing of the trouble further begets trouble.

2. Channel your 'inner support gene

Affirm and acknowledge you have gotten through trouble in the past and that you do not need to have all the answers this very moment. Recognize that no matter what it looks like, feels like, is, or might be, that you will find the support to get through this experience. Therefore, allow yourself to not prematurely come up with artificial, quick solutions or justifications just to relieve yourself of not-_knowing or of any pain or fear that may be present. Remember, now is not forever. Quick, forced answers can create its own problems.

Loosen up if possible. Go gentle on yourself. Find moments to talk quietly, and affirmatively to yourself in an earnest way. What gifts do you have and what people are in your corner that are backing you in this time of need? Why do they believe in you? Savor realistic images of you doing things well and of people supporting you. You are special in your own right. Believe it, let it sink in, while facing the potentially uncomfortable or painful reality as it is.

3. Solicit your trusted advisors

Life is not a solitary marathon but a team endeavor. Be willing to recognize you do not need to attempt to solve everything yourself. Be humble. Be willing to be vulnerable. Be willing to hear what you do not want to hear. Challenge yourself to share your more intimate, not-knowing, unvarnished self with one, two or three trusted people in your life who you respect and in whom you have faith, and they have faith in you. It does not matter what their role or status is in life. What matters is that they have only your best interests in mind; and have a capacity to:

- Listen deeply (i.e. hear the underlying intent of what you are trying to say)
- Ask good questions (i.e. will ask a lot of 'why' and 'how' questions)
- Share their honest, thoughtful opinions reflecting your interests and not theirs

4. Seek options

While there are often no quick fixes for signature challenges; explore options, ideas, or actions that may help make life better either now or later. Can you reframe the negative or the improbable to the reasonable and possible? What can you get behind that represents progress, opportunity or a better way? Recognize and consider the significance of persisting, re-occurring ideas and images. Are there any themes or patterns evolving around the trouble; or patterns around resources and approaches to address it? What's important, what's not? What is actionable that would make a difference?

Balance both the linear and logical ideas with the irrational and irritable ones. Be curious. What are you missing? What are you afraid of? What has worked for you in the past? What is new and different? What are others telling you? Be open to input and feedback. Finally, remember situational conditions, people and you may change in the beginning, middle or end of the overall experience or process. Be open to re-working or abandoning options that no longer fit with the changing circumstances.

5. Build competency

Stretch. Practice. Reflect, Do. Expanding your competency to become more effective in demanding times often involves getting better in how you think, feel and do. It is often easier to play it safe and simply do more of the same. Creating options and then attempting to move toward a better place often requires new or different practices. This may include using more soft skills that involves you or you and others (e.g. awareness of others from their point of view, not yours); and hard skills that often involves more technical or physical patterns or practices (e.g. adopting precise operating rules to implement an algorithm, a piece of equipment, or a self-defense move in the martial arts).

Solicit help in developing your competency on either the hard or soft side. Consider the following in developing competency in tough times:

- Break the developmental goal or effort into incremental, actionable steps.
- Practice the steps or skills in different settings and different ways. Alternate or mix practice patterns: hard-soft, fast-slow, interval/tempo/recovery, explicit-implicit, etc.
- Get timely seasoned feedback or coaching that simultaneously challenges and supports your progress. Address gaps clearly in a concrete and affirmative manner.
- Reflect. What is happening on a deeper level? What can you learn from the past that will influence the future? What am I doing now that is different?
- Provide yourself with little rewards along the way to reinforce choices, actions and outcomes.

6. Experiment. Take risks

Sometimes you will never know a better way of doing anything unless you take a leap of faith. Listen to your inner voice. You can spend a lot of time gathering evidence or data, yet it is often only when you commit to doing this new effort, in a new way, that you really embrace the idea or action. That is, reaching out and taking that step you've never imagined before may be the way you discover a new path in a transformative manner.

Honor your inner voice by having the courage to follow it, while testing it with trusted others. Embrace resistance appreciatively and affirm the risk or threat as performing a genuinely valuable service of discovery. As a forcing function to new, sometimes prickly insight, the risk may also unwittingly soften our rigid, hardened perspectives, when we least expect it. This shifting creates a new window on the world that can increase our capacity for impact and value. Similar to calibrating the aperture of a camera lens for maximum resolution, attentively walk through different scenarios of how a new way may unfold; and what risk mitigating efforts will make a difference.

7. Make it safe

Reduce emotional costs. Find ways to make things not seem so overbearing or overwhelming. Working in a threatening or high-demand environment can be scary. Create a safety net. Maybe it's having a backup plan or an exit route.

Sometimes you may run into difficulty with others, where it feels unsafe based on how others are treating you or each other. This implicit feeling of danger puts you on guard, on your defenses. Underneath what is being said is the underlying intent and tone of the conversation. So, there are two things simultaneously unfolding: the stated content (i.e. the words or ideas/positions on the surface) and the intent (i.e. the underlying, unstated but present attitude toward each other). The latter is what influences the former. We may hear the words, but we feel the attitude and tone often in a more potent fashion.

When there are problems with neighbors, family, friends, customers, bosses, peers, it regularly helps to detox or purify the tension. It is sharing or addressing the intent, not the content, that often matters. This can help lower the temperature in the relationship that thaws the heat and friction of the assault. It creates tolerance and perhaps the beginning of a deeper level of trust that may shift attitudes – allowing a sense of emerging safety around you and others.

Finally, there is a physical perspective regarding safety. In high demand environments, we may physically become tense, frozen, frustrated or fearful. This drains well oxygenated blood away from critical executive functioning centers of the brain when we need it most. Sometimes deep breathing can help. Or stretching limbs and muscle groups – as in yoga, can counter stress and blood depletion to the brain. Also, guided imagery of better ways and days may also soften the troubling terror of the moment. Regardless, making it safe for you and others helps to see and experience things in a new light. This is often required if we want to move forward.

8. Low expectation and high aspiration

Expect the difficult. Work to inoculate yourself ahead of time so that it is not surprising if trouble becomes a vexing companion. Remind yourself that you can move through and beyond the 'valley of despair.' For some, address the repetitive, circular nature of self-doubt or the chain of negative critique and reinforcing actions against oneself. For others, instead of plateauing at the end of a downward path of destruction and disruption; recognize that it is only part of an overall process from the preceding status quo, to the valley, to potentially higher, future ground with better results. When journeying from the old normal to the new normal, most everyone wants things to go their way without the hiccups and surprises. However, as reality creeps in with all its messiness, we need to anticipate, embrace, even be curious, affirming and attentive to the surprise, pain or disruption as part of the evolutionary-revolutionary process of transformation.

This kind of being and doing can be found in all kinds of personal and career-minded engagements where the embedded theme is considering the possible as a fools' folly, a figment of imagination, or a diamond in the rough. Aligning what we treasure and value as aspirational must also be grounded in suitable readiness for the price and terms of engagement. That is, readying ourselves for what is ahead helps to immunize us against the shock-and-awe of emerging insult and injury.

9. Only control what you can

Stay in your swim lane. Honor boundaries. Use guard rails to preserve some sense of order in the midst of chaos. We often know this already, but sometimes need reminding in the flurry of both ever-demanding and ever-aspiring interests for more. In the effort to please others or ourselves we may sometimes take on more than is realistic or even possible. In-spite of sometimes wanting it all; or wanting everything on our terms, the reality is that it just may not happen; or won't happen on our time-table. People, expectations, goals, performance and promises can disappoint--no matter how much we are counting on the contrary. That's reality.

Recognizing our span-of-control is important. There are essential laws of gravity – things in our span-of-control, and things that are not. Yes, for a variety of reasons we may be able to influence others and situations for things to go our way. In fact, some have a natural talent in working through informal networks of power to shape conditions beyond our formally designated scope or sphere of influence. But even the talented in this area can be humbled. We sometimes must remind ourselves and others we are not General Managers of the Universe. We cannot control or do everything as perfectly as we would like. Part of being a grown-up is accepting limitations while proceeding forward with high hopes chastened with reality.

10. Ride the roller coaster: embrace it, don't fight it

Embrace the moment with a light touch and a steady hand. The nature of trouble has its own trajectory. Some of it we can prepare for or course-correct. But part of it requires our surrendering to the experience. We can't force-fit or control all the elements of it. We can't predict outcomes or sometimes even our reactions, or that of others. The best we can do is float above or even through the storm clouds while anchoring to what is stable and grounded.

We may at times feel crazy, out-of-control, surreal or depressed, especially in the midst of tough times. We can even be emotionally flooded or overwhelmed by what's happening. Acknowledge our dark side. But also nurture the light side as well. That is, our source of strength and skills, our promise and potential. Spirited and enriched with this more hopeful perspective we bring a more appreciative and agile demeanor to the arena of thought and action.

Part of the ride in life is being able to lightly brace, block or bear incoming bumps in a fluid and flexible manner. On the one hand, think of what happens when you stiffen up too much—grip the rail or the relationships so tight it hurts even more. Conversely, watch someone who appears steadier and more relaxed even in tumultuous times. In the midst of swirling challenges all around them, they sometimes employ a jujitsu move, and see something magical happen. Harvesting the energy and momentum of the moment can gently re-direct the push and pathos of others.

Conversely, others may stand in the way attempting to block or counter punch, and in the process become a sitting punching bag, absorbing all the incoming blows. Literally and figuratively, these varied stances can be imagined with the all-time boxing icon Muhammad Ali. He once said of his boxing style that he: *"Floats like a butterfly, stings like a bee. The hands can't hit what the eyes can't see."* He would duck and dodge, twist and turn, be one with whatever moved until he turned his back on to the opponent.

TOP 10 THRIVE SUMMATION: Agility as Master-key

Agility is a key theme not only with #10, riding the up-and-down trajectory of trouble, but of all the preceding THRIVE tips as well. Agility, as a master-key for thriving in tough times, allows us to embrace and adjust all of our efforts and approaches for a goodness-of-fit in a purposeful, passionate and present manner.

Agility is a means of being able to go where the action is, adapt and adjust, shape and transform in some fashion that has impact and value. In the midst of shuttling between different experiences, images and events, within and outside our self, it is helpful to be able to do the following:

- In the swirl of confusion and action: step back, slow the picture down, suspend judgment, allow competing narratives, bracket buckets of meaning (compartmentalize).
- Adopt an oppositional stance. Reframe ways of looking at the same thing: is it half-full or half-empty; is it demanding or inviting; is it scary or novel; is it unyielding or re-generative. Stretch to be something larger than simply more-of-the-same.
- Embrace ambiguity by accepting the unknown as a discovery process requiring terms to be revealed by an intriguing suitor. Resist your normal responses. Stay with the ambiguity long enough to appreciate new insights (often with the help of others).
- Simultaneously challenge and affirm your senses. Be open to contradiction, to being temporarily off-balance. This requires being vulnerable and courageous at the same time.
- Renew and refresh: A rubber band will split without reducing tension. Take a break, relax, exercise, come back with a spirited rejoinder.

Final Note

We all lead lives full of surprise, boredom, excitement, fear, frustration, euphoria, ambivilance and so on. Seeking big dreams, barely hanging on, or working our way through life with mostly more of the same routines is not uncommon. What is, is a realization that at any age and in any circumstance, as extreme or comfortable as it may be, we still can control how we experience moments that matter to us.

As many of us know, Victor Frankl, the noted Austrian psychiatrist and WWII Holocaust survivor made this clear under brutally harsh conditions as prisoner in a Nazi death camp. He said in his best selling book, '*Man's Search For Meaning*[3],' (1959) that the Nazi's could torture me regularly but I get to choose how I experience the physical pain. That is, the choice to choose how I am me in the midst of such an experience regardless of what they hope I am experiencing. He said, *I am still in charge of me and I will not give up my power to be the me I want to be.*

And so today, we still have the power to be who we are and who we want to be. Yes, we can not completely control our (interenal and external) environment in all terms and times. Yet we can still move forward, backward, sideways in efforts to pivot and practice new ways of being our better self. We can reflect on ways to stretch or experiment with choices that bring us more of what we are called to be and do.

It is my hope you will find the rich array of stories, examples and developmental frameworks helpful in further embracing your purpose, passion and presence to bring more joy, and effectivenss in expressing your own personal leadership style, in high-demand, high-challenge environments. The stories include living legends, historic figures and everyday people that often have an outsized spirit, with endless determination.

---

3 Victor Frankl's classic treatise, *Man's Search for Meaning. An Introduction to Logotherapy*, was first written in part while in prison under extreme conditions. Yet he reported a certain calmness and excitement while reflecting on and scratching out key principles in the dirt and scrap paper. Later it was published by Beacon Press, Boston, MA, 2006 (Originally published in 1946 under a different name).

"THRIVE" starts with the thriving themes as they can be a guiding reference in how one may consider best positioning his or her personal leadership style for success and satisfaction. However, for some, the reverse can be true as well; that is, their personal leadership influences their thrive themes. Regardless, both the themes (purpose, passion and presence) and the styles (i.e. *protector, problem solver, optimizer, creative strategist and globalist*) are interdependent and supportive of each other[4].

I hope you find the *Introduction* as a good taste-test of what's to come. The book is built on sharing a deeper, more nuanced view of how we experience, pivot, freeze, unfreeze and/or re-engage with moments that matter - and what to do about it!

Some books provide more of a one-size fits all kind of prescription that can sometimes gloss over or minimize what is really going on; and what to do next. Universal prescriptions often disappoint. In reality we are not always the same person now or later - whether it be in days or decades. Nor do others always think or act like us, as we know.

Thriving looks very different based on how we engage with what's in front of us, between us, or in us. Hence, the five Personal Leadership Styles help to frame varied ways we thrive based on our different ways of making meaning (i.e. that is, on how we go about *knowing things*, in combination with how we *value* what matters to us).

Finally, the stories and exercises, both in the book and on the website, provide a way to bring to life a new way of knowing and doing that hopefully supports your intentions in being a better you when it matters most.

I wish you well in your continued journey to bring strength, skill, and spirit in the days ahead. May the coming chapters support and inspire your efforts along the way. Happy reading!

---

4   Later stage research will further discern the statistical significance and level of confidence between the three thrive themes, 12 capacity enablers embedded in the three THRIVE themes, agility as capacity facilitator, and five personal leadership styles. Based on this work, there will be a *Personal Leadership THRIVE Scale (PLT-S)* developed to provide summary insights into styles and strategies to consider in high demand environments.

Chapter 1

Purpose: What Matters

"It's not what you look at that matters, it's what you see."

Henry David Thoreau

"Your dreams are the blueprint to reality."

Greg Norman

"Often when you think you're at the end of something, you're at the beginning of something else."
Fred Rogers

"When you are in the final days of your life, what will you want? Will you hug that college degree in the walnut frame? Will you be asked to be carried to the garage so you can sit in your car? Will you find comfort in rereading your financial statement? Of course not. What will matter then will be people. If relationships will matter most then, shouldn't they matter most now?"
Max Lucado

Featuring

Ms. Helene Neville: Cancer survivor turn marathoner that ran through all 50 states, from one Cancer-hospital to the next to raise funds and support patients

Reverend, Dr. Otis Moss, Jr.: Southern Baptist Minister, and Civil Rights activist, partner/friend with both MLK Jr. and MLK Sr.; Marched at Selma, AL and beyond

Being our biggest, boldest, and best self both in troubled and in typical times is not easy. There is often no quick answers or silver bullets to always know how to be strong, humble, effective and respectful in terrifying or trying times. In my own life, I have had to lay people off; say good-bye to loved ones who were dying; recover from significantly disappointing results that mattered; not always know what to do next; or how to make things better when my best had already been given. Still, after six decades, these types of situations have never gotten any easier or predictable for me. However, over time, I have been fortunate to learn new or different ways to engage in a variety of difficult situations. Insights, experience and even wisdom of some of life's biggest challenges often evolved from many different sources. Through the work of this book I have been privileged to learn even more from an array of talented people who have embraced crucibles, often as an opportunity for redefining self and their embedded circumstances.

I am often amazed and inspired when I see someone who rises up against the odds to quietly, bravely confront the heat while caring for those involved. They have the competence and confidence to know, do and be with heightened ability. Some do it over and over again. Who are these people? Sometimes they are at a breaking point — with limited resolve, skill, insight or energy to step up, yet with a steady sensitive heart and head, they move forward. We know intuitively that sometimes this is easier said than done.

The good news is that there are strength-and skill-building opportunities. I like knowing there's hope; that things can always get better. Yes, thriving, or being our best when it counts, can be learned based on willingness to engage while nurturing courage, care, competence and curiosity.

For this book, I had the privilege of interviewing more than fifty notable achievers. Coming out of these deep conversations, reoccurring themes of Purpose, Passion and Presence came through as a difference-maker in thriving. The book starts with Purpose because it frames the future in spite of what may be going on.

Purpose on The Run: Helene Neville

Did you ever know you needed to do something but didn't know why? Did you ever push on when others thought it didn't make sense? Did you ever not know what to do next, but continued on anyway?

Take Helene Neville, a grandmother, survivor of multiple bouts of potentially deadly cancer, turned hard-core elite marathoner. Not just any kind of runner. She is one of the first to have run the total perimeter of the United States, followed by all the states within the lower 48 – at 58 years old. Soon after, she completed Hawaii and is on her way to doing the same with Alaska, in the winter, no less. This makes her the first person in recorded history to run the contiguous United States and Hawaii unsupported, 12,976 miles to date!

She was a natural athlete from childhood, but life's twists put Neville on her own course. When she was a little girl, Neville's father walked out on the family, leaving a loving, strong-willed Irish-American mother to support six children on her own. In one week, her mother was a member of a country club near Philadelphia. The next week, she was a waitress at the same club. Every month, the town social worker from the local family service agency visited to see if her mother would turn her kids over to foster care and sell the house. Neville hid under the dining room table as she listened to the uninvited social worker plead, cajole, and shame her mother into giving up her family. It was the 1960s, and women in this suburban, middle-class neighborhood were not to be primary homeowners, never mind being a single mom, and head of household.

The family was poor. But Neville's mother was dedicated to three things: A roof over her children's heads, food on the table, and all six children attending Catholic schools. Moreover, she aimed to protect, feed and educate all of them together as one family, one unit. This singular purpose was clear and non-negotiable. She worked three jobs to make it happen. There were trade-offs that influenced what she could and could not do based on this purpose-led, family-first approach. In spite of a non-stop schedule, Neville's mom watched all of her daughter's evening high school basketball games. To save a dollar, she watched from the gym lobby until half-time when she was then allowed in for free. She did without so that her kids could receive her three essentials. Purpose had a price, but it freed her mother from distraction or temptation to do less or to be less.

Neville learned this lesson well. Being purposeful mattered if she was going to make a difference in this world. She became a nurse and also ended up raising her kids with the mutual support of her ex-husband. All the while challenged with recurring bouts of cancer, and the cycle of chemotherapy, remission, and then more of the same. Neville spent long days and hours just staring at the window from her hospital bed. Pain was a constant, and fear of what would come of her life and her children never left her. Through all of this, she realized that her own health, her very existence, was dependent not simply on her, but also on the nurses that she had grown to love and respect. She begrudgingly reckoned with the fact that she could not do it all herself. Yet, she was determined to give something back to them and to their profession. But what, and for what reason?

> *"Effort and courage is not enough without purpose and direction."*
> John F. Kennedy

"Finding myself on the other side of the bed as a patient, I just wanted to give back to the profession that gives so much and we kind of exist on the front lines of life," said Neville. "It's a noble profession and we don't get acknowledged very well or much."

Once vertical, she realized recovery meant something more than leaving her physical ailments behind. She had changed somehow. Struggling with determining what was important to her and what she would do, first meant she needed to accept that she was vulnerable. That is, to embrace a not-knowing state. She thought most people had structure to their life, regular jobs, daily routines, and predictable plans. Neville wondered, if she could do something different, radically different, outside the box, for the nurses she so loved, that resonated with her inner voice. Could she let go of 'playing safe,' and do something a bit on the edge, where risk met opportunity? It was scary yet exciting.

This took a certain courage to have faith in the unknown self. She contemplated multiple ways that she could support nurses. There were pretend choices, such as making a small donation to the hospital, or half-way, play-it-safe choices such as participating in a local 5K charity run for cancer, but Neville chose to be all-in — running from the West-to-East Coast for the first leg of her run of the perimeter of the United States.

Once Neville gave herself to a purpose that was true to her, she realized she could let go of the externalities of meeting expectations and interests that were either not hers or not central to her best and future self. Easier said than done. How would she start? She had little money.

At first, her cross-country charity run was a multi-state trek running from one southern hospital to the next to share her cancer recovery stories with other patients. As Neville began, others got excited about her message and mission to bring hope to the hopeless. Donors stepped up and started to support her. It was inspiring about this cancer victim turned cheerleader, genuinely wanting to get up close with those needing encouragement and a potential path forward from someone who lived the same nightmare.

Others, in the health care community and beyond, started to help. They found places for Neville to stay at night and food. They set up hospital talks and radio spots in towns where she was running. Before she knew it, the raw power of purpose in action generated support from people and places she least expected. Neville slept on couches and was served meals from those who sometimes had little to offer – yet were moved by her driven spirit to serve those in pain.

> *"We make a living by what we get, but we make a life by what we give."*
> Winston Churchill

We do not always know the finish at the beginning, nor the risks involved until the dance between holding-on and letting-go begins. Sometimes, having a purpose that matters means giving up something else that is desirable. So, what is important? The safety of staying with the known can be most attractive while the unknown may be less than tolerable. The quiet courage it takes to serve an authentic purpose may not be visible, but it results in precision, utility and impact for the long run. For Neville, instead of mailing it in she chose the most of challenging of options and completed the southern perimeter run, eight states, in only 93 days.

The run was something larger than herself. The emerging planning team, the recovery wagon, the run itself, the talks and media at different hospitals and schools Neville spoke at along the road, all involved hundreds of supporters gaining inspiration and guidance along the way. This was not just a guiding coalition or community, it was purpose-driven.

The first 100 days or so of running ultimately only her first leg, Ocean Beach, CA to Atlantic Beach, FL. In Florida, she decided she needed to go farther after her brother Anthony died. She carried his ashes in an urn while running and completed the second of four legs between Vancouver, British Columbia, and Tijuana, Mexico. The other legs became more intentional and gained momentum as she completed a 9,713-mile perimeter run, coast-to-coast and north-to-south.

Along her route, Neville fulfilled her own purpose, but she also gave others a chance to become a part of her mission. "Everybody wants to be a part of something bigger than them. They just want to be included, like a team," she said. "One world, one team."

Making the Most of Purpose: What Say You?

Similar to Helene Neville and her family, many of us think about our purpose because it is central to who we are. It is also related to the promise and potential of an optimal life path with direction and engagement of our authentic selves in the world around us. Our capacity to leverage our purpose for action and impact can often lead to a rich and full life, in spite of, or because of our challenges. We can even grow to become more purposeful as the texture of our life changes with bigger or more defined fault lines in our everyday experiences.

Something we often ask is, "How do you find your purpose?" In reality, purpose is generally not something found, but rather something built or cultivated over time and with experience. John Coleman in *Purpose and Passion*[1] writes 'Most of us have to focus as much on *making* our work

---

1 Coleman, J., Gulati, D., Segovia, O. (2012). Passion and Purpose. Boston, MA: Harvard Business School Publishing.

meaningful as in *taking* meaning from it.' Purpose is not something out there to catch, but rather something deep inside of us to honor, cultivate and harvest. And it is something that can change over time. I know at 20 years old I had a different purpose in life, in work, in my family, and in my faith than I did at 40 years old.

While it is much easier to hope that somehow a neatly packaged purpose statement, customized around what is uniquely relevant for us in the moment will just show up. We know it doesn't. It can take hard work. At times, upon continued reflection and effort, our sense of purpose can emerge when we least expect it. Recognizing our purpose is a bit like horse whispering, gently and forcefully drawing out our intentions, hopes, ideas and images that describe the essence of what we want, who we are, or both.

Having Faith in Your Purpose: Otis Moss, Jr.

For Reverend Dr. Otis Moss, purpose is rooted in brutality and strong enough even to outweigh the possibility of death. A pastor for half a century, Moss was a leader in Dr. Martin Luther King Jr.'s civil rights movement, heading up operations in Ohio. He marched with King in Selma, AL and King married Moss and his wife, Edwina.

Now at 83 years of age, Moss found his purpose as a youth. Moss was 12 and growing up in rural Georgia, when a man he regarded as a cousin, Reese Gilbert, was arrested and died in jail. Then in his 40s, Gilbert was a successful, industrious black man. He worked hard and had accumulated 110 acres of land. A deacon in his local church, Gilbert was respected in his community. He was shot five times and an autopsy report found that every bone in his body had been broken. The local sheriff said he killed Gilbert in self-defense.

For Moss and his family, later acts of brutality—the killing of three young civil rights activists in Mississippi, the church bombing in Birmingham, the assassination of King and the murder of Medgar Evers — all tied back on a personal level to the death of Gilbert. That connection ignited a sense of purpose.

"There was no question in our family about the injustice, about the brutality, about the evil," Moss said. "There was an indescribable teaching that we had the responsibility of standing up as best we could or as best we can now against this kind of evil, this kind of injustice, against this kind of hate. Our faith taught us the best way to stand against it was to refuse to be a part of it within our own context."

Moss first met Dr. King at a gathering of *The National Baptist Convention, USA, Inc.* in 1956. The two had both attended historically black Morehouse College in Atlanta. Moss credits his teachers, leaders, and peers at Morehouse (1956) with helping him develop the ideas that would further influence and shape him into becoming a prominent leader in the fight for social justice and equality. King had many of the same teachers and mentors.

King's emphasis on non-violence fit with Moss' own ideals and his vision of what it would mean to be a leader in the struggle for equality and justice for African-Americans. Like King, Moss felt the best way to stand up against hate is by refusing to hate. To Moss, King represented the moral imperative that would become part of the total fabric of his being. Despite their belief in non-violence, Moss and many others in the movement could look back at their personal experience and see that conflict, and even death, could be a consequence of following their purpose.

"I cannot say that we were totally free of the fear of death," Moss said. "But, I can say our commitment was sufficient enough to override that fear. We prepared. We fought to prepare intellectually and spiritually for the facing of this kind of danger. In the next place, because we did have a collective commitment, we could encourage and strengthen each other, bringing on a daily basis hope and humor, faith, courage, and love." This over-riding purpose further strengthened the movement to face fear and the challenges of the times with renewed spirit in-spite of what came their way.

In January 1956, King received a threat that his home in Montgomery, AL, was going to be destroyed if he and his family did not get out of town. King hung up the phone and could not go back to sleep. Instead he went in the kitchen, made a cup of coffee and began to pray aloud at the kitchen table. His prayer acknowledged that he had been given the responsibility to lead the movement and do what is right, although he had human limitations. Moss said that as King prayed he heard an inner voice saying, 'Stand up for justice, stand up for righteousness, I will be by your side, forever.' Then, it seemed, the fear disappeared.

A few days later King's front porch was dynamited. His wife, Coretta, and baby were home but uninjured. Coretta King had heard a noise in the front of the house and rushed to the back with her child. The black community rallied around the Kings' house after the explosion. Some carried weapons and were ready to respond with vengeful violence. King came out on the porch and urged those with weapons to go home. His sense of purpose in creating change through non-violence remained intact.

Moss said he believed King saved members of the crowd that day in Montgomery. If they had attacked, they would have been outnumbered and beaten back by police, stalling the movement – or worse. Instead of an indication of weakness, Moss said the power of King's purpose and commitment to non-violence, even at that difficult moment, strengthened the movement.

In 2017, Moss returned to King's home in Montgomery to reflect on the work that King committed his life to and that Moss is still working towards today. Moss believes King's Civil Rights movement was drawn from an unbreakable faith in God and a rejection of violence. Instead, education and spiritual or moral commitment were the unifying forces he believed in and that shaped his purpose. In turn, Moss and so many others devoted their lives to building a just and moral future.

"We did not take non-violence lightly," said Moss. "We sought to study its meaning to understand its implications and to appreciate that kind of commitment, not perfectly but, we were willing to take the risk of believing it was the right thing to do. It was the wise thing to do. It was the moral thing to do. In retrospect, we won."

Purpose That Brings Light and Lift to Darkness: Courage, Care, Competence, Community and Curiosity

The life of Otis Moss, a lively octogenarian, civil rights activist, minister, educator and community builder is illustrative of a humble, confident, defiant, loyal man of soul and spirit. It is easy to

> "The two most important days in your life are the day you are born and the day you find out why."
> *Mark Twain*

pronounce love over evil, but to live it is another matter. Intellectually it sounds like the right thing, but in practice, we know there are often questions of pride and purpose.

Moss mentioned to me that when he has been threatened or rebuked, verbally or physically, it sometimes takes every ounce of his energy to respond in love and kindness. Not a wimpy or mealy-mouth manner, but with equal amounts of both candor and care. That is, to be straight yet thoughtful of the fear, insecurities and need for respect of the attacker. The human side of us may ask how do we face force, farce or violence with respect and still be strong? The temptation of course is to mimic the very behavior we abhor: sarcasm, insults, or name-calling. While it temporarily provides salve for the wounded spirit, it still reduces us to a lower level of being and encourages others to continue with such behavior as well. As importantly, our purpose toward a given path of being and doing may fall prey to a distracted course of action, undermining the intentions and efforts we seek in the first place.

Purpose is about shaping the future in the present. It is about reaching into the void of the undefined and giving it clothes to make it real and relevant in a way that it can be recognized. We may not always believe we are able or worthy, but we generally can recognize if we are on a path that speaks to us with honor, honesty and interest. Such a path of authentic voice may not come cheaply. There are emotional costs in recognizing and engaging our inner self as it is and fully coming to terms with all of who we are.

For Reverend Dr. Otis Moss, purpose is rooted in brutality and strong enough even to outweigh the possibility of death. A pastor for half a century, Moss was a leader in Dr. Martin Luther King Jr.'s civil rights movement, heading up operations in Ohio. He marched with King in Selma, AL and King married Moss and his wife, Edwina.

Now in his late 80s, Moss found his purpose as a youth. Moss was 12 and growing up in rural Georgia, when a man he regarded as a cousin, Reese Gilbert, was arrested and died in jail. Then in his 40s, Gilbert was a successful, industrious black man. He worked hard and had accumulated a hundred acres of land. A deacon in his local church, Gilbert was respected in his community. He was shot five times and an autopsy report found that every bone in his body had been broken. The local sheriff said he killed Gilbert in self-defense.

For Moss and his family, later acts of brutality—the killing of three young civil rights activists in Mississippi, the church bombing in Birmingham, the assassination of King and the murder of Medgar Evers — all tied back on a personal level to the death of Gilbert. That connection ignited a sense of purpose.

"There was no question in our family about the injustice, about the brutality, about the evil," Moss said. "There was an indescribable teaching that we had the responsibility of standing up as best we could or as best we can now against this kind of evil, this kind of injustice, against this kind of hate. Our faith taught us the best way to stand against it was to refuse to be a part of it within our own context."

Moss first met King at a Baptist convention in 1955. The two had both attended historically black Morehouse College in Atlanta. Moss credits his teachers, leaders, and peers at Morehouse with helping him develop the ideas that would help him become a leader in the fight for social justice and equality. King had many of the same teachers and mentors.

King's emphasis on non-violence fit with Moss' own ideals and his vision of what it would mean to be a leader in the struggle for equality and justice for African-Americans. Like King, Moss felt the best way to stand up against hate is by refusing to hate. To Moss, King represented the moral imperative that would become part of the total fabric of his being. Despite their belief in non-violence, Moss and many others in the movement could look back at their personal experience and see that conflict, and even death, could be a consequence of following their purpose.

"I cannot say that we were totally free of the fear of death," Moss said. "But, I can say our commitment was sufficient enough to override that fear. We prepared. We fought to prepare intellectually and spiritually for the facing of this kind of danger. In the next place, because we did have a collective commitment, we could encourage and strengthen each other, bringing on a daily basis hope and humor, faith, courage, and love." This over-riding purpose further strengthened the movement to face fear and the challenges of the times with renewed spirit in-spite of what came their way.

In January 1956, King received a threat that his home in Montgomery, AL, was going to be destroyed if he and his family did not get out of town. King hung up the phone and could not go back to sleep. Instead he went in the kitchen, made a cup of coffee and began to pray aloud at the kitchen table. His prayer acknowledged that he had been given the responsibility to lead the movement and do what is right, although he had human limitations. Moss said that as King prayed he heard an inner voice saying, 'Stand up for justice, stand up for righteousness, I will be by your side, forever.' Then, it seemed, the fear disappeared.

A few nights later King's front porch was dynamited. His wife, Coretta, and baby were home but uninjured. Coretta King had heard a noise in the front of the house and rushed to the back with her child. The black community rallied around the Kings' house after the explosion. Some carried weapons and were ready to respond with vengeful violence. King came out on the porch and urged those with weapons to go home. His sense of purpose in creating change through non-violence remained intact.

Moss said he believed King saved members of the crowd that day in Montgomery. If they had attacked, they would have been outnumbered and beaten back by police, stalling the movement – or worse. Instead of an indication of weakness, Moss said the power of King's purpose and commitment to non-violence, even at that difficult moment, strengthened the movement.

In 2017, Moss returned to King's home in Montgomery to reflect on the work that King committed his life to and that Moss is still working towards today. Moss believes King's Civil Rights movement was drawn from an unbreakable faith in God and a rejection of violence. Instead, education and tolerance were the unifying forces he believed in and that shaped his purpose. In turn, Moss and so many others devoted their lives to building a just and tolerant future.

"We did not take non-violence lightly," said Moss. "We sought to steady its meaning to understand its implications and to appreciate that kind of commitment, not perfectly but, we were willing to take the risk of believing it was the right thing to do. It was the wise thing to do. It was the moral thing to do. In retrospect, we won."

At times, I can be embarrassed or even defensive with my shortcomings to the extent that I consciously or unconsciously, ignore, distort or defer such reality. These transgressions cause me to be less of me. The underlying need is to be safe. Yet the artifice of such safety, of playing small or living small, cheapens my potential to fully embrace my purpose for who I am meant to be, today and in the future.

It takes courage and care to seek the truth[2]. To embrace it. This journey of seeking a deeper truth as a foundation for creating an authentically crafted purpose has its own time-line and conditions for readiness and engagement. Moving from a "knowing state" that is safe and predictable to a "not-knowing" state can present risk and uncertainty. It is much easier to often simply do more of the same than to reinvent or repurpose our future.

This is where care comes in. Care is about affirming our efforts and gifts while simultaneously acknowledging our ugly underbelly. While it may seem counterintuitive, our ugly needs to be appreciated in its own right as it often serves to protect us from the scary and the unpredictable new self. The ugly in us deserves more than denial or distortion. As noted in Gestalt[3] and other schools of psychology, once we assign functional value and genuine appreciation for our ugly habits and thoughts, we can begin to soften our rigid hold on it. (i.e. Gestalt source). The irony is that by admiring our dysfunctional ways, we can choose to experiment with new ways to engage our old, ritualistic, hair-trigger responses.

If I am on a diet, after many years of late night snacking, I may have a rigid yes-no, eat or don't eat response in passing by the refrigerator where it is calling out to me at 10 p.m. Answering the craving for sugar, salt, or butter may have served me well at certain points with comfort food that addressed momentary stress or a need for satisfaction. Cravings have been about caring for me in ways that I temporarily appreciate, irrespective of longer-term health consequences.

If I get beyond setting myself up in a battle of wills as an all-or-nothing, good-bad, heavenly-evil judgment type response and recognize the caring, I can begin to see a more pliable response to the cravings. That is to be in the moment in a more relaxed fashion. One that does not grip the self in a rigid, autocratic fashion that owns and controls the moment. Suspending judgment and being curious about my cravings, I can simultaneously be both more objective and subjective with their purpose. I can stand outside of my cravings, rather than becoming immersed in them, and marvel

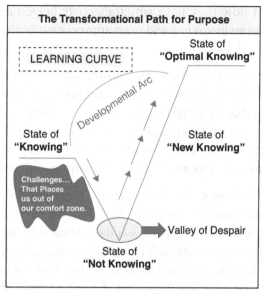

© Courtesy Mark Sullivan

Figure 1.1: Illustrates the *'Knowing-to-Optimal Knowing'* path.

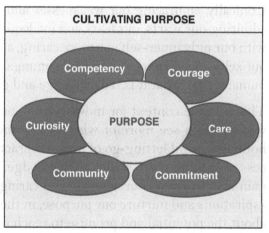

© Courtesy Mark Sullivan

Figure 1.2: Illustrates the *'Capacity Enablers'* that support the Purpose THRIVE Theme.

---

2   Boyatzis, R. & McKee, A. (2005). *Resonant Leadership.* Boston, MA: Harvard Business School Publishing. Note there are many key themes in this publication that refer to courage, care and authentic voice as critical elements to personal leadership.

3   Wheeler, Gordon. (1991), *Gestalt Reconsidered: A New Approach to Contact and Resistance,* Cleveland, OH: Gestalt Institute Cleveland Press; Ch. 5.

at how they have simultaneously helped and hurt me in many timely and distinctive ways. I can be more forgiving and even appreciative of the past while curious about new ways of embracing comfort foods.

So, for example in the future, what would it be like to temporarily experiment by substituting nachos and sour cream with cottage cheese and peaches? From an impulse control perspective, the point here is that by softening boundaries declared as the "ugly" or "weak me" with a new or "different me" in the moment, I can experiment with behavioral options, choices, or underlying intentions and perceptions. This also takes courage and competency to break the shackles of the comfortable and predictable and to seek a more effective, efficient way to embrace the unknown in seeking excellence.

Professionally, I have spent years coaching executives and entrepreneurs in readying themselves for product pitch sessions like on the television show *Shark Tank* . These very talented, bright, hard-working professionals, time and again, fear that they will not have all the answers under intense scrutiny. They may freeze, make up or overstate product capabilities, or simply argue with the venture capitalists seeking to invest in them. Often the entrepreneur is afraid to disclose, in at least a limited way, that they don't have all the answers or insights.

In some regard, fearing to "not know" has served them well in courageously redesigning the impossible into the possible. At the same time, this fear never acknowledged and refashioned, can create seeds of doubt and mistrust with the venture capitalists who are often seeking to invest in them personally as much as in their product. Those entrepreneurs who did acknowledge more work is needed often created trust and transparency in the dialogue.

Ironically, embracing our weaknesses and vulnerabilities builds strength and power. Softening or admiring our warts, our fears and inadequacies, can provide us with the safety and confidence to be with our ugly inner-self in a more caring, appreciative and courageous manner. Caring and affirming our self is not to excuse our shortcomings, but to give us an inner peace and strength to accept our humanity for what it is. To challenge and grow. It's a version of 'tough-love' applied to our self.

This sets the context for moving from 'not-knowing' to 'new-knowing.' As a learning organism, we can often see more of who we are and what we want to be if we can balance this dance of holding-on and letting-go of new-old practices with ourselves and others. Competence, or the process of gaining more skill and knowledge, plays an important part here. As we build capacity and gain insight from courageously and caring more about a bigger, better self, we also influence our aspirations and nurture our purpose, in the process. This is accelerated as we become more curious about the potential and promise to reach a continuous way of embracing 'optimal knowing.'

What does this mean? Les Wexner, the billionaire founder and CEO of L-Brands, which includes Victoria's Secret, Bath & Body Works, Pink, La Senza, and Henri Bendel, mentioned to me that when he was much younger, he lived zealously on building his business. Life was intensely focused day and night on customers, product, capital, and competitors. He was clearly very successful, but yearned for more. Years later, he started to read magazines, and then books. In fact, more recently when we talked in his office, there was a stack of more than a dozen books on his desk.

As an avid reader, he became curious about the "why" as much as the "what" and "when." His worldview expanded. His purpose did as well. Initially, he wanted to make more money than his father. Gradually, as he became more curious and thoughtful about life both in and beyond his company, his purpose changed as well. Now, he has grown into a significantly more mature, broader range of global interests in faith, community, education and, of course, business. One is not at the expense of the other. His world-view is dynamic and synergistic. His purpose is too, as he explores and integrates humanity and human nature in a broader ecosystem of commerce and community.

Going Deep with Your Purpose

Concrete Exercises to Leverage Purpose for Value and Impact

- *Care:* Lovingly appreciate who you are and what you are meant to be and do:
  - **On a big scale:** Imagine all of your friends and colleagues who care about you from *your whole life* all in one hotel ballroom! They have come from everywhere, and from all stages of your life, from childhood to now, in honor of you! One by one, they get up on the stage to celebrate something special about you.
    - What do they honor in you?
    - What are common themes?
    - What do they recognize as being different, unique or surprising about you?
  - **On a small, but significant scale:** What gets evoked in your heart or head as you hear them talk about you?
    - Based on the above, what images emerge that ring true to the person you are?
    - What is an example of a friend's description of your effort that aligns with an outcome or impact that you did which was most purposeful for you?
    - How can you take time to care for you to be strong enough to recognize and live your purpose?

- *Curiosity:* Without using a single word, draw a picture of you living with purpose? Reflect on where you are; what you look like; and how you may be different than you usually appear.

- *Competence:* Imagine it is five years from today. You are a bigger version of yourself. You have more skill and know-how. You have more people depending on you. As a result of your increased reputation and notoriety, you are watched and recognized more closely for what you do.
  - What aspirationally and concretely can you do better five years from today?
  - How does this align to what your natural interests and gifts are as you see them?
  - What one or two things can you do today to start to get closer to the person you are five years out?

- *Courage:* Name one scary thing you can try that could make a difference even though it may be a bit risky. What has been holding you back? Are you worth it? How can you support yourself while taking the first step?

Figure 1.3: Exercises for developing or deepening your 'Purpose."

Chapter 2

Passion

"There is no passion to be found in playing small – in settling for a life that is less than the one you are capable of living."

Nelson Mandela

"Twenty years from now you will be more disappointed by the things that you didn't do than by the ones you did do. So, throw off the bowlines. Sail away from safe harbor. Catch the trade winds in your sails. Explore. Dream. Discover."

Mark Twain
(Attribution is under dispute)

"The most powerful weapon on earth is the human soul on fire."

Ferdinand Foch

Featuring

Mr. Irlan Silva, Brazilian ballet dancer and soloist for the Boston Ballet Company. From a Sao Palo urban ghetto to stardom

Photo © Brooke Trisolini

Ms. Jeni Britton Bauer, Founder and CEO of Jeni's Splendid Ice Cream, a fast-growing, coast-to-coast purveyor of premium ice cream

PASSION: Leveraging Fire and Heat

Follow your passion and good things will happen. Sounds easy. Sounds like it makes sense. It also is quite deceptive. What if you don't know your passion? What if your passion keeps changing? What if you have more than one passion? What if you are too tired or not in the right space to be passionate?

I teach students at The Ohio State University who regularly come to me thinking there is a singular passion they are supposed to have captured and packaged, like lightning in a bottle. Some of them are anxious that they haven't found that bottle. The more they chase passion, the more they become anxious. "What's wrong with me?" they ask. Of course, this is similar to those who are much further along in their careers, or even later in life, wondering where is the spark now? What happened during years juggling high-density schedules, business and family obligations. Has the treadmill of life dulled the senses or skewed those moments of joy that may now be more of a fleeting, vague memory?

> "Most men lead lives of quiet desperation and die with their song still in them."
> Henry David Thoreau

We have become a society now suffering from the largest recorded number of anxiety disorders, clinical depression and suicides in human history[1]. Expectations to perform, or to be someone or something beyond who we are in the moment, fuel pressure. In part, being our real self can be co-opted by the demands of bosses, teachers, friends, parents, the media, and so on.

On top of this, some have unrealistic expectations and seek more than they have earned as a way to medicate or soothe the wounds of life. They aspire to have money, looks, power, talent, popularity quickly. Sometimes, they may even bargain half-heartedly for a "something-from-nothing" deal arguing they deserve good things right now because it is their turn. For some, in-spite of the effort not investing effort they magically hope things will change simply because they want it to change. The desire may be heart-felt. However, deep down, such expressions separate, mask or diminish the real, inner self. Yet it is in the interior where passion lives.

Passion is not an outcome, or a product, or a plan. It is a way of being. Other times, it is a way of being and doing combined. Underneath this, it is *effort, excellence* and *enjoyment* focused in a natural way that enriches our values and purpose. Passion is neither good nor bad, it simply is. Passion is something we can inadvertently block, subdue, misread or freeze. Chris Argyris, a noted pioneer in organizational psychology, detailed an array of defense routines (1978) that are used to protect self and organizations from uncomfortable truths or painful, prickly realities[2]. When emotional safety is lacking, our defensive routines often screen or distort reality. They can distort what we think and feel to the extent we are numbed by the effort

> Almost everything—all external expectations, all pride, all fear of embarrassment or failure-these things just fall away in the face of death, leaving only what is truly important. Remembering that you are going to die is the best way I know to avoid the trap of thinking you have something to lose. You are already naked. There is no reason not to follow your heart.
> Steve Jobs

---

1 Anxiety and Depression Association of America at: https://adaa.org/about-adaa/press-room/facts-statistics; GAD (General Anxiety Disorders) now affects 6.8 million adults, or 3.1% of the U.S. population, yet only 43.2% are receiving treatment. Anxiety disorders are the most common mental illness in the U.S., affecting 40 million adults in the United States age 18 and older, or 18.1% of the population every year. The annual *age*-adjusted suicide rate is 13.42 per 100,000 individuals. Men die by suicide 3.53x more often than women. On average, there is now 123 suicides per day. White males accounted for 7 of 10 suicides in 2016. Further information can be found at: *www.mentalhealthamerica.net/suicide*

2 Chris Argyris. (1990). *Overcoming Organizational Defenses: Facilitating Organizational Learning.* Cambridge MA: Harvard Business Publishers. It is foundational work that theorizes Argyris's "Mental Model," designed to protect individuals from threat or embarrassment. It is a description of a mindset responsible for setting a defensive routine in motion. He further describes a variety of routines, and double loop thinking activated as a means to keep us in control of a situation where we sense ourselves under threat.

to distort (i.e. consciously and unconsciously). Such routines, for example, led NASA engineers in the Challenger program to pass over faulty O-ring design that resulted in a horrific tragedy. The NASA management team when confronted with canceling the space flight due to below-freezing temperatures that might damage the O-ring, intentionally chose to look more at the consequences of a launch cancellation versus a launch crash[3]. This is even when the Space engineers mentioned the very real possibility of a launch failure. Similarly, we can pass over, dull or distort our passions as much as we can information stripped or immersed with emotion.

What helps? Connecting and embracing our true passion or passions in an authentic manner? How do we leverage passion to more fully engage our energy with purpose and value? Start with heart. Start with being open and respectful of the moment. Ask where is our gentler, appreciative self? How can we look at our self with new eyes? How can we feel and forgive ourselves for shortcomings and genuinely treasure the gifts with which we are so abundantly blessed?

With my students, I ask them to do an exercise that requires them to find five people they trust and who know them very well. These individuals are asked to each write five, one-paragraph stories that catch the students at their best. Some of the students are uncomfortable with the exercise. Yet never have any of their requests gone unanswered by their friends, family and colleagues. Often, to their surprise, they are flooded with rich, detailed stories that reveal their best selves, full of passion and spirit.

However, they are required to hold off from reading the stories until they get to class where we explore how to be open to the themes and underlying messages. I ask them to do this in class, in part, to fully appreciate the story observations from their trusted friends, and not deflect or minimize or discount such feedback.

> "You don't have to be great to start, but you have to start to be great." (Found on a painted stone in a beach stone garden in Wellfleet Bay, MA)

Readily the students find emerging questions: Where is your excitement, your passion? What makes you so strong, so powerful? They also see answers, themes, bits and pieces of what matters to them. More than a few times, they have read stories through tears. They have caught a true piece of themselves, unvarnished, and in an appreciative context supported by not one but by five people they trust deeply[4].

On a deeper level, passion is about meaning and purpose. Martin Seligman[5], a noted psychologist, refers to meaning as extending beyond one's own interests in service of others. First lady Barbara Bush once said, if you want a better life then focus your time and attention on others. Similarly, both as a professor and as a former executive I found students and employees who focused on solving problems of value often more readily cultivated a sense of passion in the process, rather than the other way around. This particularly has happened as competence and confidence grows in their purposeful efforts to make a contribution.

---

3 Allan McDonald, the director of the Space Shuttle Solid Rocket Motor Project for the NASA engineering contractor Morton Thiokol was so concerned about the O-rings and the predicted below-freezing temperatures at launch that he refused to sign the launch recommendations over safety concerns, the night before the fatal space shuttle tragedy. More details of this classic example of 'selective denial of reality' can be found in the article: "Engineer Who Opposed Challenger Launch Offers Personal Look at Tragedy," at Nasa.gov.

4 Similar variations of this exercise has also been done by NTL: National Training Laboratories in the 1960's in their Maine Retreat Center; and in varied commercial, academic and religious workshops, under a variety of names. Mine is referred to as the PBS or Personal Best Self Exercise.

5 Martin Seligman, a pioneer of Positive Psychology has done extensive research in meaning, meaningful life and happiness. See Pursuit-of-Happiness.org.

At Honeywell International, and later at Battelle[6], I was the executive co-lead and founder of a corporate business accelerator. Its' objective was to develop both new business opportunities (i.e. high margin revenue streams); while developing leaders with deeper, market-facing, critical thinking skills. Each wave of four business development teams competed against each other in a 100 day period. Their objective was to create and preliminarily test new product or service offerings that could be funded, if promising enough, as determined by the management team. Over an eight year period, I ran over 150 of these 'pre-seed' Honeywell and Battelle business development project teams through the 100 day business accelerator. It generated an aggregate of over $950 million of projected or recognized revenue from the market-place.

The exciting part of this project was not the money. It was the people and the process working together. Most of the team members were senior-level engineers, scientists or technologists viewed as 'high potential' executives. Many of them had limited serious business experience where they could craft, price and deliver sustainable value to paying customers. Now they had been hand-picked by Officers running billion dollar businesses to compete with three other business teams, from three other divisions, to see what they could come up.

This was an immersive, signature career experience where on top of their day job; the employees went through an intensive five day strategy boot camp; and follow-on weekly team sessions for 90 days. This was all under the close supervision of world-class business strategy team consultants and their division officer. They conducted customer buying experiments, pricing schemes, and varied routes-to-market strategies. Each team, in the presence of the competing teams, needed to report back at the end of 100 days, on stage, to the Chairman and the Executive Committee in a TV reality show, *Shark-Tank* pitch-like environment.

Many of the participants said they had never worked so hard in their life. Many felt the pressure of performing in a high profile competitive environment. They not only learned about products and about business. They learned about themselves. Many of them learned how to think and learn in a new way—with new questions to ask, and new ways of listening; how to ask for help; how to address conflict; how to build trust and deliver results to team members they had never worked with before. In the process, the teams consistently transformed old, sleepy businesses into new, hot, customer-buying market segments.

Today, years later, I regularly get calls from these participants. They have so regularly talked about how it was one of the most exciting, scary, rewarding experiences in their careers. Seeing it up close, I would say it was passion-rich experience. The company was placing bets that these talented yet largely unproven individuals could deliver in the marketplace. The employees were betting they could accelerate their own knowledge and skills under a highly curated action-learning environment.

Passion, it seems, often follows purpose and problem solving. Conversely, those who start by trying to find passion in isolation have few moorings to anchor or guide energy and effort. Staying focused in building meaningful moments and monuments creates the fire, the spark, to engage a deeper self to be "all-in." This is particularly illustrated in the story that follows.

---

6 At Honeywell, the business accelerator was named SMP or the Strategic Marketing Program. It was jointly supported and co-led by the CMO, Chief Marketing Officer, Rhonda Germany; myself, and the Honeywell executive team under the leadership of Chairman David Cote, starting in 2004. At Battelle, it was referred as the BELL / Battelle Executive Leadership Lab and was singularly started by me and supported by the executive team under the leadership of Chief Executive Officer Jeff Wadsworth, starting in 2009. The Battelle accelerator version, BELL, included the 100 day report out competition between the teams on stage in front of the Executive Committee. The format was a precursor to the TV network show "Shark Tank."

Irlan Silva Interview: The Power of Passion

Take Irlan Silva; he is part athlete, part entertainer. He is a Brazilian ballet dancer and soloist for the Boston Ballet Company. He is featured with critical acclaim in the *Tribeca Film Festival* documentary *Only When I Dance*. It is a true-life story of being raised in the most violent favela, or urban slum, of Rio de Janeiro.

One cold Boston April morning next to the tall, cast-iron black entry gates to the ballet, Silva was standing next to me with gym bag in hand. Up close, as I talked to him, I could see his strong, but refined muscles under his attire. He was starting another typical grueling nine-hour day of stretches, drills, dance routines, and recovery exercises. He looked as fit as anyone could be.

I asked him how he could continue this rigorous routine day in and day out. He told me what you did that really mattered happens long before anyone comes to see you on stage. "What matters is what you have in your heart. You can't pretend to like ballet. You've got to love it." Later, I asked him how that happened for him. "Well, over time, it found me," said Silva.

"People from the favela at that time, and still to this day, don't have that much connection with art," Silva said. "They don't know a lot about dance, so they think that the classical ballet is only for girls."

Despite a low level of understanding or respect for the arts in the community, Silva proved to be naturally gifted and his mother nurtured his passion. Silva's father took some time to come around to the idea of his son dancing but was eventually convinced. The first time he saw his son dance he cried and Silva said his father is now his "number one fan."

"Just having someone you love saying 'Yes, do it. Do what you love to do. Do what you like to do,' this means more than anything," Silva said. "Because just to have someone next to you means you're not alone. It's very important for the artist to have someone supporting you, and if you have anything that you don't know you can always go to that person and ask, 'What do you think I should do?' Especially if it's your parents."

There were many barriers for Silva to dancing in Brazil and actually making a professional career out of dance in the United States. He started jazz dancing and picked up classical ballet when he was 11 years old. He took classes and began competing in solo competitions. Soon first-place prizes began rolling in. "The first time I realized that's what I want to do for my life was when I came to New York City for the first time when I was 14. I got first place in this competition, the Youth American Grand Prix," Silva said. "So, when I was there they called the first prize for Irlan Silva, I couldn't believe that was me. It was in New York City in front of the full house and everyone was clapping for me, and I would never forget that feeling that I had in that moment, getting my medal."

His first exposure to dance was watching his family dancing at parties as a child. He remembers admiring the way they moved to the music. He was inspired after his ballet instructor brought him to watch Brazil's national classical ballet company perform in Rio de Janiero. "I was mesmerized from the ballet," Silva enthusiastically said. "I remember it was a ballet called *Giselle*, and it was very romantic. I was like I want to jump like that guy, I want to hold the girl like that. I was kind of mirroring me on him.

Silva's ballet instructor brought him to the national theater because she recognized in Silva the qualities and behaviors of a great dancer. "She has the eyes to see who has the physique, the body to dance," Silva said. "There is one thing that she always told me, and that is you don't choose to dance, dance chooses you to be part of it, because it's not everyone who can have the body to dance, because everything that we do is not totally normal for a human body—we do the opposite. So, I'll never forget that."

Silva had opportunities to be exposed to professional dance and began to develop his passion for dancing, but he had to deal with the hardships of crime in his community and the fact that many kids his age weren't like him. They didn't understand why he cared so much about dancing, and they made fun of him for it.

"It was very hard, I'm not going to say it was easy, because there was so much going on with the police and all the gunshots and shootings all around," Silva said. "There were some days that at night I was going back home, and I couldn't get inside my house. I had to sleep over at some friend's house out of the area, because it was impossible to go home."

Silva moved to the United States when he was 16. He said this was the first real challenge in his life, because everything was new and unfamiliar, and he had to go through it alone. "I kind of felt like an animal. I was looking at everything and staring because everything was new. Even in classes, because the steps are the same but the way they explain it is a different language. I tried so hard to accomplish everything they were asking me, but it was super hard."

Worse, he also had to acclimate to the weather in New York, which was a stark contrast to what he was used to in Brazil. "The winter for me was the worst. It's still one of the worst parts; it is like my sacrifice to be in this country, because the winter is something that I don't like at all. The first month that I had the winter I was like I want go back home right now because I can't feel my toes and fingers. I thought my hand was going to fall off."

Despite the homesickness and culture shock, Silva knew that he was in the right place because he finally had the opportunity to do what he loved in an environment where it was respected and appreciated, and he was able to grow as a dancer and as a human.

"I had to change my whole life to be what I wanted to be," Silva said. "I came here because I wanted to be here. I knew there were going to be a lot of changes, but when you imagine something it's not exactly what you could have thought it would be. It's a shock. I was calling my mom and saying I don't know if I still want to be here. And she was like, 'Well, you chose to be there, you know what you're doing, that's your passion, you're doing everything that's possible to be dancing the way you wanted to.'"

Today, Silva's dance schedule is demanding: he dances six hours a day. He dances on holidays and works from August to May with a week-long break in January. However, Silva said the work is worth it. "You have to feel it; just be grateful to the hard work that you have been doing for weeks, and the special night that is like the opening night or the day you're going to dance that piece. It happens to me a lot,'" he said. "I don't say any words when I'm bowing, I just start crying because it's so many feelings at that moment, because your body and your mind know how much you've been working for it and once it's done you gave it to the audience, to the people who were watching you. When everything is done, it's done. It's past. It's the grand finale. To have the audience clap for you, for me is the best thing. It's the best way that you get paid for your hard work—it's when the audience likes your work."

Silva's success as a dancer did not come easily, and it did not come overnight. It came from long hours and long distances, it came from emotional and physical sacrifice, and it came from staying true to himself and to what he wanted to become instead of listening to what others thought he should be. "First thing, you really need to know what you want, and you have to work for it and have to have focus and patience," Silva said. "If it doesn't happen in the time you want, it's going to happen—you just have to be mentally positive in your mind, and just imagine yourself doing that and you're going to get there and get what you want. If it's not in that time that you want, it's going to be later, or the next day or the next month or the next year, but you have to keep trying because whatever you have in your mind that you imagine to do, it's going to come to you."

Needless to say, Silva is an amazing talent in his field. He has been recorded by critical acclaim for his technical precision of complicated dance routines; but not without a hearty acknowledgement of a memorable, passionate heart that transforms the moment from the mechanical to the sacred, from structured and scripted to the spiritual.

Passion – A Close Cousin of Purpose

Passion is rarely present in isolation. Passion is not a plan but rather something that is lived. Scott Adams, creator of the cartoon strip *Dilbert* once said, "Success fuels passion rather than passion fueling success." Passion is the shaping of energy to amplify the moment to get something done, eventually perhaps for meaning and purpose.

In his early days Silva had a simple interest in being able to dance. Before he had a dream to be a dancer he wanted to simply find a safe, private place where he could dance uninterrupted deep in the heart of his ghetto neighborhood. His neighborhood roof tops became his dance studio. He didn't know where it would lead, but he found joy in working hard and getting better at his dance. He didn't know that it would lead to becoming an accomplished ballet performer.

The effort over time led to a burgeoning skill, then to a talent, and, finally, to a dream. The progression was never quite so linear, and the passion-filled dream was not something that just showed up like magic. Hard work, joy, pain, excitement and anxiety were all bundled up in it. Eventually a path, a goal, evolved that supported an emerging dream. This dream to be a dancer—eventually on the world stage, was converted into a goal. This intersection of purpose and passion became the glue to face the many challenges thrown his way.

Passion, while sometimes discounted or misunderstood as secondary to purpose, is at times the difference that makes the difference. Purpose without passion may lead to a variety of outcomes such as loss of interest in a goal or relationship, declining commitment or wayward standards of excellence, and finally, distracted, fragmented attention. With passion, purpose can often be sustained in a more full-bodied, focused manner.

Passion also has several characteristics that influence the look and feel, or aesthetics, of the energy itself. We know when someone is excited or not. They look different than others in the same setting. These characteristics of passion are pace, intensity, alignment, and form. They are the aesthetics of energy. Pace speaks to the duration of an effort over time while intensity addresses the depth or lightness of the emotion or energy.

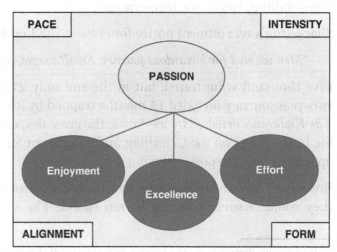

Figure 2.1

The notable achievers in this book and accompanying website spoke in a more multi-dimensional manner about passion. It was about shaping their own energy which translates to form. They described being "all in" which speaks to intensity. They said they stepped it up, or increased pace. And they talked about gathering themselves up to face a crisis or align their efforts for the challenge at hand.

As a marathoner, when fit, I run at a ten-minute pace. In this context, intensity is the level of effort needed to climb hills or deal with cold and rain. I often look at a marathon as 26.2 miles divided by heat and hills. Alignment is about awareness, calibrating or adjusting to conditions in the moment. If I am running on an icy trail in the winter I will need to run heavy, at a slower pace, while negotiating the ice. Form relates to a range of options before, during or after a given moment. Running on ice requires good form to readily shift weight, speed, and posture in an agile fashion.

Of course, this applies to any setting. Referring to someone who is "steady," often means intensity. When there is a rush to meet a new near-term deadline, we are usually talking about pace. Someone in an office yelling with gusto that things "are crazy around here" may be in need of a calibration-check, if their energy is not in alignment with others around them. If someone is described as being in rare form, it could be because they have not shifted to a more acceptable state of being. These characteristics obviously show up every day, as well as in extraordinary times.

When looking at notable high-achievers, passion is present in many ways that often has a goodness-of-fit with purpose. When it is said that one is "comfortable being in his or her own skin," there is usually an integral connection between purpose and passion. What someone seeks and who they are in the process supports both purpose and passion. Great individuals start by being great at personal leadership. Their purpose and passion build on each other. They resonate, and they enrich their authentic and powerful self. An example is Sir Earnest Shackelton, noted British maritime adventurer and explorer.

British Mariner Sir Earnest Shackelton: Purpose-Driven, Passion-Fueled

In 1914, during the heroic age of Polar exploration, Sir Earnest Shackelton led what many claimed to be the most daring expedition of his time. It was a 1500-mile, cross-continent trek across mountainous, ice-capped Antarctica. This had never been attempted before given the arduous, inhumane conditions just to get to the start line. The British expedition would have to navigate the uncharted Weddel Sea off South Georgia (Antartica), full of deadly ice flows, menacing gale and bone-chilling, sub-arctic temperatures.

Shackelton's recruitment notice for crew at the London dock read[7]:

> *"Men wanted for hazardous journey. Small wages, bitter cold, safe return doubtful."*

Five thousand volunteered, but in the end only 27 scientists, officers and seamen set sail. Their two-year journey included 15 months trapped by ice when the open sea froze over. With their boat *The Endurance* crushed by ice-flows, the crew desperately attempted to race to Elephant Island in life boats. Short on food, clothing and equipment for months on end, Shackelton kept their spirits up, with a new purpose—staying alive.

Reaching Elephant Island, after months of being tossed around at sea and on ice caps, they realized they couldn't survive on the barren island. The story ends with Shackelton taking a desperate

---

7 Recruiting message in *Shackelton's Imperial Trans Antarctic Expedition 1914*~With Sound! Centenary Edition; 1:24 minutes on YouTube.

gamble to shoot for a South Georgian whaling station in a small sailboat, some 800 miles away, across the roughest seas on Earth. His sense of purpose and success in getting everyone home was just short of miraculous.

But the real story was how Shackleton kept spirits up by nurturing passion and hope through personal leadership. He found big and small ways to bring joy, excellence and meaningful effort to daily life as polar explorers. He built camaraderie and care among the shipmates with assigned chores and team games played on the ice flows, nurturing a continual effort to bring camaraderie and care to their fellow mates nurtured their spirits under horrific conditions. Shackleton never gave up on his men, so the men never gave up on themselves or the journey. Once safely back to homeport, Shackleton wrote of the journey[8]:

> *"In memories we are rich. We had pierced the veneer of outside things. We had suffered, starved and triumphed. Groveled, yet grasped at glory. Grown bigger in the bigness of the whole. We had seen God in his splendor; and heard the text that nature renders. We had reached the naked soul of man."*

While Shackelton's story lays claim to the power of passion in extraordinary times of yesteryear, it is as relevant today as described in the life events of Jeni Britton Bauer, a nationwide purveyor of premium ice cream. Shackleton, like Bauer, are examples of great leaders fueled with passion's ingredients: Excellence, effort and even at times, enjoyment blended to create possibilities out of the impossible.

Jeni Britton Bauer Interview: Passion in many flavors

© Courtesy Mark Sullivan

Figure 2.2

Jeni Britton Bauer's passion is impossible to miss. She is known in some circles as the entre-preneurial artisan turned rock-star of premium ice cream, with a spirited cult following. While visiting her downtown Columbus office, I was impressed by the renovated hip, open-office setting. Jeni's corporate headquarters was intimate, with cozy, new-age work spaces, a test kitchen off to the side, and a soda fountain bar adjacent to a slew of high-energy, millennials. Jeni popped out of her corner office giving me a lively handshake, a big smile with colorful dangling teal and purple earrings swinging side-to-side.

In 2002 she founded Jeni's Splendid Ice Creams which specializes in creative flavors, among them Bangkok Peanut, Brambleberry Crisp, Cocoa Curry Coco, Juniper & Lemon Curd and

---

8 Shackleton's *Memories We Are Rich* narrative can be found in *Shackleton's Imperial Trans Antarctic Expedition 1914~ With Sound! Centenary Edition.*

Wildberry Lavender. Jenis creates and markets its ice creams, but it also manufacturers them without relying on standard industry ingredients such as preservatives and emulsifiers.

"The hardest part was figuring out how to get the fresh strawberries and all of the water they bring to work into ice cream," she said. "How do we make them into ice cream without making it icy because there is so much water in them? Every year, we tweak the recipe because every year, they have a different water content depending on how much rain we got. Those are really important questions for us. Most companies are going to use a strawberry paste or a base with a couple of fresh strawberries. This is the reason our ice cream is so good."

Continuously adjusting the process to create new flavors and production techniques is nothing new for Britton Bauer who, personally, has been seeking new alignments throughout her life. As a child, she moved frequently and never had a ready-made set of friends to sit with on the first day of school. She never complained about moving and embraced it. "Having a new blank slate, getting to become whoever I wanted every year with a new group of friends didn't bother me a bit. I loved it."

Naturally shy, she adopted a strategy to fit better into the service industry when she was 15 starting her first job at a local ice cream shop. Her mother told her that Meryl Streep also was shy and adopted a new persona whenever she had to face an uncomfortable situation. Britton Bauer tried it. "I put on a character and that character was whoever I wanted to be, and it was different," Britton Bauer recalled. "I found that I loved service for that reason because I could put aside all of my fears and hesitations to make somebody else feel good and that made me feel really good."

Today she is always adjusting the business to make sure she can take advantage of all options to develop the right form for the future. "I love that we always say we are going to make better ice creams. 'Best' is the most boring business mission you could ever have," she said. "When you say 'best,' every time you say it, you're comparing yourself to somebody else. But 'better' is this slow process of inching forward and cutting the path with a machete. It's reflecting on what you've done, it builds. It gives yourself time and the space to think and do and react to that. The idea of 'better' is never dead nor moving forward. If you're on better, one day you're going to be better than the next best."

Passion in Perspective

After our conversation, I was energized by Bauer's office warehouse and by her spunk and spirited outlook on living. For me, Bauer's business, was not as much about building a corporate monopoly as it was a life calling, curated to share with friends and family—and many satisfied customers. The passion was not simply an artificial overcoat for show but was a blend of a free-spirited head-set anchored in a mature expression of meaningful values. Passion, or energy expressed in a variety of ways is a deeper reflection of our inner self.

Deeper passion is linked with purpose in what Mihaly Csikszentmihalyi[9] (1975) describes as being in a flow state. This is the immersive self, deeply engaged and absorbed, yet free-floating. Think of Karl Walenda, the grandfather of dare devil stunts physically working into his 70s. He conquered the impossible as a high wire aerialist leading his family with four, and then seven-tier human

---

9 Mihaly Csikszentmihalyi. (1990). Flow. New York: Harper**Perrinial** Modern Classics. While figures 2.3 and 2.4 were developed in 1975, they were more robustly described by Csikszentmihalyi in his later publications.

pyramids unbelievably cycling on a high wire. They were often described as being in the zone, or in a flow state while performing with no safety net, often hundreds of feet above rocky river gorges or dangling in the wind on slippery, wet wires straddling city skyscrapers at high altitude. Yes, passion with purpose has many forms. It is often intensity with metered pace and alignment to shape energy as a spontaneous or planned expression in the moment or for purpose-driven outcome. As you can see in figure 2.3, there is a constellation of shaped energy, in a continuum, as described by Csikszentmihalyi.

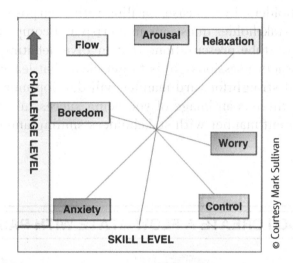

Figure 2.3

Passion that is a contributor to thriving in challenging times is not reckless, or unchecked actions, feelings and outcomes. It is a mixture of focus and free-spirit, a balance of excellence, effort and enjoyment in the now and what can be. It has its own rhythm of energy that ebbs and flows with both intention and spontaneity, knitted with authenticity in the moment. An integrated balance of energy, intent, expectations and in-the-moment outcomes will often create what Csikszentmihalyi refers to as a *flow* state. He further describes that we do our best work, even in high demand environments, when we are in a flow state.

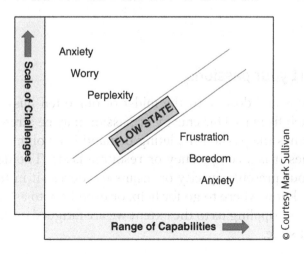

Figure 2.4

Below is an exercise in cultivating a flow state. See figure 2.5.

➤ *Step one* is to focus on a strength that can be cultivated in a concrete and direct manner.
➤ *Step two* is to explore learning opportunities, approaches and rationale for getting better using your identified opportunity from step one.
➤ Step three is linking a fun or pleasant image associated with step one and two.

An example might be preparing for an important high profile briefing session or presentation with key stakeholders. In this case, for illustrative purposes, step one might be an intent to answer tough stakeholder questions in a crisp and compelling fashion. Step two (a) could be to review youtube presentations that involve debating; and solicit coaching feedback in your own practice sessions. (b) is to get clear that learning how to engage in an authentic, skilled and straightforward manner will develop more trust and credibility with stakeholders. Step three is an image of you being successful in answering questions in a comfortable, competent manner with stakeholders smiling and clapping at the end of your engagement.

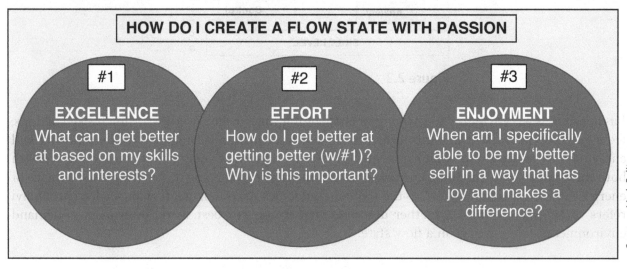

© Courtesy Mark Sullivan

Figure 2.5

Things to do to support your passion:

We all know life has its ups and downs. In the midst of our often busy lives there are demands and deadlines that ask much from us. Our energy or passion may be stretched, drained or distilled now or over time. Sometimes the passion-depleting demand is a volume issue: too much to do in too little time. Other times it is a competency or resource issue. The demand is challenging us to do something beyond our present capacity or means to address it in the moment. We may not have the support we need; know where to go for help; or even how to ask for help. Other times the energy-depleting demand is crippling us to the extent we are fatigued or numbed into complacency, exhaustion or a depressed state.

> **Here are a few suggestions on how to nurture your passion:**

- **Rest:** Sleep is important. Catch up on it or take 'power naps' to physically restore your body.
- **Set Priorities:** Know what is important. Determine what your daily and weekly goals or activities are and revisit them in the beginning and end of the day. Establishing boundaries provide a sense of self-control that can be useful in leveraging your energy.
- **Stay Strong:** Keep physically active. Walk the stairs instead of using the elevator. Park the car at the end of the lot for a longer walk to your work site. Get up and walk around regularly, if not exercise, in some consistent fashion. The endorphins from the exercise will energize your physical presence.
- **Be Kind:** Be mindful of others best interests. Be helpful or provide a 'random act of kindness.' It often creates its own energy as others genuinely appreciate you for who you are.
- **Express Gratitude:** Appreciate others as well as yourself. Intentionally express the good works of others. Share a sincere complement without expecting anything back in return.
- **Renew:** Refresh with positive thinking or imagery. Imagine you being in a successful or satisfying place. Consider scheduled daily guided imagery or meditation. Picture people and places that are happy, relaxing, supportive of you.

The Passion Premium: Making It Real

Example of ways to enrich life with focused energy (passion) using an experimental stance with any of the five domain's during a 90 day period.

Life's Domains	Experimental Goal	Success Criteria	Action Steps
Work	Increase impact and value with a key stakeholder	Client (people) are excitedly asking for more of your involvement	■ Listen to pain and opportunity points to their level of satisfaction ■ Seek best practices; reach out to mentor for modeling new behavior ■ Take a risk; apply effort in a new, creative way ■ Refine or improve skill in a high value manner ■ Actively provide and solicit positive and constructive feedback ■ Demonstrate genuine gratitude
Home	Deepen a key relationship in a meaningful manner	The significant other wants to spend more time with you	■ Start from a point of appreciating / affirming a specific aspect of them ■ Make more time to be 1-1 with them ■ Re-learn what is most important to them now and why ■ Be vulnerable; be willing to share a weakness ■ Help them out by regularly offering to do one of their unpleasant tasks ■ Check-in with them in the middle and end of the day ■ Inquire and acknowledge what makes the two of us special together ■ Carry or post a photo of them for looking at as interested
Health	Increase capacity to be more physically flexible	Able to attend a yoga class and be active the rest of the day without significant recovery needed	■ Regularly stretch a minimum of three times a week ■ Attend a yoga class twice a week ■ Warm up and cool down in an extended manner ■ Use 'Deliberate Practice Methods' in exercise regimen: ➤ *Increase intensity; mix type of exercises; solicit timely feedback* ■ Increase hydration and recovery periods as needed

Life's Domains	Experimental Goal	Success Criteria	Action Steps
Faith	Understand how someone of a different faith tradition finds value in life	The other individual invites you to participate in a special holiday meal, tradition or practice	▪ Reflect what and why you want to be fluent in another faith tradition ▪ Find someone willing to share their practices ▪ Go deep with understanding why their faith is important to them ▪ Suspend judgement; Explore how faith enriches their life ▪ Learn rituals apart of holiday tradition and its related significance ▪ Share an appreciation for the intent behind some aspect of their faith ▪ Research notable leaders in their faith that have made a difference
Community	Coach a youth athletic team for a season	The participants regularly attend practices (and games) along with a number of the parents; team members improve performance and enjoy being with each other	▪ Seek previous coach to learn past history and practices ▪ Review rules, challenges, operating conditions and responses ▪ Ask for help from a variety of sources ▪ Practice teaching and coaching methods (i.e.: 'Deliberate Practice') ▪ Stay physically fit; eat smart, exercise and rest ▪ Keep it fun ▪ Build relationships with parents, team, referee's, administrators ▪ Host extended team (i.e. family, parents, neighbors) celebrations

Presence: Engaging, Under-the-Skin Impact

"We convince by our presence."

Walt Whitman

"What you are speaks so loudly I cannot hear what you are saying"

Ralph Waldo Emerson

Featuring

Dolph Lundgren: Starred in over 40 Hollywood movie roles including Rocky 4's Ivan Drago

Tommaso Boddi/WireImage/Getty Images

Francois Durand/Stringer/Getty Images
Entertainment/Getty Images

Valerie Plame: Former covert CIA ops officer who focused on nuclear proliferation issues.

What is presence? Why does it matter?

It started like a regular meeting. Yet I could tell there was something special in visiting with David Gergen. We were at his Harvard Kennedy School Office where he is Professor of Public Service and Co-Director of the Center of Public Leadership. The night before I was watching Gergen on CNN, where he regularly serves as a political analyst.

He looked tired, but I got him at the end of the day, and I could only imagine what his travel schedule is like. I was not sure what town he was flying to next. He has a team that backs him up on many fronts: research, scheduling and logistics, communications, media. They are on call 24/7 trying to keep up with him. In spite of his schedule, Gergen was now sitting up close to me, in a small private room, looking deep and directly at me. It was as if I was the most important person in the world to him. This is a guy who was an advisor to four U.S. presidents. Now, 100 percent of his attention was on me. It was humbling and affirming all at once.

He asked me how the book was going? Where was I taking it? What was I learning? I thought ever so briefly I was the one being interviewed. But his questions were conversational, full of care and curiosity. He was being helpful before we could even start. He was already collaborating, connecting and cooperating and he had been with me for only a few minutes. I thought to myself, this is a man who gets under the skin. You can feel his presence. You can tell when he is in the room.

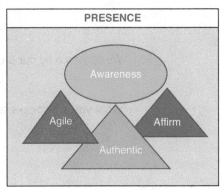

© Courtesy Mark Sullivan

David Gergen has presence. In a spirited, partisan debate of panelists on a talk show, it is Gergen who is the adult in the room. He is the one everybody listens to. Presence may sometimes be viewed as a sophomoric, light, inconsequential ingredient in dealing with challenging moments. Yet, time and again, the way one shows up can be the difference that makes a difference, as difficult times are being addressed.

Leveraging a Gestalt View: A Platform for Presence

Some of the theory related to presence can be found in the Gestalt school of psychology. In German, Gestalt means whole or completion. It is a systems approach to presenting self, focusing on our presence or self in context with the larger external environment. It aims experientially to bring the present and future into the moment. It is in the present, where we experience and live life, make choices, create memories, and so on. This is where we define one's presence as it unfolds in the moment as "me" and "not me." This is different than other schools of psychology that draws more heavily on the past.

Presence is about engaging, influencing and shaping our energy, in the moment, in hopefully a meaningful and memorable manner. It focuses on relational (i.e. people-to-people) boundaries or a way of embracing and working with self. One may say of another that they grabbed the attention of everyone in the room, or that they crossed the line on something. They are referring to the degrees one is on which side of an acceptable boundary line, as defined by a set of norms. Presence is about connecting with self and others in an everyday kind of way that enriches and energizes the relationship, where one is taken more seriously. In a challenging context where doubt or despair exists, presence can be the social accelerator that knits and mobilizes very different people together on issues and actions.

I used to train a lot of sales representatives in negotiating skills[1]. The better sales agents had presence. Ironically all the very successful negotiators I worked with were about ways to create

---

1 Between 1983-1986, I trained roughly 840 senior sales representatives and purchasing agents in negotiating skills at the United Airlines Executive Sales Institute, Chicago, IL and Tokyo, Japan.

a safe, non-threatening environment to build enough real trust to help both sides to drop their guard and function as genuine business partners. Most seasoned negotiators already knew many tips and tools to seek advantage or leverage perceived value. However, they were less about power, intimidation, manipulation or social control. The good negotiators were as interested in helping the other side to 'win' as well. They knew a good relationship was rarely one-sided. A sustainable, long-lasting deal would not come undone if it was shaped to have enough value that improved life for the customer on their terms and not simply on one's own terms.

These seasoned negotiators went into the 'conversation' (i.e. as opposed to calling it a negotiation') knowing that both sides would need to change their positions sometimes in challenging ways for themselves for the deal to stick. Early on, they would help the other side to learn that like themselves, they too would need to change and adapt as well if they were going to get something out of this jointly-crafted arrangement. The good negotiators were genuinely *authentic* in their efforts to connect with others. They were *agile* in adjusting or calibrating their engagement. Some negotiators were very *aware* that their customers were initially guarded or defensive. They needed to be agile enough to stop talking; slow down and start asking questions about their clients hopes and fears behind their formal opening positions. They needed to *affirm* or support their clients in a genuine way signaling they cared about their success. In so doing, these superior negotiators built a special relationship where they had presence and were present in their client's lives.

Below is a brief sample of a buy-sell dialogue that reflects early elements of *awareness*, *agility*, *affirmation*, and *authenticity* being incorporated into the natural give-and take of a commercial exchange.

(C/Client): Okay, so I hope you have something good for me on price and terms because no one has come close to what I need before I can even consider getting serious with any of you suppliers.

(ESR/Enlightened Sales Rep): It sounds like you have had a frustrating experience with us suppliers. What have you heard that was particularly annoying?

(C): The numbers of course have been extraordinarily high and the term sheet requires payment in 30 days in-spite of the volume where talking about here. Ridiculous!

(ESR): It sounds like you have some very clear boundaries of what's in and what's out; what's acceptable and what's not. Is that right? I'm also wondering what else is on your mind. Can you talk a little about what an understanding yet realistic product discussion would be about? One that recognizes you have to go back to your boss with a win...but also realistically realizes the supplier has to also go back to his boss with some kind of margin so that it's worth it to provide the kind of service and quality you deserve?

(C): You need to get in the X minus range for me to take you seriously.

(ESR): Can you say more about what is behind that number? What are the soft and hard ingredients that make up that range?

(C): We run a cost-driven shop here which is why numbers matter so much. Price and payment matters because of the degree of competition that has increased in the marketplace. So, for example, if we can get 60 days on the payment side of our invoices we can optimize our cash-flow which is real money to our balance sheet.

(ESR): That makes sense. Thank you for sharing that with me. It helps to better understand what matters to you and to your company.

(C): So…what can you do for me?

(ESR): It's hard for me to say this, but unfortunately, I can't go as low as the X minus range. However, I truly want to prove to you that you are important and worthy of our most extraordinary attention. We may be able to show some flexibility on the term side, something perhaps beyond 30 days, but, there needs to be some flexibility on price or I really can't fight for you with my boss. I would hate for that to happen. I really want to be in a position where I can prove to my company that you are worth it. I want to build a meaningful relationship that goes beyond the typical posturing at the front end of a sales discussion. Does that make sense?

What we know about our self or others is often telling. Someone may say they get anxious in having a difficult or challenging one-on-one conversation with someone. Presence in Gestalt is about paying attention in the moment to what we think, feel and do as our true self. It is about recognizing and honoring what is going on inside of ourselves while still simultaneously engaging and embracing others in our outside world, in an under-the-skin fashion. This integrating and differentiating of our ways of being and doing in the moment requires growing a 'third eye' to simultaneously being aware of 'us-inside' and 'us-outside.' This third eye is like a control tower at an airport mediating inbound and outbound traffic using the glide path (for dissenting traffic) and tarmac (for accelerating, accenting traffic) in an interdependent fashion. Becoming more present in an impactful manner requires practicing what we see for real and what is not seen but is present. As an outcome, *when you change the way you look at things, the things you look at change.*[2]

An executive once asked me why no one would ever ask him questions after his staff meetings after he realized his executive-peer had a great deal of interaction with employees after his staff meetings. When the first executive was told he scowled, raised his voice and pointed assertively at his team when he asked for questions, he was confused and not happy to receive the feedback. He didn't quite know what to do with it. I asked him in private to act out how he looked in staff meetings and would role play the employees. Then I did a role reversal and I played him and he, played his team. He was shocked to experience me as a strong, heavy-handed, finger-wagging boss, loud and in his-face. We did more role playing where he had a chance to soften his voice, experiment with a smile, welcoming hand gestures and a chance to show deference and respect. He tried out this new engagement approach with his team when asking for feedback and was amazed at the favorable response. He proudly declared later to me that he was late for our meeting after his staff met because there was so much discussion.

Awareness of self helps us to embrace our in-the-moment knowing and not-knowing of self. How quiet or loud in volume we are, how animated or stiff our bodies are, how conceptual or concrete are minds are. Our capacity to be aware and enrich our ways of engaging, as observed by many notable high achievers in this book, was further articulated through their agility, and flexibility, emotionally, intellectually or socially; and affirming or genuinely appreciating oneself in the moment. Interestingly, the executive who was working on his engagement style with his team

---

2 This reference has been noted in a variety of ways in contemporary times by the former American Psychologist Wayne Dyer (1986) and by others dating back to the ancients in both Greek and Roman times.

started to adjust as we talked about what goodness lies in his heart, and in what he truly wants for his employees. As he could genuinely affirm and support a new image of himself and of his employees, on both a feeling and thinking level, he was able to be more aware, affirming and agile, in his engagement practices.

Affirmation, like agility and awareness, is interdependent and supports efforts in being authentic. In Gestalt, authentic change in how we present ourselves occurs more from being who we are than from trying to be who we are not. It is an honest, appreciative stance of our self without ignoring elements that are not in service of our better selves. This whole-hearted appreciation of self and self-with-other, is not an arrogant, cocky view, but a humble realistic awareness of the big and small ways we bring gifts and grit to our challenges in high-demand environments.

This brings us to an extraordinary story of a bright, talented MIT Fulbright scholar and Hollywood movie star featured in over 40 films. However, he had a rough start in life. Through a series of courageous acts, he became more aware, agile, affirming and authentic—transforming his life and the relationships around him.

Dolph Lundgren Interview: Presence through vulnerability

Dolph Lundgren is an imposing physical presence. A towering, white-blonde Swede, Lundgren played the menacing Soviet superstar opponent of fictional Rocky Balboa on screen in *Rocky IV*. Lundgren has built his buff body with martial arts, but he also cultivated and nurtured his presence with therapy and meditation.

As a child, Lundgen suffered physical abuse from his father. To retaliate Lundgren refused to cry or show that he was in pain. "I don't know if I developed toughness through the beatings because I couldn't go anywhere or if I already had it. I guess I had some of it prior to that."

In his late teens Lundgren met a British Karate instructor who became a mentor and introduced him to life in the dojo, a training space for martial arts students. "I learned a lot from him about being a man, being humble, being respectful, and being tough in the dojo and having good manners outside of the dojo."

Lundgren said he worked hard and went on be Karate champion in Sweden, Europe and Australia. He decided to move to the United States and studied at the Massachusetts Institute of Technology in Boston. Then, by chance, he met another mentor, Sylvester Stallone who picked Lundgren from cattle call to play Soviet boxer Ivan Drago, launching an accidental career in Hollywood.

Although Lundgren was successful in work, he faced problems at home. After 18 years of marriage, Lundgren and his wife divorced, and she moved to Spain with their two daughters. "I was going through a lot of escape behavior; drinking, having extramarital affairs, and basically not being a good husband. My kids were suffering from it, too, and that was the hardest thing, when I had to talk to my wife and kids about it."

Lundgren had hit a low point until a woman he knew suggested he try psychotherapy. He told her "'Are you kidding me? Why would I go to that? It's for weaklings.' She suggested meditation and I thought that was a bit mumbo-jumboish, but it turned out that I tried both and they sort of changed my life."

Psychotherapy helped Lundgren move on from his violent past. He learned that for him drinking, taking drugs and other damaging behaviors are a way to escape emotional pain. In therapy he managed to revisit his past. Gradually the abuse he had suffered lost its grip on him. Lundgren realized that inside he was still a frightened boy fearful of dying in a beating. He needed to step up, embrace that boy, and take care of him. He began to drop his air of invincibility and his need to be perfect to convince his father that he had been wrong in telling Lundgren that he was worthless.

Lundgren, an actor known for his portrayal of a tough, violent fighter, became vulnerable. Each day he practices Southeast Asian Vipassana meditation. "Usually I start with the love and kindness meditation where basically you forgive everybody that you've hurt or has hurt you. For me, I do it every day and it's like 'Who did I hurt yesterday? Was it that guy in traffic that I was mean to? Was it someone I didn't sign an autograph for? Was it my girlfriend? Or that I didn't call my daughter and ask for her forgiveness?' I just ask it to myself. Then I forgive myself for things I've done to myself. I also forgive people for having hurt me. It could be in business or personal things. Then, I kind of just wish love and kindness on everybody."

Lundgren has risen to great heights. Yet it was in life's struggle, his pain as eventually experienced and appreciated from deep within his soul, that reintroduced him to a new beginning and a new life. It takes work to be more present with our true self while simultaneously expressing it in presence with self and other. And so was the case with Lundgren and of course with the rest of us. Being vulnerable enough to see who we really are, and how we show up, or present ourselves, often takes courage. This courage to recognize and face the elements is most poignantly portrayed in *The Princess Bride* as Westly declared to Buttercup in the midst of the danger and dark odds of the bewitched forest, "The only way out is through."[3]

As with Lundgren's journey of discovery and transformation, there are five Gestalt layers of engagement which move closer and closer to actualization. This process of deepening awareness is referred as peeling the onion[4], and was first developed by Bud Feder[5] (1982) and Jorge Rosner[6] (1990). As mentioned earlier, presence is about an under the skin connection with others. It is also about our own awareness of what we are experiencing in the moment. Each layer has value and can function in an everyday manner.

Feder and Rosner essentially describe it this way:

1. **Cliche Layer**: Reacting to others in stereotypical and sometimes inauthentic ways; involves interacting with others in a patterned, mechanical fashion. (*Example: A brief hallway or elevator engagement. Small talk. It can also be for a longer period where for example one is being nice to others to get something from them.*)
2. **Role Layer**: Hides behind a policy position of powerlessness, or protective mask (i.e. "Don't ask me, I don't make the decisions around here."), as it provides safety and security in the midst of potential conflict. Avoids or denies emotional pain. This serves to protect us from facing a truth that may be too painful to embrace at the time. In some ways it is a kind of social armor. Readiness is critical. (*Example: Denying or not admitting that an important*

---

3   The phrase "the only way out is through" was originally made famous by Gestalt pioneer Fitz Perls as he described a way of engaging how we are to experience the moment.

4   'Peeling the Onion' refers to how we embrace the moment from a broader experiential scope (i.e. cliché, role and phobic perspective or layer to a deeper more inner (personal or core) layer.

5   Feder, Bud. (1982). *Peeling the Onion: A Gestalt Therapy Manual for Clients.* Bud Feder & Ruth Ronall Publisher.

6   Rosner, Jorge. (1990). *Peeling the Onion: Gestalt Theory and Methodology.* Toronto: Gestalt Institute of Toronto. More in-depth information from a coaching or counseling perspective can be found in the following publication: Zinker, J. (1991). Creative process in Gestalt therapy: The therapist as artist. *The Gestalt Journal, 14(2),* 71-88. Also, one may go to the Gestalt web-site at: http://www.gestalt.org

relationship with someone has changed or ended.)

3. **Phobic Layer**: Person feels stuck and afraid of being viewed in a particular manner. They come face-to-face with their fears in some direct or indirect fashion and becomes paralyzed by such fear. (Example: *One has a major difference with their boss, or a key customer, but yet is fearful of addressing it for what it is—and therefore not willing to do anything about it.*)

4. **Personal Layer**: Aware of one's real self, feelings and experiences

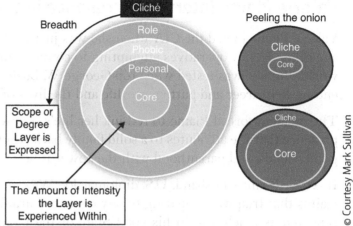

including areas of being frozen or paralyzed. This is a point of emerging self-discovery at a deeper level. (Example: *Awakening to a richer more real and robust view of self but still defers from telling the boss as to what is really going on till another time.*)

5. **Core Layer**: Where the person is more authentic and real; without pretense, experiences feelings fully. (Example: *Publicly willing to share a vulnerable moment that will provide a deeper connection of trust and intimacy.*)

When we are not connecting with others it is helpful to reflect on what level of engagement we are at. The earlier levels (i.e. Cliché level; Phobic Layer or Role level) reflect an interest in being safe or finding protection or security. If someone is not opening up to you, as you are interested in, then it may be useful to not only focus on what they are doing but also on what you are doing or are not doing on your end. So, for example, I have found when a group or team is holding back from candidly sharing what is going on, I will often do any combination of the following to create what may be a need for more of a safe (i.e. less threatening) environment:

- Shift to asking the team to review what successes or progress they have made recently, and how that happened?
- Ask what challenges they see ahead and what ways they think they will be able to support each other in being successful?
- Share selectively a challenge and/or failure I (you) have had in the same area and what I learned from it.
- Ask them to aspirationally dream what a perfect solution or path would look like if there were no constraints?
- Probe deeply, but gently, in what can the team do different that is difficult but necessary. Then what can you individually do that is difficult but helpful. What resources or support would you need to sustain any new behavior in-spite of the challenge?

Later levels of engagement (i.e. Personal or Core levels) reflect more confidence and readiness to face reality as is – within self and between others. The focus is more on acknowledging the opportunity area for change and supporting the exploration around different options, risks and ways forward in a concrete, actionable, appreciative manner.

These layers of awareness are often critical as we are confronted with life's challenges when answers are neither clear nor immediately forthcoming. With that in mind, the other story in this chapter is of a talented, dynamic, former government field operative betrayed by a peer government official. What is she to do? How does she make sense of a world turned upside down? How does she rebuild her future?

Valerie Plame Interview: Presence in the midst of betrayal

Valerie Plame joined the CIA when she was just 21. She worked undercover and went on to manage other agency operatives attempting to contain nuclear proliferation in rogue states around the world. But she was tested when top George W. Bush Administration officials outed her, effectively ending her career and putting her life and the lives of her husband and two small children at risk.

The incident forced Plame to rethink her life's course. She was able to move forward with strong presence that she attributes to a solid family background, mentors, nature walks, a wide network of good friends, and parenthood with the power it brings to fiercely protect innocent young.

In 2002, Plame's husband, U.S. diplomat Joe Wilson, was sent by the CIA to Niger to investigate claims that Iraq was preparing to buy enhanced uranium from the country. He found nothing and reported as much. But in his 2003 State of the Union Address Pres. George W. Bush said that Saddam Hussein "recently sought significant quantities of uranium from Africa." Wilson rebutted the President's statement with an opinion article in *The New York Times*, titled *What I Didn't Find in Africa.*

One week later, Robert Novak, a conservative columnist at *The Washington Post*, with information supplied by Bush officials, fired back and outed Plame as a CIA operative. Plame's career was over. Worse, her family was now in jeopardy. "How do you navigate that?" asked Plame. "Sometimes all you can do is put one foot in front of the other and having little kids makes you do that. You have to check your impulses and be selfless sometimes which is what parenthood is all about."

She asked the agency for additional security but was denied. "I was a little bit in shock at trying to navigate this, but I wish I had been more assertive and less of a good girl. That just comes with time and maturity. I just wish I had been more assertive than let the chips fall as they may. I didn't want to in any way jeopardize the people I worked with. I was really concerned about them," said Plame.

She officially resigned from the CIA in 2005, and Plame and Wilson moved their family from Washington, D.C. to Santa Fe, New Mexico. She had a strong network of friends from college and soon fell in with a supportive and empowering group of women that she said is essential to her well-being. "The list of strong smart women in Santa Fe is just unbelievable. Maybe, I didn't know that moving here, but I found it out right away. It is crucial," she said.

Plame also said she has a need for quiet privacy, as well. "For me now, it's very important that I am in nature and that could just mean walking my dog on a leafy street. You don't have to be camping in the wilderness, but just being outside and being alone—I'm a very gregarious person, but I also have deep needs for solitude to collect myself."

Plame was tested again in the past year, with the death of her mother and separation from Wilson. "This time I learned the importance of taking care of yourself physically and spiritually. I didn't know that the first go-round and I tried to gut it out. It's really crucial," she said. "When kids or other people are depending on you, you have to take care of yourself. It's easier said than done. For myself, I felt very responsible and that can be really self-defeating."

Plame is now an author and has become engaged in the community, serving on the board of the United Way of Santa Fe County and volunteering with her children at shelters. She said public service was important in her family when she was growing up. Giving to others, she said, is good for her. "How many times are you walking on the sidewalk feeling sorry for yourself and you see some person in a wheelchair or something and you go, 'Right, I'm not in a wheel-chair.' It's more valuable for you than whatever service you give, whether you're working in the soup kitchen or in a board meeting. I get way more out of it than what I ever give. It helps anyone feel connected and that of course, is a critical component of one of the things you have to do in living in this world."

Service, she said, can be spiritual. "The fact is, you feel connected to something larger than yourself. That is what religion and community do for you. All of a sudden, you're not at the center of the universe for at least a few moments." She said a rabbi recently described an exercise that resonated with Plame. "'Write your own eulogy,'" Plame said he told her. "'Write one as if you died today and write one as if you died in thirty years. What do you want that to say about you in your short time here?"

Perspective: Growing Awareness to Be More Present

In both stories, there was much to celebrate as these individuals showcased a broad range of agility, affirmation and authenticity in their own personal leadership within demanding environments. Perhaps though, what was foundational was their growing capacity to leverage awareness. Awareness leads to being able to make choices and then to take on responsibility. Awareness, choice and responsibility go hand-in-hand as we seek to grow and have more impact and influence in our world. Our capacity to shape a powerful presence is central to what we do with our efforts to be aware and attentive to the feedback we give and get.

Below is a popular awareness model referred to as the *Johari Window*[7]. It was created by Joseph Luft and Harry Ingham (1955) based on two factors: (1) What we know about ourselves and (2) What others know about us. This model is divided into four quadrants or windows and convey a certain level of understanding about ourselves. These windows include the following:

Window #1: Open or Free Area

Anything you know about yourself and are willing to share is part of the open area. Individuals can build trust between themselves by disclosing information to others and learning about others from the information they in turn disclose about themselves.

Window #2: Blind Area

Anything that you do not know about yourself but others with in your group or team have become aware of, is in your blind area. With the help of feedback from others you can become aware of some of your traits or characteristics as perceived by others and overcome some of the personal issues that may be inhibiting your efforts and dynamics with in your group.

Window #3: Hidden Area

There are also aspects of yourself that you are aware of but might not want others to know. This window is referred to as the hidden area.

Window #4: Unknown Area

This area is unknown to you and others. This is referred as the unknown area.

---

7 Luft, J.; Ingham, H. (1955). "The Johari Window, A Graphic Model of Interpersonal Awareness." *Proceedings of the Western Training Laboratory in Group Development*. Los Angeles: University of California, Los Angeles.

The size of each of the four windows can change. You might want to tell someone about an aspect of your life you had previously kept hidden. For example, maybe you are not comfortable contributing ideas in large groups. This would increase your open area and decrease your hidden area.

It is also possible to increase your open area by asking for feedback from people. When feedback is given honestly it can reduce the size of your blind area. For example, maybe you interrupt people before they have finished making their point. Sometimes you don't realize these aspects of your character until they are pointed out. By working with others, it is possible for you to discover aspects that neither of you may have appreciated before.

Below is an exercise you may consider that can further enrich your awareness in pursuit of cultivating more insights and information of a more intimately known and appreciated you. Remember presence starts with Plato's age old dictum, "Know Thy Self."

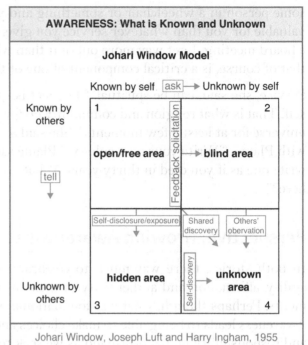

Johari Window, Joseph Luft and Harry Ingham, 1955

© Courtesy Mark Sullivan

Johari Window Awareness Exercise

Step One: Window #1 *(Known by Self and Known by Others)*

Start with the 'Open Area.' Make some notes about yourself.

- ◼ What are your strengths?
- ◼ What are some developmental areas?
- ◼ What are you comfortable with and willing to share with others?
- ◼ Try to be honest and clear about what you know about yourself already.

Step Two: Window #2 *(Unknown by Self and Known by Others)*

The 'Blind Area:' Involve other people and ask for feedback about yourself. Be prepared to seriously consider. information you have heard about yourself from before, even though it may be somewhat threatening.

- ◼ Take a breath. Pause. Reflect. Suspend judgement. Repeat what you heard.
- ◼ Thank them for making the effort to share feedback for you.
- ◼ Remember that giving feedback is a skill and that some individuals may be better at it then others.
- ◼ When receiving feedback, be curious. Ask why this is important from their standpoint. Ask if there are different ways that this shows up?
- ◼ Ask what you can say and do differently. Repeat back to their level of satisfaction.

Step Three: Window #3 *(Known by Self and Unknown by Others)*

Embracing the 'Hidden' area. Make some notes about yourself.

- Build safety. Describe why others are important to you or to a cause or effort.
- Select a weakness or deficit you can self-disclose to help others to know you better.
- Share context and rationale for why this has been less than public information.
- Describe what they are to do with this information; and/or how they are to support you given this revelation.

Example:

Business Team: I want you to know that while there are many things I am good at, numbers are not one of them. While I can do basic balance sheet math, I am soft on more advance mathematics for calculating analytics or statistical ratios. Therefore, I will need you to really bring your quantitative expertise when we do higher order financial analysis. In fact, at certain points, I will be looking to see if some of you can selectively tutor me on some specific valuation scenarios.

PRESENCE AWARENESS INDEX

Rank yourself on a one-to-five scale (i.e. 1 = *Least Like Me*; 5 = *Most Like Me*), being as truthful as possible in responding to what is the real you. Do not overthink the statements. Move quickly, answering if possible at an intuitive, or gut level.

		1 Least Like Me	2 Infrequently Like Me	3 Occasionally Like Me	4 Frequently Like Me	5 Most Like Me
1.	I get people's attention by sometimes telling a really good story, joke or recent event that is captivating or compelling.					
2.	I am often invited into conversations with people intentionally seeking my participation.					
3.	I am curious about new or different ideas, positions, practices or trends that are not part of our current accepted operating context.					

(continued)

(*continued*)

		1 Least Like Me	2 Infrequently Like Me	3 Occasionally Like Me	4 Frequently Like Me	5 Most Like Me
4.	I can intentionally be playful or expressive in the moment to further energize individuals around a given topic.					
5.	I am aware of a range of differences within and between people in a group I am addressing.					
6.	I am comfortable in sharing feelings that provide a more personal connection.					
7.	I can suspend judgment (i.e. bracket off my opinions) when I deeply listen to differences.					
8.	I will naturally adjust how I (socially, physically, emotionally, or intellectually) engage with a group, if need be.					
9.	I am told that sometimes my body language (non-verbal behavior) can be animated.					
10.	I sometimes share things about me that are somewhat personal.					
	Sub-Total Score					
	Net-Total Score	**Add all above Sub-Total scores together to get your Net Score:**				

Source: Dr. Mark J. Sullivan, Ph.D., 2018

<u>Score Interpretation:</u>

40-50 = Prominent Presence:
Capacity to connect with others in an intentional and personal manner in a variety of ways on a regular basis.

30-39 = Felt Presence:
Can reach out to and engage others when it matters.

0-29 = Intermittent Presence:
Shows up with presence in a less-than-frequent manner.

Chapter 4

Five Ways of THRIVING In High-Demand, High-Challenge Environments

Five Personal Leadership Styles: Transformational Stages of Capacity

Making the Best of Where We Are At; and Exploring a Line of Sight For Growth and Opportunity

"Many men go fishing all their lives without knowing that it is not fish they are after."

Henry David Thoreau

"Knowing is not enough; we must apply. Willing is not enough; we must do."

Johann Wolfgang von Goethe

"Knowing others is wisdom, knowing yourself is enlightenment."

Lao Tzu

Featuring

Mr. Jim Tressel: 10th President of Youngstown State University and 22nd Head Coach of The Ohio State University Football Team

Icon Sports Wire/Getty Images

Photo © Kerry Boyle

Mr. Cameron Mitchell: Founder and CEO – *Cameron Mitchell Restaurants* (CMR), 32 restaurants under 13 different concepts, within 12 states. The company also oversees the Rusty Bucket Restaurant and Tavern, which operates in 23 locations in six different states

We Approach Challenges Differently At Different Times.
We Often Embrace the Same Demands
Differently in High School, College, Early Career,
Mid-Career, and Later in Life.

❖ Doing more of the same, or in just in a different way, does not always address the underlying dynamics of tough times.

❖ It often requires deeper insights in how to look big picture at our self in the world, while also looking at near term concrete choices, emotional costs, tools and trade-offs.

© Courtesy Mark Sullivan

Figure 4.1: The Case for expanding maturity and capacity as we age.

The Story of United Airlines Flight #232: Tragedy and Triumph In the Sky and On the Ground

"Know thy Self," is a big calling. Most of us lead busy, high-density lives. We are looking to get things done with minimal drama and maximum payback for our efforts. We realize the currency we use, time and talent, does not always get us to where we would like to end up. Sometimes, life is not fair. Life is hard. Life can require going uphill, time and again.

We can incur high emotional costs on a given challenge and still end up less-than-satisfied with a certain part of our life, the impact or outcomes. The way we engage tough times, is often very telling of who we are and where we are in our life. Sometimes what leads us into a difficult space can unwittingly be of our own making. It is easy to describe our crucibles as something cooked up outside of ourselves and then claim to be helpless victims. This face-saving dynamic is like a sweet tart that tastes good going down but is full of empty calories. Truth can be so inconvenient.

Sitting with truths about ourselves can offer an awakening to new insights about our internal capacity, or how we think and feel about things, and our capabilities which are the ways we function and perform. Such truths can affirm our strengths and gifts, as much as signal developmental opportunities to expand capacity and capability. This matters for most of us. The individuals

I respect and admire most have not simply been through the heat of the fire but have significantly invested in the shape and form of themselves during and after the heat; like shaping molten ore into the more functional form of steel when it is soft and pliable.

The stance we take toward life is consequential. We can view growth and development as an inconvenient, one-and-done affair. An episodic look at the give-and-take of challenges. Or conversely, as an on-going trek of life-long learning. The latter positions us to leverage our curiosity, and a reflective, active stance to adapt and mediate for deeper and broader ways of engaging and learning. This can happen as often at the end of life as in early life. My 95-year-old mother in her retirement home, a nurse through-and-through, still read the Physician's Desk Reference (PDR) on her bedside table, as nightly reading, "for fun" in spite of its very dense scientific prose. Curiosity was her friend. Conversation was her playground for trying out ideas and actions. Life's trek is full of hidden surprises and secrets of new possibilities, even in little ways, if we are open to it.

In so doing we often need fuel and food for the journey. Humans need capacity to foster knowing, doing and staying power. There will be a closer look at what this means in this chapter. This will include viewing how we make sense of things from two combined continuums or perspectives. Specifically, this includes: *Life-Valuing Orientation* and *Knowing Orientation*. This way of *knowing* and *valuing* is embedded in any and all of the five *Personal Leadership Styles* (i.e. *Protector, Problem Solver, Optimizer, Creative Strategist* and *Globalist*) that will also be reviewed at a high level in this chapter.

The five Personal Leadership Styles have a *knowing* and *valuing* continuum embedded in each of the leadership styles. These personal leadership styles actually reflect developmental stages of capacity – early-to-later stages. Each stage (or alternatively, *style* as in personal leadership style) builds on the preceding stages or styles of personal leadership. The later stages (i.e. Optimizer, *Creative Strategist* and *Globalist*), provide more emotional and social fluency in which to address challenges—easier said than done. However, each stage, including the early stages can be powerful and represent individuals that have a great deal of success and satisfaction based on how they leverage their personal capacity. In fact, a mature early stage personal leadership style (e.g. *Protector Style*) may have more satisfaction with less capacity than other stages (or styles) due to their sage use of what they do have and use. More on this later. Overall, obviously none of us is perfect regardless of where we are on the continuum; nor do we get a pass on all things that shouldn't come our way. We aren't born always knowing what we should do as live unfolds.

Over and through time, a range of experiences deepen our insights and actions to potentially provide a more mature response to life. In-spite of this, none of us have figured it all out, even if our more recent times have been relatively stable and sound. Some of us learn more than others based on how we reflect and act from varied experiences[1] (Sullivan and Kolb, 1995). We use our head, heart and spirit to address the world around us. Each of us does this differently[2]. This is particularly exemplified in the following airline story of United Airlines Flight #232. It poignantly highlights

---

1 Sullivan, Mark & Kolb, David (1995). *Do it…and Understand: The Bottom Line on Corporate Experiential Learning: Turning Experience Into Learning.* Concord, NH: Kendall-Hunt Publishers.

2 In Chapter 4: A description of a two factor continuum is detailed that further illuminate's differences in our meaning making (Knowing and Valuing) out of our lived context. One continuum is based on levels of concrete-to-conceptual orientation. The other orientation is focused on a value continuum of self: me-we or we-us.

how the same tragedy was perceived and experienced by the airline recovery team and survivors in significantly different ways. This story further introduces a stage model of functioning as personal leaders of self in our own high-challenge ecosystem.

Tragedy Defining Character and Capacity in Different Ways: Flight #232

I remember working for United Airlines when UA flight #232 from Denver-to-Philadelphia crash landed in the cornfields of Sioux, City Iowa on July 19, 1989[3]. The DC-10, developed an "in-flight mechanical" at 30,000 feet in the air. Never before had all three hydraulic systems controlling the direction, altitude and pitch of a commercial jet been simultaneously compromised. With the loss of hydraulics, the crew was unable to control air speed or the subsequent sink rate of the aircraft. The yoke, or steering wheel, would soon be rendered useless. The throttle was in questionable form; the fluid levers jammed; ailerons and spoilers disabled, landing gear inoperable, and two of three engines were blown out. The instrument panel was lit up with multiple flashing red and amber lights. This flight would never make it to its intended destination. Sadly, 111 of 296 passengers and crew on board would die.

With little-to-no control, the plane's wings clipped, lunged toward the tarmac sideways, at 245mph – 100 mph faster than normal. Gyrating side-to-side, with two belly flops and a rollover, the main fuselage and cockpit ripped apart in multiple sections while traversing 200 square feet of cornfield adjacent to the landing strip at Sioux City Airport. Smoke, fire, oil and metal scraps blanketed the area.

United immediately went on "red alert" and company officials were busy assembling key personnel. At the time, I was only one of fifteen members belonging to the UAL / United Airlines Situation Team, known euphemistically by some internally as the "Crash Cadets." As a group, only seven others and myself, had previously worked together through United's only other crash during a 10-year period. Up until then, United had been touted as having one of the safest and most reliable fleets in the industry. In some ways, we had the good fortune of not knowing each other that well. We had been previously dispatched only for a brief time in what turned out to be a relatively smaller incident with much less complexity and intensity.

Now things were radically different. We were about to live and work together as the Sit-Team managing the nerve center for the recovery, day-and-night, non-stop for six weeks. Our assembled team would work the first 96 hours without relief. There was unrelenting, external pressures from reporters demanding a story under deadline; outside lawyers pitching their services; corporate executives seeking constant updates; families demanding the status of their loved ones; crash site recovery personnel, hospital and coroner officials needing to trade much needed timely information between us on everything from baggage remains, human effects, and treatment protocols to death certificates.

We were about to discover who we really were and how different we were individually and collectively, from the inside-out. As physicians, psychologists, pilots, emergency specialists, gate agents, lawyers, insurance agents we were clearly a very mixed group of professionals. Actions

---

3 Details of UA Flight 232 can be reviewed extensively by multiple internet sites including: *Flight 232 Wikipedia.org, The Crash of United Flight 232 – Popular Mechanics, Plane Crash Sioux City, Iowa – Unite Airlines Flight 232:* YouTube

would be at a premium – particularly meaningful and coherent ones. Ideally, we needed to be able to talk to each other and understand our differing professional languages, assumptions and perceptions. We would need to be able to work with each other in crisis mode. Would we have the maturity, the presence of mind and heart to appreciate our unspoken and in-your-face demands? What could we tolerate? How is it we could draw conclusions on the same data in such different ways? What kind of temperament would work day-in-and-day-out? How would we take care of ourselves and each other in the enduring press of conflicting data, fraught emotion, mixed levels of expertise, and differing ways of engaging and dealing with stress, uncertainty, and relationships between grieving families, survivors, press and team members.

Six of us were hand-picked and temporarily dispatched to family-relations duty. This meant we had to quickly fly around the country to personally visit each family affected by their loved ones, who did not survive the crash - all 111 of them. Telling family, face-to-face they lost a brother, mother, infant, dad, sister, or in some cases, multiple family members, was gut-wrenching. It went on for days. The media watched as we went up too many front porches to personally deliver both the tragic news, and occasionally remaining luggage and effects from the crash-site.

It became clear that this was more than just being in the people business. We were wrestling with hearts and souls. At a fundamental level we needed to connect with others, understand their pain and in some small, humble way recognize that everyone's mental and emotional way of functioning were all so different, yet at a base level, universal.

There I was, in one such case, on the front porch of a Northern New Jersey household – one of many that had lost a family member. Behind me, several feet back, was a United security escort. He was a very big man with broad shoulders. He had undoubtedly been in a weight room more than a few times. His job was to discretely offer me protection in the unlikely situation that it was needed.

Upon knocking on the door, a man came out to the porch. Surprisingly, he was huge. Truly, the largest man I ever met. It shook me a bit. My six foot structure barely reached up to his massive chest cavity. I was a mere midget in the shadow of this bodybuilder (I learned of his profession much later after spending hours with him and his relatives at their family wake). I had already visited with six families that day and was exhausted. After quietly, solemnly telling him he had lost his brother on the flight, he looked at me, straight-in, eye-ball-to-eye ball. There was something in there for both of us to read—fear, grief, sadness, pain. Upon hearing the news, he leaned in on me, extending his bulky arms at which point my now seemingly smaller escort quickly stepped up beside me. The bodybuilder could crush me in a heartbeat. For an instant, I stiffened thinking this was it for me. Then he closed in – giving me the biggest bear hug ever, almost suffocating me. Then, as if his body went limp, he fell to his knees holding my legs shaking. Shaking uncontrollably he thanked me incessantly for the news he was so desperately seeking. To an outsider, his words may appear to betray his grief. He was in a state of shock. I was a mere momentary safe-haven for his soul and spirit to cling to.

Clearly each family drew on the early themes described in the preceding chapters: *purpose, passion and presence.* The struggle to make sense out of their new and tragic lives often involved revisiting their life's purpose; drew on sources of energy (passion); and often found themselves, connecting in an under-the-skin fashion in new and different ways as they tried to get through their days (presence). Some of this was intentional. Most of it was not.

Moments of awareness of what now really mattered not only shaped the evolving nature of a potentially new purpose, but such a path of pain and insight often re-calibrated their authentic self. One survivor told me and others later that something happened to him when he climbed out of the burning, gaseous, smoke-filled, crippled plane - capturing a glimpse of the cornfield crash-site, draped in Iowa summer sun and blue skies. It was surreal. But then the moment was punctuated upon hearing the god-awful screams of a mother in the cornfield shouting, she had lost her baby in the plane. One glimpse of her in agony, instinctively without thinking, caused him to sprint it back into the dark, death-trap, hole of terror—the remaining mid-section of the plane. Somehow, while crawling through the smoke, twisted scraps of metal, burning flesh and live dangling wires, he miraculously heard the screams of a crying baby in the pitch dark. Without being able to see more than inches in front of himself, his lunge forward paid off. He scooped up and carried the infant to safety under terrifying combat-like conditions.

Some said it was truly a courageous act of selflessness. I couldn't agree more. Later, I understand he was to say he did it as much for him as for the screaming mother. He said he could never live with himself otherwise. This courageous act of care was said to inspire so many of his fellow survivors to re-dedicate their lives to something larger than what was lost by some in the flailing fog of life - the busyness of treadmill schedules and rituals. I wonder how much he was aware of how his purposeful act influenced a community of survivors and their family, and employees at United, to be something bigger in their everyday life. Clearly, his presence influenced the purpose and passion of many from all walks of life.

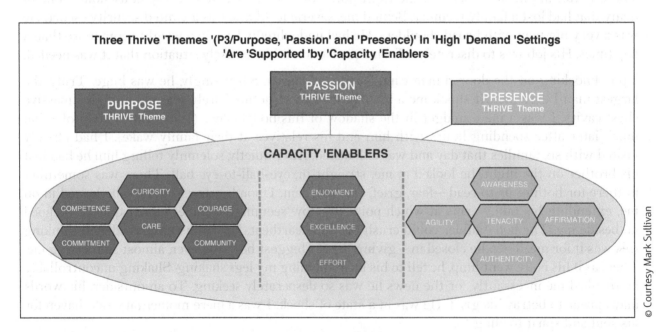

© Courtesy Mark Sullivan

Figure 4.2: *Purpose, Passion* and *Presence* are THRIVE themes that help individuals to address challenge in high demand environments. These three THRIVE themes have embedded ingredients or "*Capacity Enablers*" that support ways to THRIVE. The 14 Capacity Enablers embedded in Purpose, Passion and Presence show up differently within each of the 5 *Personal Leadership Styles* (i.e. Protector, Problem Solver, Optimizer, Creative Strategist and Globalist).

How much are we aware of others watching us? Of others being influenced by our presence in big and small ways. Research suggests we only use about 10% of our potential[4]. Can you imagine what our lives can be like if it was a bigger number?

As mentioned earlier, the capacity enablers (see figure 4.2) below suggest ways we can further seek to leverage our purpose, passion and presence in addressing big challenges. The notable high-achievers featured in this book and accompanying website used these enablers very differently to thrive in sustainable fashion. Helen Neville, three-time cancer survivor and grandmother, turned cross-country marathoner, re-fashioned her life's purpose for struggling fellow cancer patients. She used capacity enablers such as athletic *competence, care, community* and the *courage* to reach out to those in need in hospitals across America, literally by running to them, without money or places to stay. Jeni Britton Bauer, founder of Jeni's Splendid Ice Cream, brought passion to confront competition and a major business disruption in her up-scale premium ice cream shops across America. Her commitment to *excellence* and *effort*, went far beyond FDA government standards and helped her solve an almost intractable problem, surprising doubters who gave her business little chance of coming back. Or to Dolph Lundgren, one of Hollywood's favorite tough guy action thriller movie actors who brought the presence of tenderness and spirit to those close to him needing love and kindness. His emerging *awareness* and *affirmation* of a better self, showed and shared a softer side of him where forgiveness and redemption was possible.

Personal Leadership: Stages of Capacity Based On Experience

These capacity enablers are not free-standing elements on their own. They connect to something larger; to a way of making sense of the world and to a way of living in the world. These capacity enablers connect to what I am calling Personal Leadership Styles[5], as defined by a means to shape and influence behavior based on stages of adult maturation - of valuing and knowing[6]. This connection that ties our capacity enablers to our interior adult stages of maturation or Personality Leadership Styles is based on what we *see, sense, feel* and *do*. This dynamic interaction of elements between what we are experiencing in our interior and exterior world is described in the Gestalt literature as being in the 'here and now.'

What we *see, sense, feel* and *do* can happen in milliseconds. And in no particular order. In trauma, such as a plane crash landing, passengers have very different experiences. Some may emotionally freeze and only be full of what they *see*. Or they may be full of *doing* energy even while belted in, bent over with head between legs. They also may rock back and forth uncontrollably, another form of *doing*.

---

4 Robynne Boyd, February 7, 2008. *Do People Only Use 10 Percent of Their Brains?* Scientific American. Note multiple sources suggest optimal potential to be between 10-20%, based on varied conditions, with no one specific amount agreed by all scientists.

5 There are many sources on personal leadership but one that provides a broad overview of the topic includes the following source: Christopher P. Neck, Charles C. Manz, and Jeffery D. Houghton. (2017). *Self-Leadership: The Definitive Guide to Personal Excellence.* Thousand Oaks, CA: Sage Publications.

6 Personal leadership is often described more in a behavioral or clinical terms. Here, with an adult developmental continuum being used, the THRIVE personal leadership model features more of a developmental psychological approach. An example of a developmental leadership approach can be found with the following source: David Rooke and William R. Torbert. (2005). *Seven Transformations of Leadership.* Cambridge, MA: Harvard Business Publication.

In a less stressful, more routine kind of demand, where, for example, one is uncharacteristically required to make a big formal presentation to a challenging group, sensing energy may kick in.

While one may go through all four elements even in a somewhat linear fashion, from seeing, to sensing, to feeling, to doing, one may experience the four elements in a more emphatic manner. For example, a novice communicator takes a quick look at the huge audience in the hotel ballroom before their speech. That would be seeing. They may then start to sweat as they tell themselves "this is a problem," *sensing* trouble. Then they might *feel* nervous and begin to stiffen or pace in a *doing action*. In this case, the speaker may be spending an undo amount of time and effort sensing in an unconstructive manner with the other three elements quickly confirming what they are experiencing.

This is where awareness and agility are critical mediators for a constructive, supportive intervention. Recognizing in the above example that sensing is signaling destructive messages one can reshape both the image and message. The awareness and agility to recognize such an intervention can be developed through practicing *guided imagery, Neural Linguistic Programming (NLP)*, or *meditation*. One can concretely reconfigure thought structure or affective experience in a more positive and productive manner. My work coaching executives and leadership teams often involves helping individuals practice spotting and substituting ways of re-framing a challenging engagement into a more constructive, productive experience. This often requires shuttling what you see, sense, feel and do both with the content and with the underlying intentions. This can require focused, deliberate practice.[7]

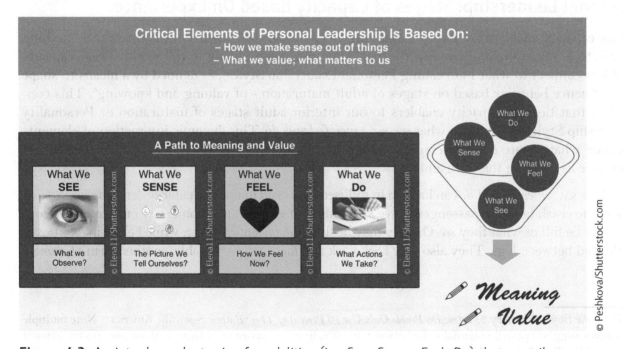

Figure 4.3: An interdependent mix of modalities (i.e. *See, Sense, Feel, Do*) that contribute to making sense out of our experiences.

---

7 Deliberate practice is a method used by athletic coaches and now other types of performance coaches to accelerate performance outcomes. It involves targeting specific areas of improvement with a mix of different practice regimens: repetitive, interval, chunking, etc. A key part of deliberate practice is getting timely skilled feedback and increasing the overall intensity of practice mixed with recovery at the strategic time.

Personal Leadership: Knowing and Valuing Embedded in Five THRIVING Transformational Stages of Capacity

We'll look first at the foundation that shapes the *Personal Leadership Styles* (PLS). As mentioned, it involves a two-factor model, or continuum composed of a *Knowing Orientation* (or meaning making) and a *Valuing Orientation* (or life-value orientation). Collectively, these two continuums (i.e. knowing and valuing) help to shape a way of individually making meaning and valuing out of one's day-to-day interactions, particularly in a high challenge context. It also helps to shape one's personal leadership style within each of the five stages.

As mentioned before, these stages, alternatively referred to as personal leadership styles, include: *protector, problem solver, optimizer, creative strategist and globalist* (see Chapter 5 for an overview of each style and chapters 6-10 for a detailed review). Later, we'll summarize an operating model that describes how Purpose, Passion and Presence thrive themes, with twelve embedded capacity enablers, relate to the five personal leadership styles within a fly-wheel construct (i.e. see Chapter 12).

5. Transformations in Personal Leadership:
➢ Adult behavior can be organized around these personal leadership styles or stages of development
➢ Preceding stages set the developmental capability for increasing levels of functioning and impact in successor stages or styles of personal leadership

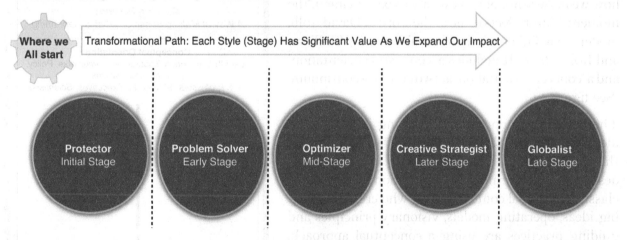

© Courtesy Mark Sullivan

Source: Original research is influenced in part from the original work of Eric Ericson, Bob Kegan, Harry Lasker, Jane Leovinger, and Suzanne Cooke-Greuter who had more stages in total. The above five stages have varying levels of thought somewhat similar in areas to some of the seven to nine stages of development of previous research in developmental stage theory. However this is additionally based on qualitative theming from 62 Adult Life History Interviews and surveying 620 undergrad and graduate Ohio State University students. 2000 more students will be part of a larger pilot in 2018–2019.

Figure 4.4: An adult developmental continuum of capacity from *Protector* to *Problem Solver* to *Optimizer* to *Creative Strategist* to *Globalist*.

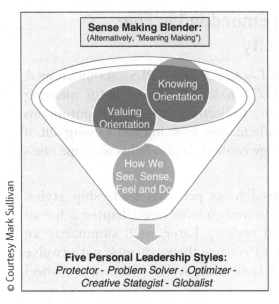

© Courtesy Mark Sullivan

Figure 4.5: *Sense Making* ingredients that influence the 5 Personal Leadership Styles

What we *See, Sense, Feel* and *Do*, influences both the *Knowing Orientation* and *Life-Value* Orientation and fundamentally shape who we are. What we value and what makes sense to us is blended with the mix of what we see, sense, feel and do. This mixture co-creates each of the five styles or stages of adult development.

Each PLS (Personal Leadership Style): *Protector, Problem Solver, Optimizer, Creative Strategist,* and *Globalist* is based on varied degrees of integration and differentiation of what we value and what makes sense to us. This differentiating and re-integrating of self, based on the interplay of knowing and value, is what makes us unique and yet common and characteristic to a particular PLS.

Knowing Orientation

The Knowing Orientation is a continuum that reflects how we make sense of what we are experiencing in the moment. This reflects some of the work of David Kolb, modern day father of experiential learning (Sullivan and Kolb, 1994). It includes a 'conceptual orientation' and a 'concrete orientation' at two ends of a continuum. (See figure 4.6).

The conceptual approach to knowing is focused on ideas, theories, or a framework of abstract but relevant theses arguing a particular point of view. This description of the Knowing Orientation is framed in a classic conceptual context. Those who create original big ideas, operating models, visionary principles and guiding practices are using a conceptual approach. Individuals who prefer to make meaning in this way would tend be scientists, executives in large organizations, researchers, professors, economists, strategists, amongst others.

The concrete approach to knowing is rooted in action, outcomes, and process steps that describe or express what is happening at a given point. Diagram 4.6 is in itself, an example of what a concrete learner or per-

KNOWING ORIENTATION
A Way of Making Sense of What is Happening

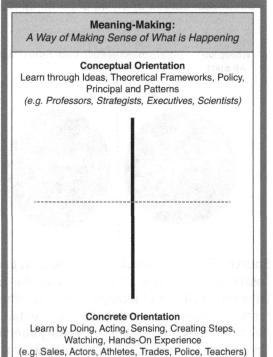

© Courtesy Mark Sullivan

Figure 4.6

former would prefer to use as a way of further making sense of a particular concept, in this case the knowing orientation. Existing models, pictures and frameworks are preferred and can assist the concrete execution or applying of a concept with great fluency. While a conceptual approach emphasizes thinking, a concrete approach features doing and experiencing. Individuals who prefer to make meaning in a concrete way would tend to be sales representatives, counselors, craftsman, artists, athletes and teachers. While a blend of both is possible, individuals tend to have a dominant style in how they determine meaning. (Kolb, 1993).

Public performing artists and influencers such as, composers, politicians, sales reps, clergy, executives, teachers are best if they can blend both conceptual and concrete approaches in a mixed audience. This would include a combination of theory, and big ideas (conceptual); and stories, examples and executable steps (concrete). Shakespeare's plays were uniquely noted as one that could reach the masses and the nobles and elites of the day given his combining both in a rich and dramatic form.

Valuing Orientation: A Me-We Perspective

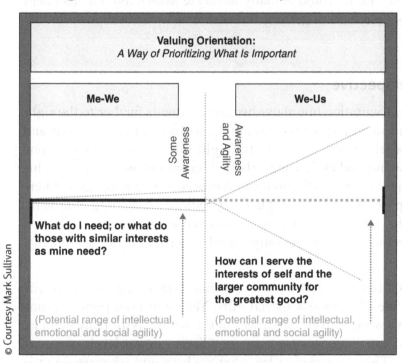

© Courtesy Mark Sullivan

Figure 4.7: Illustration of the *Valuing* scope and breath

The second of two factors that contribute, at a base level, to the five PLS is the Value Orientation (as opposed to the knowing Orientation). It focuses on "Me-We" or "We-Us." That is, whether we resonate by default, with a self or us orientation, when we are challenged. Specifically, *Me-We*, guides and gauges satisfaction based on how much one's individual needs are being addressed. This also includes an awareness of others who are in a same or similar type of group, "like-me," and an effort to protect or preserve their interests as well. There is somewhat of a family, clan or tribal-like way of framing interests and actions. In this perspective, the "we" are those like me, or an extension of me, and as such, also need care and attention. There is an ever-present concern or even fear that external forces may overwhelm or undermine the not *me-we* interests, particularly when we least expect it.

At the extreme of the continuum, the far left, the *we* part of *me-we* is viewed strictly from the self, in a first-person perspective. That is, viewing other not as differentiated from me and others, but rather as a form of me.

There is some capacity to flex but for the most part, a lot of energy is invested in protecting one's thoughts and feelings in a more immutable stance. There is less curiosity about how others are experiencing life from their perspective; but rather selectively reinforcing one's own way of seeing things. Extending beyond boundaries into the *not me* can appear confusing, circular, threatening, imposing or in some circumstances, as an assault on the senses.

I remember a good airline friend of mine, David, who worked on the airline crash-site in Sioux City. His job was to pick up and tag human remains, such as limbs and blood samples, near the plane. Four days after the crash, while I was immersed with family-relations work, I asked David, by phone, how he was doing. He was involved in gruesome, solitary work to be sure. Yet he said, after a day or so he had adjusted, and he was okay. But then he asked the same of me. He said, you have the harder job working with grieving families. I was surprised by his comment. I asked him to say more. "Mark, on your end, they actually talk back at you. I could never do what you're doing." He was referring to an ability to flex or align one's heart and head with where victims were in the moment.

David is a very smart, seasoned gentleman with talent. However, he is more gifted in working in a defined, structured setting where tasks are for the most part clearly set. Within a *me-we* orientation he excels. As an extremely successful airline sales executive he could provide superior service to his travel accounts knowing pre-existing, externally imposed limits on operating costs, service, and other criteria. Within such parameters, he could actually advocate assertively for his client accounts and, by extension, himself as a partner, in getting the best structured deal possible that suited their collective interests.

Valuing Orientation: A We-Us Perspective

Now, as we look further at the Valuing Orientation line above, we see it extends further to the right of *me-we*. As it does, its trajectory widens in awareness and agility within and between self and other. This expands or broadens one's self in the world. On the right side of the continuum, one is more open to different ways of engaging and embracing others who are not *me* or *me-we*. This requires having more porous boundaries and the ability to be with others who may be quite different in a respectful and perhaps even appreciative manner. This may require suspending judgment, to be curious rather than critical of the differences. This is not to excuse or diminish one's own principles and preferences, but to potentially expand the range of what is comfortable and normal within our self.

For some of us, this is not easy. It requires a level of maturation that at this moment in our life may not be fully intact. This is okay. We still possess special gifts. Yet we are not perfect. Some have more or less capacity in how we view our selves and others in the world. With truly genuine confidence in our real assets we can accept that as humans we are different in our levels of capacity and in different stages of maturity. This appreciation for what we have and what we don't is requisite for being honest and authentic for us in the moment. In a staged model of maturation, of personal leadership, it is easy to strive for some later stage of development that is really not us in the moment. Or to artificially claim to be something we are not.

The important idea is that we need to start where we are and not where we think we should be. Growth and development of our better self always starts where we are now, not where others are, and not at some aspirational distant place that lays hollow to the beauty of who we are at the moment – with all our shortcomings included.

Putting It All Together: Knowing and Life-Valuing Orientation

Below is a model of my construction of the key ingredients that go into each of the five personal leadership styles (Figure 4.8: THRIVING In High Demand Environments). It includes the *conceptual* and *concrete* approaches to the knowing orientation and the *me-we* and *we-us* valuing orientation. It reflects a natural way of being and functioning that is hard-wired like a set of algorithms.

These orientations are based on our implicit, or unconscious, response to everyday moments and interactions, within and between our self and our external environment. In a stimulus-response exchange, our orientation to a particular way of being and doing is in part based on the level of interest or importance associated with a why prompt. If I am a *concrete, me-we* learner for example, and I am listening to someone telling me to do something, I may be more attentive if they are giving me a story or an example of how it will benefit me or someone in my interest group. If I am a *conceptual, we-us* learner I may be more open to the request if it is framed as a provocative question, novel task or idea that stretches the curiosity, for example.

The Optimizer would be able to excel at creating actionable ways to execute and customize policy in an operational manner. They would be able translate the complex into the simple being mindful of exceptions and efficiencies at scale. A protector would be able to effectively crisis manage

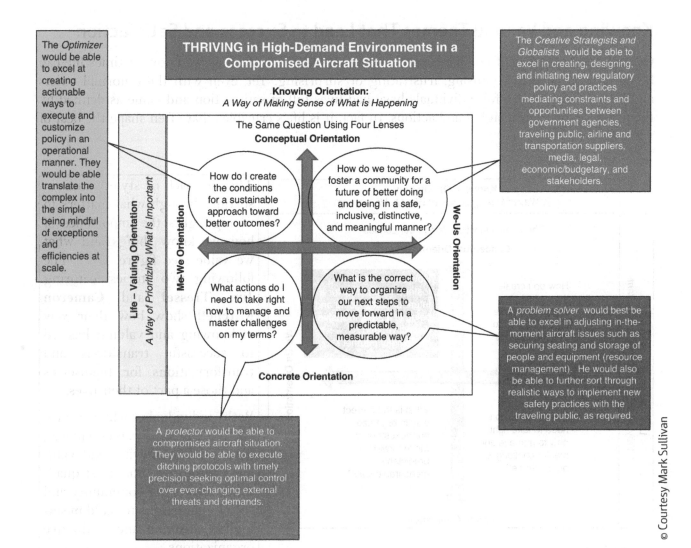

Figure 4.8: Illustration of the *Valuing* scope and breath

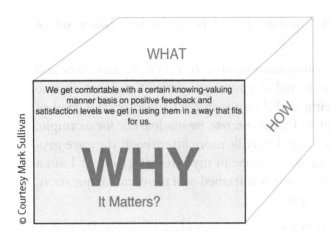

© Courtesy Mark Sullivan

Figure 4.9: Our knowing-valuing is reinforced by fit & feel

Knowing and Value = WHY It Matters

Why do we do things the way we do?

Why do we embrace the world in a concrete or conceptual manner or in a *me-we* or *we-us* way? What we pay attention to and how we engage are often about our finding satisfaction in embracing the world in a given manner. We reinforce this orientation as we get more comfortable and competent in this way.

We are often motivated by the "Why" of things. If I naturally look for and remember stories and examples, I will often repeat and reinforce such a concrete practice as it *provides stability* or *balance in my efforts to be me*. Sometimes these operate on an implicit or unconscious level and at others times in a more intentional manner all in the service of addressing need-fulfillment.

© Courtesy Mark Sullivan

Figure 4.10: What we do is often answered by why

Knowing and Valuing Themes That Lead to Success and Satisfaction

Overall, the trajectory of our life is rarely static or smooth. In fact, as we know, at times life can be more than chaotic, confusing, frustrating or surprising. Yet, even with these normal twists and turns, many successful individuals have had lives full of satisfaction and value as defined by themselves—by their insights and actions. In fact, it is life's crucibles that often shape the best of what we become.

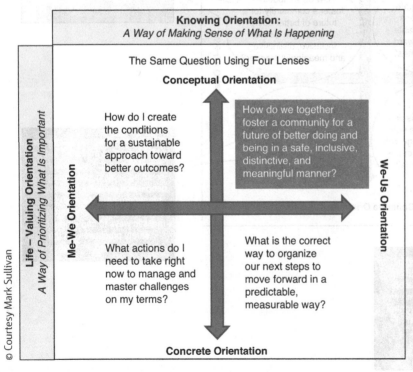

© Courtesy Mark Sullivan

Figure 4.11

The approach or style we use in sorting through what matters to us highlights the importance of how we know things and what we value (see figure 4.11). The following two stories featuring **Jim Tressel** and **Cameron Mitchell** show how their way of knowing and valuing has led to successful transitions and transformations for themselves and those a part of their lives.

Both individuals, while representing different career choices, have similar knowing and valuing trajectories (northeast quadrant), leveraging community and social interactions to build meaningful, satisfying and distinctive organizations.

Jim Tressel has done many things in his life, the most recently being a university president and a former Big 10 head football coach. Regardless of what he has been involved in, he mentions that to really have a good life, with all its ups and downs, one must consider what he describes as his five non-negotiables. They include: 1) strong work ethic, 2) talent, 3) curiosity 4) grit and 5) selfless service to others.

His knowing-valuing perspective in the northeast quadrant (see figure 4.11) is typical from a valuing perspective of someone with a strong *we-us* orientation. As a side-bar to our conversation for this book, Tressel described how he had recently run into a number of relatively new students from Nepal on his university campus. They were very homesick for a good authentic Nepalese dinner similar to what they would find back home. Tressel asked the young men if they would like to cook an authentic Nepalese -style dinner in his house. They were startled but very excited that the president of their university would make such a personal offer on something that meant so much to them. Tressel said, "You give me a list of all the Nepalese ingredients you need to cook up a great meal, and I'll go out and buy it. Then I'll give up my kitchen for you to have a special night with you cooking the ingredients in the tradition of your homeland." These young men, far away from family, ended up having a memorable evening cooking for hours in Tressel's kitchen. Those that have a *we-us* orientation tend to do things like this. More on this as Tressel tells his story about making the best of what stage you are in life.

Jim Tressel Interview

Jim Tressel is the current president of Youngstown State University, and former head football coach at The Ohio State University. His tenure as head coach came to a sudden end in 2011 after National Collegiate Athletic Association (NCAA) violations by players. After this unexpected development, Tressel was forced to reexamine the remainder of his career.

His entire professional life had been guided by hard work and helping others, and as he moved forward, Tressel remained committed to his core values. "I always wanted to have that opportunity to think what was next, now it ushered in a little bit more quickly," said Tressel. He lost his coaching position over Memorial Day and within a week, "I kept getting all of these calls asking me to come do this or that with other people and I said, 'You know what, I'm not doing anything until I read 100 books.' I started that, and I got up to about 30 books and I didn't want any of them to be about sports."

Some companies respected his plan and suggested some reading about their own industry. "I had gotten calls from Chesapeake Energy. They had wanted me because they were going to start getting this plan into Ohio. They thought I might be a natural with them to develop it. So, they gave me three books. All of a sudden, I got into energy. I got to about 32 books and I was feeling good about what I was learning."

But in August, he got a call from Jim Caldwell, coach of the Indianapolis Colts. "He called me and said, 'Hey you know, we're not going to have Peyton Manning, we're going to be challenged without him. Could you come and help me a little bit? I'd like to win a couple games.' What's funny is that Jim is a voracious reader. Riding on the bus to a game, he'd be reading a book. I asked him how he became such a reader and he said that his parents demanded such good grades, and he went to the University of Iowa and played football." Tressel explained. "There was no question he was going to have good grades, but he wanted to go out with the fellas occasionally at night. He came up with a way to get all of his homework done whether he was riding the bus on the way to class," said Tressel.

Tressel hadn't reached his 100-book goal yet, so he had some reservations. "Jim said, 'You can work from home and just come three days a week.' Columbus and Indianapolis aren't far. I asked him to let me think about it, then I asked my wife because I had made this commitment. She said, 'Do it. I'm tired of you being around here seven days a week. Get out of here. If you ask me one more time, 'What are you doing today?' For our sake, it was time. So, I did it."

His decision became pivotal. "It made it clear to me that one, I didn't have a passion for the NFL," Tressel said. "And two, it really affirmed that it was time to take on something new and grow. But I had no idea what that was going to be. As the season was going on, I was pretty clear at the end of the season that after I had this experience it was time to move on."

Tressel had a lot of opportunities to consider. "In December I was getting calls from head hunters about small college presidencies." Tressel had attended a small Ohio School, Baldwin-Wallace College, where his father was the football coach. "I was a small college guy, in fact. David Boyle from Connecticut stopped at my house in Columbus and he was on the Board of Trustees at Wittenberg University. I had never thought of that, but I knew I wanted to be in education. He told me he wanted me to interview with their committee in Columbus and they would be downtown in a hotel with 22 people." He interviewed for the job and said, "When I got home, my buddies from Baldwin-Wallace called me and said that they heard I interviewed with Wittenberg, who was their rival. They said, 'Our presidency is open, you better come interview for ours.'"

So Tressel interviewed at Baldwin-Wallace. "I went back to Columbus and got a call from the president of the University of Akron, where I had got my Master's. He called and asked me to come and meet with him and that I ought to work with them." I said, "That's funny that you mention that because I just interviewed for these two. I don't even know if I'm going to make it to the next step." I agreed to visit with him. Northeast Ohio was home, and Akron was the one that gave me my first chance and there was some sentiment there. I went and met with him and he asked me to come on as a vice president. I went home and that night, the two schools called back and said that I was in the finals, the next step was an on-campus interview. Now, I'm scared because I didn't know if I could do this." However, he chose to take the opportunity at Akron. "None of it was orchestrated," he said. "It was all studying what is next."

From here, even though he was learning what the university needed, he didn't feel like he was under what he calls duress. "What I think we need in life is for the game to slow down and not feel the duress so that we can do what we have to do and stay focused. Execute what we have to and not allow the duress to affect our performance. I remember William White who played at Ohio State, telling me when he was with the Atlanta Falcons. He talked about the key to being successful is to just slow the game down. Slow it down and understand what's going on. He said that the same thing is true in life. Slow the game of life down so that you can make good decisions and execute."

Tressel learned and improved in this new venture. After two years at the University of Akron, Tressel became the President of Youngstown State University. One of his biggest frustrations from coaching, the NCAA scandal, followed him to higher education, too. "People would talk about my players that did this or that. So often, not publicly, I would be like, 'If you would have grown up where he did and had the same role-modeling, or lack thereof, would you have gotten to the point where he is now.' I said to my department chairs, 'Colleagues, the only thing I'd like you to be willing to do is make sure you and your faculty treat every kid exactly the way you would treat your own children with those expectations because I know all of your kids are brilliant."

He urged the faculty to be more hands-on. "Make sure they are managing their class schedule while involved with internships and extra-curricula's. Don't wait three weeks to find out if they went to class. If they are five minutes late to the first class, you'll nip that right there because that is not what is expected or what it's going to take to be successful. If you just do that with all of your students, you'll be fine.' There are some faculty that do just that. But there are some faculty that think, 'Hey, they're big boys, they're adults.' There are some students that think they're adults and don't want to be told what to do. It's not easy for us. There are some, at our college, that feel as if those habits should have been developed by now and that's not our job. Our job is to take them to the elite intellectual level. If they don't want to do it then, that's their problem."

During a guest lecture on the economics of sports, a student asked Tressel, "'What's different about what you did all those years in coaching and what you're doing now?' I said, 'There are so many things that are similar, but one observational difference I have is as a coach, if we succeeded it was because we had a really good performance by our players. If we didn't succeed, it was the coaching. That was just our mentality. What I've learned in some cases in higher ed is that if the students didn't succeed, they weren't prepared, and it was their problem. If they did succeed, it was the brilliance of the faculty member. So, it's just the opposite mindset.'"

Growing up, Tressel said, "There was nothing more important in my life than education and college education." He said he was heavily influenced by his grandfather. "I watched my grandfather, who was a farmer, herd dairy cattle, and there was no such thing as a day off. We were up at 5 o'clock to milk cows and then we were up again in the early evening and worked in between, and that was seven days a week. My father went on and became a teacher and coach. My grandfather never had a chance to watch him coach. My dad left the farm environment, but he wanted to make sure we understood the farm environment. So, our vacation when we were little kids, every summer, we got sent to the farm individually and we worked for a week to understand. They assumed it would be a great experience. So, just to watch the work ethic that it takes. My father wasn't a farmer, but he had those exact same qualities in his work. My mom, who was not a professional, spent every day of her life serving somebody, whether it was us, the PTA, or the community. Every single day, she was working extremely hard to make it a better place."

From his upbringing and his professional experience, he has distilled his learning into five guiding principles. "There are five non-negotiables and I always give them to them in descending order. The fifth important one is work ethic. I've never seen anyone great that didn't work extremely hard. I've never seen a great team that didn't work extremely hard.

"Number four in my list is talent," continued Tressel. "You've got to become competent in what you do. You've got to have some talent. I could practice basketball all day long and I'm not playing for the Cavs," he went on. "My number three is curiosity. I've seen people work hard, develop their competencies, have capable talent, but they've lost the curiosity to get better and someone ended up beating them. Curiosity is a non-negotiable and it's even more important than work ethic and talent.

"My number two is grit. I've seen teams who worked hard, who were talented, who were curious, constantly studying the films and trying to find ways to get better, but they got hit in the mouth and they couldn't handle it. They didn't have that ability to deal with adversity. They hadn't thought about it in advance. The one thing we talked a lot about to our teams was that I say, 'I'm old enough now that I can predict the future and I guarantee you, here is your future. It's going to be combination of things you hoped for, trained for, and wished for, going exactly the way you thought it would and some things that you can't believe the way that they happened. It's going to be a combination of the two and it is the ones that you didn't plan for that twill determine how close to reaching your potential you can get." Tressel's number one non-negotiable is, "You have to be selfless. That's hard as humans. We're all selfish by nature, but you have to work together as a team. You have to work hard at trying to be selfless and that is difficult. It's not just something you say, 'Well, I hope to be selfless.' You've got to think about ways to be selfless. You've got to have constant dialogue and recognize selfless activity.

"Those are kind of my five non-negotiables," Tressel concluded. "In education, sometimes I'm afraid that we spend so much time trying to give temporary knowledge. They don't need us for knowledge, they need us for 'What's it going to take to make it in this tough life?' It's difficult for us, as educators, because chances are that most of us had no problem in school, most of us had a pretty good life with not a lot of duress. Yet, we're being assigned to help someone along, but we've never been in their moccasins," Being selfless is a start, he said, because it generates empathy and the compassion necessary to understand others who come from different circumstances. "To feel it," he said. "To recognize their opinion and where they're coming from.

****

Similar to Jim Tressel, Cameron Mitchell is extraordinarily talented on many fronts. Mitchell grew up with a home life that was quite challenging. Yet this did not deter him from sorting through what his purpose and passion were and then, against incredible odds, excelling on many levels to eventually build one of America's finest chain of upscale restaurants. While he was ranked 592 out of 597 in his high school class, he was also the senior class president and touted as most likely to succeed.

His journey from disruptive dishwasher to CEO of a high growth, nationally acclaimed restaurant company is noteworthy. Similar to Tressel, he is in the northeast quadrant of the *Knowing-Valuing Grid* (see figure 4.11). While he is hands-on (concrete) enough to literally stay close enough to know what is going on in the kitchen and the dining room; he is also a visionary and big idea (conceptual) oriented entrepreneur. That is, enough so to develop over a dozen creative and competitive restaurant concepts. His capacity to read trends and changing tastes in the market place and translate the "so-what" into actionable offerings has kept his restaurants in the upper quadrant of successful, in a notoriously high-churn business, where bankruptcy is a common sight. Also, his capacity to shuttle comfortably from the board room to the kitchen and back demonstrates an agility (i.e. socially, emotionally, intellectually) most frequent of one in the northeast quadrant of the *Knowing-Valuing Grid* as well.

Cameron Mitchell Interview

Cameron Mitchell built his restaurant business from the ground up, beginning his career as a dishwasher in a Columbus, Ohio steakhouse. Mitchell is the founder and CEO of Cameron Mitchell Restaurants (CMR), with 32 restaurants under 13 different concepts, within 12 states. The company also oversees Rusty Bucket Restaurant and Tavern, which operates in 23 locations in six different states.

Mitchell said the probability that he would succeed with his restaurants was "the equivalent of someone handing you a water bottle, a pair of tennis shoes, and a pair of shorts and saying you're going to cross the Grand Canyon. It was very, very difficult, but I knew it was possible."

Mitchell struggled as a teenager. "My troubled youth was really about my parents splitting and doing drugs and alcohol and then running away and dropping out of high school," he said. But he didn't let his background stop him. "Even back in high school when I finished 592 out of 597 in my class, I was senior class president. I was voted most likely to succeed and most absent."

For Cameron Mitchell, "High school was all about the 'will do' not about the 'can do.' I had the 'can do.' I always had the brains, it was always just the matter of applying myself. The whole thing turned when I graduated high school. I lived in Upper Arlington, Ohio. All you can do is drive around Upper Arlington in June and see all the kids are going to college. That's 90-some percent of kids go off to college. I was working for beer money, 18 years old, not knowing what I want to do, living with mom, really not a man, not a boy, just lost."

He kept coasting like this until he stumbled upon a passion that changed his life while bussing and washing dishes in restaurants. "I had a transformation one Friday. It was a shift change, and it hit me. It was pandemonium in the kitchen, and I had an epiphany. I said, 'This is what I want to do for the rest of my life. I love it.' I went home and wrote down my goals. I want to be the president of a restaurant company by the age of 35 and all the interim steps along the way. I had been on three days suspension and in the middle of 30-days probation; I was the laziest guy in the kitchen, going nowhere, on a Friday, working for the man and working for beer money. Then I woke up on Saturday and everything had changed. I was working for my career, my future, and I was the hardest working guy in the kitchen. I had the worst attitude on Friday and the best attitude on Saturday, a 180-degree turn overnight."

He immediately got started on his goals and began working towards his education. "I applied to the Culinary Institute of America. I had that epiphany, this is what I want to do for the rest of my life, and immediately I knew I had to go to that school. I knew it was the Harvard of culinary schools, it was immediately where I wanted to go," said Mitchell.

His high school grades, however, made things difficult. He recalled. "I'm still 18 at the time, this is right before my 19th birthday, I got a letter that said, 'Thank you for your application. I regret to inform you that we can't accept you as a culinary student. We liked your resume, and we know you've worked hard in the business. We'd be willing to reconsider your application if you went to your local university or college and took math and English courses and get good grades and reapply.'"

Mitchell told his friends, "This is going to cost me a six-month delay and at least a half a million dollars. And mind you I'm making five dollars an hour. They said 'What? It's going to cost you a half a million dollars?' And I said, 'I want to make at least a million dollars per year in my life, and if I have to spend another six months making $20,000 a year that's another six months less than I'm making a million dollars a year, so that cost to me is half a million dollars.' At 18, those words came out of my mouth in that exact manner."

When thinking about what caused his epiphany, he said, "I think I was searching. People ask, 'How did you find the restaurant business?' Well I didn't really find it; it found me. I could've been sweeping car lots at a bunch of car dealerships and gone into that business, but restaurants just happened to be where I landed. I'm sure you see it all over, I just happened to be blessed. At 18, to know what you want to do and to be able to choreograph your entire future towards that was a huge blessing. So, I was searching, it's no different from my wife. I dated a lot of girls along the way but then, I was ready to get married, I wanted to get married, so I was searching for that right girl. I found her, and I was madly in love with her; I am madly in love with her. I couldn't think of anything else – that's all I wanted to do was to marry this girl. So much like this epiphany came along when I was ready."

After working in the same restaurant for six years subsequent to graduating from Culinary Institute of America, Mitchell was ready for something new. "I was already thinking about moving on ," he said. "'What am I going to do, what's my future going to hold, and that's when the next epiphany hit me," he said. I was out at a restaurant and observed the chef owner working the dining room when the restaurant was packed, and I said, 'You know, I'm going to start my own restaurant company.' I think it's that my mind was in the right place and open to doing that because I wanted those things for myself. I always wanted to be successful. I can tell you another story, I always envisioned myself successful, even when I was struggling as a kid. "

Even as a teenager, Mitchell never doubted he would fulfill his passion. He was aware that he already had leadership ability. "Whether it was president of my class or group leader in school. Everywhere I've been ever since I was a little boy, I've always become a leader. It was always innate. You know, leaders: Are they born or bred? I believe wholeheartedly that I was born a leader with entrepreneurial skills."

He said childhood experiences gave him this motivation to succeed. He remembers visiting an aunt and uncle who were wealthy and had a swimming pool. "I always wanted that, but my mom couldn't even give me lunch money. We'd go to their house at Christmas time and they had a housekeeper, and two refrigerators. Back in those days, it's the '70s, who has two refrigerators? I always coveted that, so that gave me the drive to attain more for myself like they had."

Once Mitchell had his second epiphany, he found people to look up to. "I've always studied people. I've always had idols. I like to say that Rich Melman, who is the top restaurateur in the country, out of Chicago, is one. I met Rich once in Chicago when I was a restaurant manager, and it was like meeting God. You're going to remember that. I watched him, he was always a mentor of mine, even though I didn't personally know him. There were a lot of guys like that. Eventually, I won the Rich Melman leadership award and was on the cover of a restaurant business magazine with Rich. That's when I really met him, and he and I sat and talked for three hours and we were like kindred spirits, almost identical, in our thoughts about the business and everything else." He listed other entrepreneurs he admired in the restaurant business and Herb Kelleher from Southwest Airlines. "All those guys I've watched from afar and read about and studied."

Aside from his experience, Mitchell said his success comes from doing what he loves. "My story is really simple in that regard. Sure, I had to have some brains, no doubt about that. But a lot of people with a lot of brains fail. It's not just that; it's the leadership and the people. I'm an entrepreneur in the truest sense of the word, I don't know failure, I don't even think about failure, it's really not an option."

That doesn't mean that Mitchell hasn't faced setbacks. But he said he remains positive when facing trouble, and he knows he can surpass any obstacle. "I have had a few sleepless nights along the way, but I've also learned over the years, I've always overcome. I've always persevered. In essence, that gives you a lot of confidence, not cockiness by any means, but confidence. The sun will rise eventually, the dark is not the end of the world, and sometimes that is where the most clarity is, in the darkest moments."

Fear is also a motivator, he said. "It's the fear of failure, it's the refusal to fail." But that also has its drawbacks. "I'll tell you another thing about being an entrepreneur, it's almost my biggest strength but it's also my biggest weakness, this unbridled passion for growth."

Through struggles, Mitchell said he maintains perspective. During periods of adversity he has told himself, "'Go stand at the front door of the 'Columbus Nationwide Children's Hospital,' you know if you think you're having a bad day. It's easier for me to draw out those experiences." He tells his children, "You got to understand that you can't change the way you were born or what you were born into. You need to accept that because this is who you are. But the best way to heal yourself and feel good about yourself is to apply that and don't take it for granted. Do something, do good with what you've been given."

Mitchell believes that working from the ground up was necessary for his success when he finally decided to start his own restaurant. "When I look at my career, I opened my first restaurant when I was 30. I had a pretty good resume built in the twelve years I had been doing it. I think to what I knew then, to what I know now, it doesn't even compare," he said. "Most of my friends who are all first-generation and starting their own business worked for somebody else. They saw a niche and went and jumped on it and got it. They learned entrepreneurism on the job. It's almost like the chicken versus the egg. They had a lot of core skills, and were able to see this niche, and had education—life education versus teaching entrepreneurism."

He did not realize how much his 'life education' had benefitted him until he reflected on it. "One of the most rewarding days of my life was I guest lectured in an Executive MBA class at The Ohio State University with 200 people. When you're doing your role in the presidency of your own company, you're working, you're running, you're gunning," he said. "When I walked out of class, they had peppered me with questions for over an hour, and I answered every single one of them with authority. I walked out of there thinking, 'Yeah, I kind of do know what I'm doing.' That was very enriching."

Thinking back to his youth and what led to his success he said, "A positive attitude is the key to everything. You can't just say, 'I have a positive attitude.' You've got to believe you've got a positive attitude. It has to be real. You have to discipline yourself to try new things and put yourself out there. Your life experience will come and therefore your life will come. Don't sit there and wait for it to come to you. You have to be involved. Be active. Get out there and see what you can see and do what you can do. Eventually, you'll find your way."

Chapter 5

Personal Leadership Styles: An Overview

"Personal leadership is the process of keeping your vision and values before you and aligning your life to be congruent with them."

Stephen Covey

"Knowing the edge of your competency is important. If you think you know more than you do, you will get in trouble."

Warren Buffet

"The challenge of leadership is to be strong, but not rude; be kind, but not weak; be bold, but not bully; be thoughtful, but not lazy; be humble, but not timid; be proud, but not arrogant; have humor, but without folly."

Jim Rohn

Featuring

General Stanley McChrystal: Retired Four Star General: Commander of Joint Special Operations Command (JSOC).

© Ban Gabbe/Getty Images
Entertainment/Getty Images

© Splash News/Newscom

Governor Steven Beshear: 61st two-term Governor of Kentucky (2007–2015)

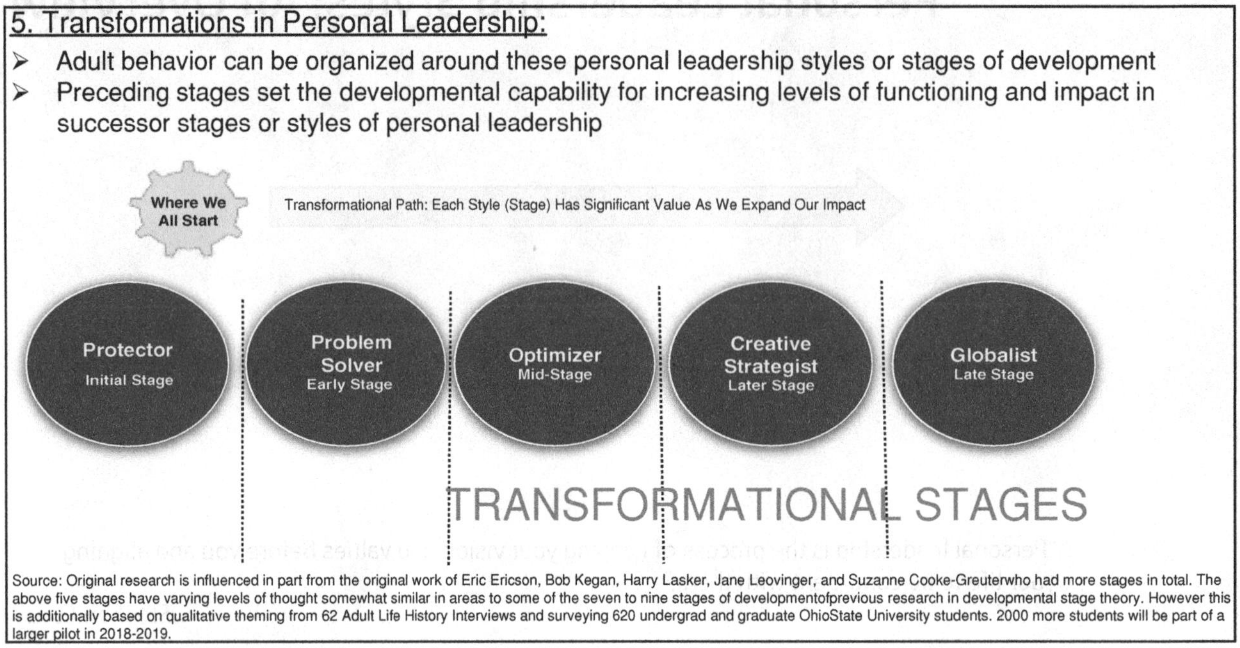

Figure 5.1: Five styles for knowing and valuing

This airline tragedy, now decades past, has stayed with me. Faces, voices, memories all intertwined to form a respectful residue of the human spirit caught by trauma and terror. It sparked my interest in developing a continuum of how we personally lead and live our lives in a period of trouble. While on United Airlines family relations duty, I recall each family visit was different.

As I trudged up and down many front porches along the East Coast following those early days after the crash of Flight #232, I saw, time and again, families mapping tragedy through different and common lenses. At the early stages of this nightmare, it was obvious that we collectively had serious, common questions around life and death issues—status of passengers, health and well-being of the survivors, support and care on multiple levels.

Beyond these common, consequential topics were differences in how survivors, victims, rescuers and support teams experienced the trauma and what kind of healing they and their loved ones needed early on and later. The trajectory of their experience, and how they proceeded was based on what they valued and how they made meaning of the moments leading up to, during, and after the accident.

In so doing, as mentioned previously, I have created a framework[1] that expresses a range of capacity in high-challenge contexts, indicating five styles for personally leading oneself and others through a knowing and life-valuing process. These styles are highlighted below (see figure 5.2).

---

1   Figure 5.1 and 5.1, et al. is my continuum of personal leadership in high demand environments? It reflects a transformational process of being and growing within our own life-space. It is based on the interviews of the notable high achievers and my on-going research of *thriving in high demand environments.* I am particularly appreciative of my book contributors as well as my research colleagues, partners, coaches, preceding pioneers and professors at Harvard, OSU and elsewhere: Susan Cooke Grueter, Bob Kegan, David Kolb, Mary Ann Krauss, Jane Leovinger, and Harry Lasker. Some of their work has deeply influenced my own thinking and construction of my PLS (Personal Leadership Style) model.

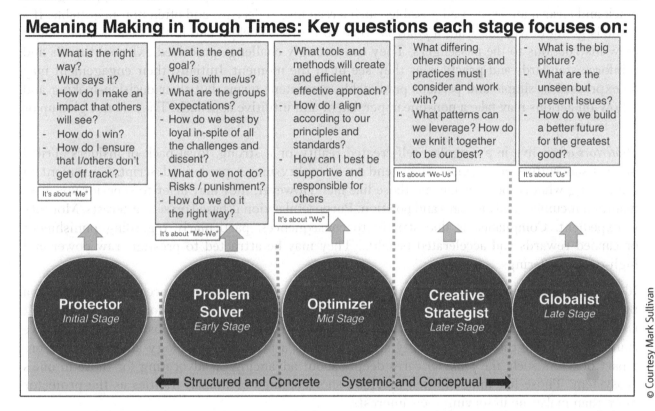

Knowing & Valuing in Tough Times: Key Questions Each Stage Focuses On

Meaning Making in Tough Times: Key questions each stage focuses on:

- What is the right way?
- Who says it?
- How do I make an impact that others will see?
- How do I win?
- How do I ensure that I/others don't get off track?

It's about "Me"

- What is the end goal?
- Who is with me/us?
- What are the groups expectations?
- How do we best by loyal in-spite of all the challenges and dissent?
- What do we not do? Risks / punishment?
- How do we do it the right way?

It's about "Me-We"

- What tools and methods will create and efficient, effective approach?
- How do I align according to our principles and standards?
- How can I best be supportive and responsible for others

It's about "We"

- What differing others opinions and practices must I consider and work with?
- What patterns can we leverage? How do we knit it together to be our best?

It's about "We-Us"

- What is the big picture?
- What are the unseen but present issues?
- How do we build a better future for the greatest good?

It's about "Us"

Protector *Initial Stage* — **Problem Solver** *Early Stage* — **Optimizer** *Mid Stage* — **Creative Strategist** *Later Stage* — **Globalist** *Late Stage*

◄ Structured and Concrete   Systemic and Conceptual ►

© Courtesy Mark Sullivan

Figure 5.2: Each style has its own way of thinking; its own inner logic to make sense out of their everyday world

Personal Leadership Style: PROTECTOR

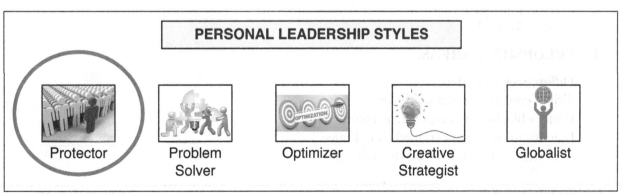

PERSONAL LEADERSHIP STYLES

Protector — Problem Solver — Optimizer — Creative Strategist — Globalist

© 3DConcepts/Shutterstock.com

Figure 5.3: Illustrates the Protector in the PLS continuum

The ***Protector*** is a PLS that is often of tremendous value in the heart of a crisis. Their role in providing immediate contribution to their teams will often influence others like an echo chamber in the social terrain. When immediate action is required they are often there to respond. They may have a shorter, but intense, focused-to-free-floating attention span.

© 3DConcepts/ Shutterstock.com

The *protector* views the world in concrete, black-and-white, structured and defined terms. They are committed to reinforcing their world view, or how they interpret what is happening, in a quick and clear manner, if at all possible. Such a response is decisive and often non-negotiable. If a plane is going down, you want a *protector* to be both in the cockpit and in the cabin leading flight crew instructions to the passengers. They can strongly challenge perceived external threats and reinforce standards and practices as they see fit in the moment. Initially, their engagement may be expressed in simple and perhaps predictable, consistent terms, but their decision-making and follow-on actions may take a non-linear, persistent and intuitive approach. They do not give up or give in easily.

Protectors often live in a singular, self-created reality, or a strong, loyal pack of insiders. Tribal or partisan culture may exist. They tend to fit reality into a predefined script, convenient in reinforcing what is "best for me and those like me." However, they may defer to superior power to maintain incumbent advantages and position. Purposeful action is based on self–interests. Morality is expedient. Compliance is due strictly to consequences, particularly regarding punishment or earned rewards and accelerated benefits. They may be attracted to prestige, raw power and high-quality offerings.

Ideas, images, positions or actions not in alignment with the protector's stance is often viewed in a threatening or adversarial manner. Defensive routines involve conflating, distorting or demonizing issues and adversaries to distract or disrupt offensive arguments and positions. Appreciative routines, or strengths, involve loyalty and support of a prescribed ideology and those that are a part of it. As such, the *protector* cares deeply about advancing or advocating for those in one's ecosystem. Those like-minded often overlook shortcomings or human frailties as the protector more than makes up in serving their interests.

STRENGTHS:

■ Speed
■ Decisiveness
■ Action-oriented
■ Clarity of purpose
■ Results-focused

DEVELOPMENT AREAS:

■ Differences viewed as a threat
■ Tribal energy: Us against them
■ Prefers black-or-white; Gray is insufficient
■ Loyalty means unquestioned compliance
■ Attention and focus can be short-lived

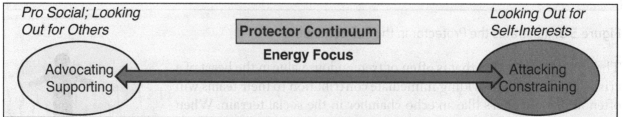

Figure 5.4: How our energy is used for self and others as a Protector

Personal Leadership Style: PROBLEM SOLVER

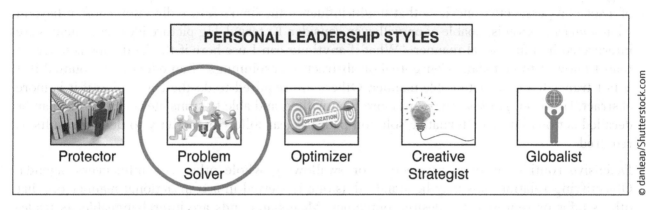

Figure 5.5: Illustrates the *Problem Solver* in the PLS

The ***Problem Solver*** is the "Go-To" person to get the job done. They pay close attention to expected norms and procedures in following orders; or somewhat creatively figuring out how to best work trade-offs with conflicting interests. They are the "company man (or woman)" as they demonstrate loyalty and dedication through delivering concrete actions and desired results, and are appreciated by key leadership, and influencers.

They strongly identify with the "in-group" as they are keenly aware of working within operating rules and perimeters of authority and existing hierarchy. They rely on "in-house" procedures, established book knowledge or methods institutionalized by the organization. For example, large companies with strong Six Sigma[2] cultures, or robust quality and efficiency practices, will have a deep bench of *problem solvers* managing the initiative at all levels; on the front-line to work with individual contributors on execution or implementation; to mid-management in balancing resource trade-offs such as effective utilization and deployment of capital, hardware, process flows and staff mapped against milestones and ever-changing requirements on volume, speed, service, output; and at the executive level to plan and manage deliverables and prospective orders as mediated through customer and competitive value.

Unlike the *protector*, they have some emerging interests in differing from others, but it is more from the standpoint of how to work with others to get results. They live in a utilitarian world of transactions, of "You scratch my back, and I'll scratch yours." Given they are ever vigilant on the right and wrong ways of doing things they are attentive to differences in thought and action as there is on-going behavioral and organizational calculus in determining if the math is adding up, or if corrective action is required. If need be, deals and IOU's are crafted to get the job done.

---

2   *Six Sigma* is an efficiency-oriented methodology pioneered in the 20th century by Edward Deming, used to establish "lean" or effective processes to get work done. Generally, it is particularly found in a manufacturing environment as a data driven methodology to eliminate deficiencies and to accelerate speed and quality targets. There are five basic phases including: *Define, Measure, Analyze, Improve* and *Control.* This very structured process is also referred to as DMAIC (pronounced as "duh-may-ik). It works best in environments requiring repetitive, mechanical steps; and less so in creative, organic, improvisational contexts. GE, Motorola, Honeywell, and most auto manufacturing companies extensively use six sigma and have a supporting culture around it to reinforce actions and decisions at all levels from the front-lines to management. More information regarding methodology and certification processes can be found at the American Society for Quality (ASQ), Institute for Industrial and Systems Engineers (IISE), and Chartered Quality Institute (CQI).

As a "utility player" you can count on *problem solvers* to speak and act on the interests of the in-group in multiple roles or scenarios. However, a broader view of the enterprise, or a macro view of a societal perspective and how that might influence the firm's future direction is often beyond what a *problem solver* is capable of or, will even consider. External, big picture ideas and themes are interpreted in a functional manner: "What if anything can I use here if the landscape is different than I know it to be today." Conceptual or abstract underpinnings of an effort is discounted if it is not translated in an actionable manner. Others are required to do the translating if it is more abstract. However, *problem solvers* are more than willing and able to translate concrete, off-plan or derailed actions into an alternative solution path of clear follow-on activity to deliver results as required.

Defensive routines involve introjecting or swallowing whole other key influencers' agenda. Objectifying relationships may be standard as one is viewed in a transactional manner of what others offer or represent for desired outcomes. Means-and-ends are interchangeable, as trade-offs are still somewhat oriented in doing whatever it takes, regardless. Morality is situational and often explained away as being for the good-of-the-cause. Appreciative routines or strengths involve being committed and creative in supporting process, practice and people according to other's overriding leadership and operating objectives. They can differentiate between me and the "not-me" in others and will recognize and appreciate their differences to some extent. They bring passion and heart to their efforts and genuinely care about the results that others may give up on when hurdles mount.

STRENGTHS:

■ Focuses on process
■ Results-oriented
■ Recognizes key differences from others standpoint
■ "Smoothes" gaps
■ Resourceful

DEVELOPMENT AREAS:

■ Means-ends orientation
■ Minimal tolerance for nuance
■ Accepts artificial ways to collaborate
■ Avoids conflict; dismissive of feelings
■ Accepts tribal norms without questioning
■ Focus only on facts and things

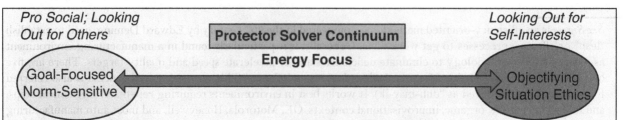

Figure 5.6: Continuum that describes the *Problem Solver* focus from a self-other perspective

Personal Leadership Style: CREATIVE STRATEGIST

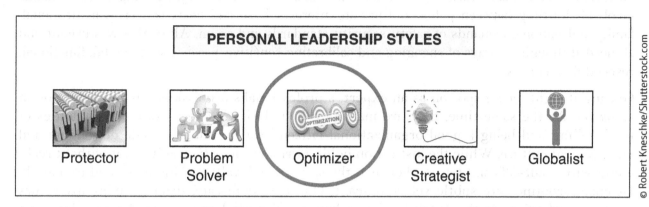

Figure 5.7: Illustrates the *Optimizer* in the PLS continuum

The **Optimizer** is about excellence. They bring high standards, keen analysis and recognition of deeper, broader complexity to relationships and issues. They are also the bridge between the concrete and conceptual world. As such, they leverage a more mature rigor in diagnosing underlying dynamics, appreciative of root cause analysis, interaction effects, and third person perspectives. With a  multi-dimensional view of the world, they can recognize and act on a collection of differences: self, other, and system or organizational stakeholders each from distinct points of view. Through natural inquisitiveness, they can make the invisible visible by bringing what is less-than-apparent to the surface with deep, penetrating questions about the "as-is" and "to-be."

Given the above, *optimizers* can differentiate between self and group interests and goals in a more intentional and confident manner. They can invite criticism and are open to subsequent feedback. Instead of disconfirming contrarian positions, they are able to explore purpose and intent behind opposing or conflicting issues.

Somewhat like the *problem solver*, the *optimizer* prefers conventional forms, routines, rules and order in which to provide fair and expedient outcomes. Knowing and doing the right thing in a traditional manner is still important. However, while external dictums still prevail, they are softening. Unlike preceding leadership styles, *optimizers* can clearly think for themselves in an original way and may willingly offer controversial or differing opinions. However, they are cognizant of norms and the status quo and therefore often raise issues only tentatively while seeking to maintain respect and support for self and one's embedded groups.

Optimizers demonstrate a broader sense of responsibility and obligation to others, in a more well-rounded manner, while still honoring one's own agenda. They have a growing interest in social consensus. They excel in a more complex setting where multiple conflicting interests converge. Individuals in United Airline's Operations Recovery Center staff often had qualities of an *optimizer* as they were regularly in a shock absorber position. Physicians, psychologists, pilots, lawyers, journalists, clergy and others were immersed with families legitimately demanding status or remains and effects of their loved ones by the hour or minute; coroners and funeral homes requiring numbers and dimensions on coffins; hospitals seeking death certificates, family medical records;

crash-site personal needing lab reports and dental records to identify bodies; safety officials looking for aircraft maintenance records, and finally, the media seeking a story. Meeting these demands involved shuttling between public and private interests, head and heart concerns, institutional, family and national demands of safety, security, standards and so on. All of this was urgent and all needed thoughtful ways of engaging and calibrating sensitive, precise, sentimental, functional, respectful responses.

Getting it right, being spot on as an expert, a professional's professional, is the nature of an *optimizer*. At the same time, they are managing boundaries between conflicting realities of truth telling and being a good organizational citizen loyal to informal code of conduct and management culture. While the institution holds a grip on the *optimizer* it is not without reckoning with trade-offs and tension between the *optimizer's* loyalty to "the man" and to oneself. Defensive routines are subtle yet significant. One may obfuscate, defer or minimize issues requiring attention, at the expense of spending social capital and personal reputation, that may reduce standing and stature with the embedded group. Conversely, appreciative routines highlight developing clarity and consensus when the *optimizer* is fully empowered to leverage analysis and insight, to knit together higher functioning in a social and resource-constrained environment. *Optimizer's* are less about speed and show and more about the right path and precision. They make a difference when they begin to listen as much to themselves as they do to their colleagues.

STRENGTHS:

- Standards of excellence
- Shuttles between different worlds
- Recognize and work with some nuance
- Efficiency based on recognizing patterns
- Some use of conceptual thinking, analysis
- Open to feedback and practices that challenges the status quo; engages conflict

DEVELOPMENT AREAS:

- Accepts key organizations norms while recognizing constraints and repressive ways
- Situational authenticity: ability to see and engage beyond pretense yet struggles with trade-offs
- Tolerance for controversy until it threatens to reduce stature, reputation or position
- Truth is relative to the expense of future conditions
- Avoids conflict
- Accepts tribal norms without questioning

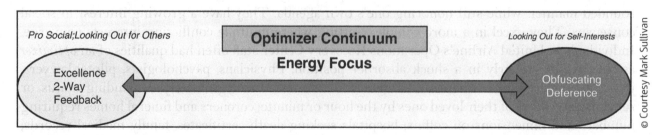

Figure 5.8: Continuum that describes the *Optimizer* focus from a self-other perspective

Personal Leadership Style: Thriving as a GLOBALIST

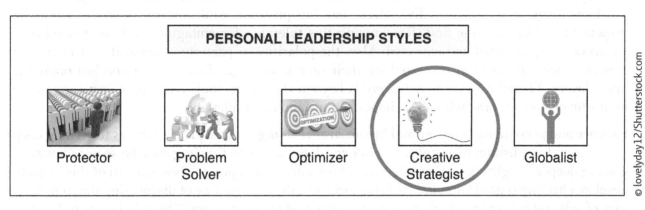

Figure 5.9: Illustrates the *Creative Strategist* in the PLS continuum

The *Creative Strategist* is in a dramatically different place then preceding leadership styles. Rules and perspectives are no longer absolute. Here one is principled and supportive of greater causes that seek to benefit others even if it runs counter to incumbent rules or ways of doing things.

The *creative strategist* uses a broader lens to view and appreciate competing values, interests and obligations. As such, one has moved from self as me, to self as me-we, to self as we-us. The aperture of life's window has broadened, and is more inclusive in thought and action, on all levels, individual, team or group, organization, community and so on. One is more open and innovative so diversity of tools, practices, race, experience is re-defined to create new possibilities, solutions and opportunities in a more engaged, creative, expansive and advantageous manner.

The *strategist* side of this style is essentially conceptual as one asks many "why" and "what-if" questions; and shuttles comfortably between macro, meso (i.e. middle or interim) and micro perspectives–the big picture, the details, and everything in-between. One moves beyond linear logic to a more systemic, organic, holistic approach to seeing and sensing issues iteratively, end-to-end, close-up, or in distant abstract fashion. The *creative strategist* further begins to use peripheral vision in looking around corners where limited or conflicting data is present, or worst yet, present, but not visible. This is fortified through keen critical analysis, the wisdom of experience, and the visioning - hypothesizing of the potential, the promise of the unknown, with the stability and certainty of the known present.

The *creative* side of this style does have some concrete energy and interest in seeking optimal ways to apply ideas and practices in a tangible, sticky, distinctive manner. They can think, organize and frame images and actions with the design tapestry of a movie trailer or a good murder mystery traversing asynchronous, multi-dimensional, memorable and impactful journey. However, *creative strategist* never stray too far from the conceptual as they embrace paradox and contradictions as multiple realities. Understanding things are rarely as they initially seem to be for a *creative strategist*. They use the intellectual dynamism and rigor of addressing a complex business school case for translating common and disparate themes into meaningful, actionable patterns. They scan for inconsistencies, test assumptions, hypothesize options and pathways for new ground - for planting opportunity, nurturing resilience, growth and functioning for a better way.

The *creative strategist* recognizes that not all issues and challenges can be understood with quick or simple answers. The context may continue to shift. The 'Whac-a-Mole' arcade game effect can loom large as we successfully address one big problem, while several others pop up as a response to addressing the first. Recognizing this tolerance for ambiguity and unintended consequences is appreciated and expected. Also, the polarities of partisan or oppositional forces are expected, accepted or even respected for their own inner logic. Life when un-packed often has many layers. Therefore, a *creative strategist* is beyond the secure static comfort of certainty, to the multi-dimensional future, with all its imperfections and contradictions.

Patience and persistence is recognized by the *creative strategist* as frequent partners to seeking deep learning and acquisition of insight, and informed action. In fact, failing may be seen as a way of gaining deeper insights into what follow-on experiences could provide benefits. All of this helps to develop a healthy regard for emotional and social intelligence – a way of discovering different realities of self and others in new, deeper, appreciative and inclusive ways. This allows one to be open and empathic and accepting of changing conditions and threats while working from contrasting vantage points. The pool of shared meaning is nurtured with a collective ground, often lumpy yet fully fertilized for seed planting.

When United Airline's Situation Team first organized in the early hours after the Flight #232 tragedy much was needed. This was 1989, before cell phones and digital everything. Initially, there were only 15 of us (seven of the 15 from the original standing team sponsored by Corporate), however we grew to many multiples of that in 72 hours. There was only paper, writing utensils, some early pre-desktop, 'luggable' IBM computers, and land lines. Only seven of us had done something in the disaster recovery area before, and what existed were only checklists in a few spiral notebooks. There was no play-book, no operating model, no off-the-shelf portable campaign to deploy. It was more than 10 years since there was a major United Airlines plane crash. What we primarily needed was deep improvisational learning, leveraging the energy and leadership of *creative strategy*.

Our original Situation Team was a diverse group of individuals. We represented multiple personal leadership styles. This was helpful as we had many different skills and tasks required which played to different styles. Fortunately, our *creative strategist* were able to visualize and transform an old cinder block and tiled airline building reminiscent of the Kennedy Cold War bomb-shelter days into a workable multi-purpose operations headquarters with a control room, in-bound call center, family relations desk, press room, mini chapel, break room and government coordination hub.

Next, as a self-organizing team, we agreed our first priority would be to serve the families involved in the crash, and the second priority would be to learn how to do that. Later, we realized we had to make ourselves individually and collectively a priority as well, or we would not have endured through this tragedy. This strategic focus helped us to sort through competing facts, methods, goals and values—from a head, heart and spirit perspective. Without this, it would be easy to be sucked into the swirling forces of unchecked human drama lacking a sense of balance, or collective grounding, for situational learning and performing. With it, we were able to train 300 case workers in 48 hours to work with the 184 families related to passengers; organize 200 meeting planners to arrange for air and ground travel itineraries, hotel rooms, limousine services, flowers, receptions, and religious services for the affected families. This strategic focus would allow us to arrange for more than 500 gate agents and flight crew personnel to personally escort the 2000 people that were related to passengers as they were enroute to the crash site, memorial services, or family hometowns.

Organizing and shaping the vision of what could be, hyper-accelerated into the present, was not without challenges. Truly there was much to celebrate, yet there were shortcomings. The defensive routines of a *creative strategist* is elitism, arrogance, detachment, denial and intellectualism. As such, we had our moments, the 15 of us. Some good people momentarily lost their way as they led in an all-knowing way, violating well-earned trust when it mattered. Complexity, often got the better of some in this style as their predictive powers fell short at times. Denying the unfolding, ever-changing reality as it was, caused mis-steps and re-work of effort when we could least afford it.

Yet the counter-balance, as it is so often referred to in many schools of thought[3], is the appreciative stance helping to propel us forward. The power of *creative strategist*, at their best, is a co-creating a new and better reality through inquiry and action. The energy they put to extracting unforeseen possibilities and insight[4] creates a "third eye." Their visioning and prototyping a way forward, based on individual and collective intelligence, provides options that yield legs and lift when we most need it.

STRENGTHS:

- Creative, flexible, innovative
- Comfortably engages dramatically different social terrain in a constructive, productive manner; embraces multiple realities
- Empathic; emotionally elastic in expression
- Values are more global and generative
- Third person perspective: sees things from multiple perspectives – yours, mine, others
- Skilled at pattern recognition and conceptual analysis; proactively sees second/third order effects; in problem solving applies strategic thought experiments/principles as found in chess

DEVELOPMENT AREAS:

- At times can be over-confident, elitist or arrogant
- Appreciation for legitimate gifts and talent can get In the way of others offerings or authentic voice
- While flexible in many ways, can also be stubborn or determined to have things go one way – my way
- May deny or distort reality to fit an aspirationally desired image or prototype
- Can over-think or delay action at the expense of implementing at the opportune time
- Can bring more theory than practice further confusing *what, how or why* for others seeking to understand next steps

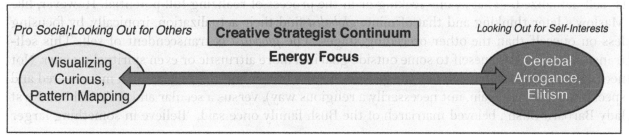

Figure 5.10: Continuum that describes the *Creative Strategist* focus from a self-other perspective

---

3 There are many of the seven global faith traditions and philosophies, particularly the eastern ones (e.g. 'Ying-Yang'), and schools of psychology and their practices (e.g. 'Appreciate Inquiry') that offer an appreciative and balanced energy force for awareness of relationship between self and other. In Organizational Behavior field, Kurt Lewin developed a *Field-Force Model* reflecting a broad dynamic relational or people-to-people field, as an example.

4 Related to *insight*: Eurich, Tasha. (2017). *Insight. Why We're Not as Self Aware as We Think, and How Seeing Ourselves Clearly Helps Us Succeed at Work and in Life.* New York: Crown Business, an imprint of the Crown Publishing Group.

Personal Leadership Style: GLOBALIST

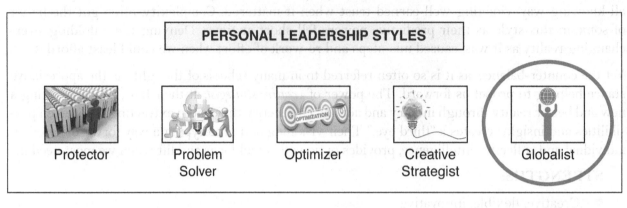

Figure 5.11: Illustrates the *Globalist* in the PLS continuum

The ***Globalist,*** the last stage of capacity on the personal leadership continuum, is focused on developing and leveraging a broad range of interdependent relationships for the greatest good. The Globalist often acts as a catalyst in shaping others' lives and organizations. They can make others genuinely feel worthy and whole given the dignity and deep respect they have for them. As such, they foster a community sense and inspire others to be a better self.

The focus is on us - doing the greatest good for the greatest number. So, the attention has focused from the early stages of self as me or me-we, to later stages of self as we-us and *us.* With each shift there is more appreciation for the significance and majesty of self as part of other.

Globalists are comfortable in their own skin, appreciative of the blessings they have received and committed to providing greater value while giving back and paying-it-forward in a way that makes a difference. They are the institution builders, community organizers, activists and contributors, in the public and private arena. They are dedicated to expand the network of human good, service, value and need-fulfillment. Abraham Maslow[5] (1943), with his own 'hierarchy of needs pyramid' of varied stages of development would say the *globalist* is "self-actualized." That is, one seeking or in the process of realizing full potential. However, like Maslow's later thinking and that of mine, *globalist* find their actualization, ironically, by focusing less on oneself than the other preceding stages. The *globalist* is transcendent of self. This self-transcendence gives oneself to some outside goal in a more altruistic or even spiritual manner. Not necessarily religious (but can be), the *globalist* honors others and their causes in a more sacred and special way (i.e. yet again, not necessarily a religious way), versus a secular and stoic fashion. First lady Barbara Bush[6], beloved matriarch of the Bush family once said, "Believe in something larger

---

5   Abraham Maslow's classic hierarchy of needs includes: ***Physiological-***basic need (i.e. food, water, rest), ***Safety-***basic need (i.e. security and safety), ***Belongingness and Love-***psychological needs, ***Esteem-***psychological need (i.e. prestige and feeling of accomplishment), and ***Self Actualization-***self-fulfillment need (achieving one's full potential, including creative and community activities). More can be found in a related article providing a primer on the topic: Saul McLeod. (May, 2018). *Maslow's Hierarchy of Needs:* Simple Psychology (on-line at https://www.simplypsychology.org/maslow.html).

6   Barbara Bush, the only women since Abigail Adams to be both a wife and mother to a U.S. President offered this quote on March 11, 2010. More can be found at goodreads.com.

than yourself…get involved in the big ideas of your time." Mrs. Bush also went on to say, "Some people give time, some money, some their skills and connections, some literally give their life's blood…but everyone has something to give."

Beyond individual giving, our culture and history honors independence more than it does interdependence. However, in light of the millennial's interest in social enterprises, a more collaborative, and for many, a new paradigm is to pivot from individual sovereignty over issues to one of shared stewardship. Peter Block[7] (2009) describes stewardship as balancing one's own interests while embracing the deep consideration of others' perspectives, needs, rights and interests. In his terms as well as mine, it is something catalytic, not commanding; facilitative rather than dominating.

As a *globalist* and as a steward, there is a relational responsibility (i.e. people-to-people) to respectfully challenge others as much as support them in being their better self. This is not an attempt to change them for your own purposes, but for theirs. *Globalists* respect the essence of others at a base level, so they do not need them to be different for their sake. It is rather about what is best for others and the community or the ecosystem they create and exist in.

> "We cannot live only for ourselves. A thousand fibers connect us with our fellow men; and along those fibers, as sympathetic threads, our actions run as causes, and they come back to us as effects."
>
> *Henry Melville*

Like the *creative strategist*, the *globalist* tends to primarily be conceptual in orientation. They not only see, but often create the big picture; and more interestingly, tie or make relevant the salient piece parts in the vision. They recognize the different personal leadership styles not as competing, but as differing ways to mediate reality, often in an appreciative manner. There is an effort to simultaneously suspend judgment at times so as to be open to contrarian views, and innovative options. This is while not giving in to core beliefs and principles. They are flexible, yet focused; visionary, yet respectful of history and the tried and true.

What extends capacity further for the Globalists than preceding leadership styles is that, by default, their base interests are in the broader community. Yes, at a deeper level, there is psychic gain in being purposeful and serving others, but the differentiator here is that it is principally done in the authentic spirit of investing in others-for them and not for self-aggrandizement or personal affirmation. The *globalist* wins by helping others to be more powerful and present in a way that makes sense for them. Their interests in seeing others profit is on a more enduring and grander scale: personally, socially, financially—lifting standards and practices for all.

At the time of Flight #232, United Airline's Chairman and CEO was Stephen M. Wolf. He had finished roughly five years of managing significant growth through acquisition and horizontal integration of key market assets, including Hertz Rental Car and Westin Hotels. He was by all accounts respected for overseeing the successful profitable operation of what was at the time the world's largest and safest airline, in a complex, ever-changing, hypercompetitive industry.

Then came this unforeseen tragic accident. The corporate lawyers sequestered Wolf. He was told to maintain a low profile as they and the communicators would be the go-between with the media[8]. Wolf was a strong personality, but also understood that when confronted by the media he would immediately be challenged to account for, apologize, and accept full responsibility and culpability legally and fiscally for the tragedy. Regardless of who was at fault. Certainly, he had heart and was

---

7 Block, P. (2009). *Community: The Structure of Belonging.* San Francisco, CA: Berrett-Koehler Publishers, Inc.

8 Based on personal discussions of status and near term actions between Corporate staff, colleagues and myself.

genuinely concerned like everyone else. Interestingly though, many months later, the National Transportation and Safety Board (NTSB) determined through its own rigorous investigation that it was General Electric (GE) and not United Airlines that was at least partially culpable, if not the primary factor in Flight #232's troubles. A GE parts supplier provided a defective fan blade in a key engine that was the determining reason in cutting the hydraulic lines in three places[9] on flight #232. This made the plane inoperable within a short period of time. Of course, blaming the airline in the absence of facts would be far more convenient and timelier in assigning guilt.

As time went on, the press was prosecuting Wolfe in the court of public opinion for not being more publicly present. Yet the lawyers were relentless in putting a firewall around the Chairman. The press was still ever vigilant in demanding access. The battle went back and forth. Hours seemed like days. I learned that Wolfe was agitated with the stand-off, as he grew wary of not personally address-ing the unanswered questions from families, victims, employees, the traveling public and the media. He reached out to some of my colleagues as I was on family relations duty at the time with those grieving victims. He became quite concerned, touched by the level of pain and trauma on multiple fronts. "Damn the lawyers," he was said to have thundered. To the surprise and disdain of his legal counsel, he shifted course, left the corporate compound in Chicago (Mount Prospect, Illinois). While he did not hold press conferences, he became very accessible to employees, and the surviving passen-ger community. He directly engaged more than a few difficult, emotion-charged, pointed questions. Through it all, he was most concerned about the families; but also, more broadly with the employees and the traveling public. He wanted our country to know that not only United, but the industry-at-large, was genuinely motivated and committed to safety. That it was not just rhetoric and United would do whatever it would take to find out, pay for, and fix the problem for good. Easier said than done, but he did it. This was a Globalist in action. He cared not just for his company and its profits. He put both aside when he went public for the good of people everywhere. He took on the wrath of more than a few investors and shareholders, but it didn't matter. He put values first, and many fami-lies and employees who he personally visited with grew strength and support from what he did.

Globalists often rise to prominent positions due to their mature presence while being tested in big and small ways. They think about what a better future looks like from outside-in, public interests are an overriding priority. What is our legacy, and the legacy of this generation and the institutions a part of it? They think about the truth at the heart of the matter and about universal principles in action.

In crucibles like the one described above, defensive routines may reflect a certain detachment or distance from center stage. *Globalists* may be a bit taken back by what is perceived as unfair or disrespectful treatment; and less aware, cognizant and reflective of their own role in the mess-making. On occasion, they can be charged with abandonment. That is, abandoning a key position or platform for action when needed. From an appreciative stance, in challenging spaces, *globalist* often build safe and supportive social environments to further build confidence and competence with others. Candor and care at a community-industry level matters. They seek a fully engaged, prosperous and profitable future, distinctive, relevant and of great service to those that follow. They are humanists, visionary, responsible for the problems of today and are engaged in leading a bigger tomorrow with value and velocity that makes a sustainable difference.

---

9 Note: Multiple sources document the compromised GE manufactured fan blade as part of the problem with the DC-10 Flight #232. However, the NTSB also raised questions about the role and timing of United's maintenance and certification process for this equipment as well. See, *Part of Flight 232 hydraulic system found.* (Oct. 21, 1989): UPI Archives.

STRENGTHS:

- Seeks greatest good for the greatest number
- Visionary: Thinks big picture about a future far reaching, aspirational and hopeful
- Values inclusion, differences, excellence, performance, creative distinctions, and principles based on respect and dignity
- Strong work ethic, high standards, persistent
- Affirms and inspires communities and communities of thought
- Willing to take risky, public positions on principle, but may be strategically measured in timing and approach

DEVELOPMENT AREAS:

- May deny or distort reality to fit an aspirationally desired image or prototype
- At times may be over-invested in one's own ideas at the expense of a better way
- May occasionally be quietly or boldly arrogant or elitist if challenged; 'My way is the best way-period'

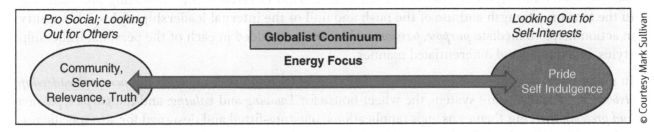

Figure 5.12: Continuum that describes the *Globalist* focus from a self–other perspective

The Five Transformations of Personal Leadership©

—The Central Question at Each Stage —

Stage 5	**GLOBALIST** (Self as Us)	How do we make today and our future better for all of us?
Stage 4	**CREATIVE STRATEGIST** (Self as We/Us)	How do we create new innovative ways of functioning that transform our way of doing and being (Leveraging stability and flexibility, sameness, and difference)?
Stage 3	**OPTIMIZER** (Self As We)	How do I use the right tools and processes to work with others to efficiently build conventional forms of progress and impact?
Stage 2	**PROBLEM SOLVER** (Self as Me/We)	How do I leverage options and opportunities to address practical issues for me and my key stakeholders?
Stage 1	**PROTECTOR** (Self as Me)	How do I control, predict, and promote the outcomes I need for what I want?

Each stage has its own inner logic and can reflect its own success and satisfaction within the arc of its own operating assumptions

Figure 5.13: View of key messages framed in question form for each of the five Personal Leadership Styles

■ While deeply curious and thoughtful, can sometimes readily abandon a position/investment without fully doing due-diligence if it is of a personal matter
■ Embraces or initiates conflict from a principled or global perspective based more on the interests of others—but may do so when it is too late or at a time that is less than effective

Summary

The five personal leadership styles as described in this chapter are part of an overarching operating model. Their way of making meaning or '*knowing*' and *valuing* from a big picture conceptual perspective, and a self-as-me to self-as-us is the foundational powerhouse in expressing individuals' purpose, passion and presence in many different ways. Purpose is further enabled through effective use or expression of *competence, care, curiosity, courage* and *community*. Passion is further enabled through *enjoyment, excellence* and *effort*. Presence is further enabled through *awareness, agility, affirmation and authenticity*.

Agility is a critical role in the presence thrive theme in particular but is also strategic enabler to varying degrees that assists the facilitation and integration of purpose and passion as well, within the five leadership styles. Agility is like the elastic band in recognizing, mediating and adapting to the tension, strength and use of the push and pull of the internal leadership styles. This agility in action helps to mediate *purpose, passion and presence* embedded in each of the personal leadership styles, in a unique and differentiated manner.

In many ways, one can visualize this operating model (See figure 5.14) with the *personal leadership styles* being the operating system, the wheel-house for *knowing* and *valuing*; and the *purpose, passion and presence* thriving themes as apps (applications), custom-fitted and designed for site specific use in bringing to life the full value of self in high demand settings. *Agility* is a key contributor in the flywheel in calibrating speed and direction of energy and effort.

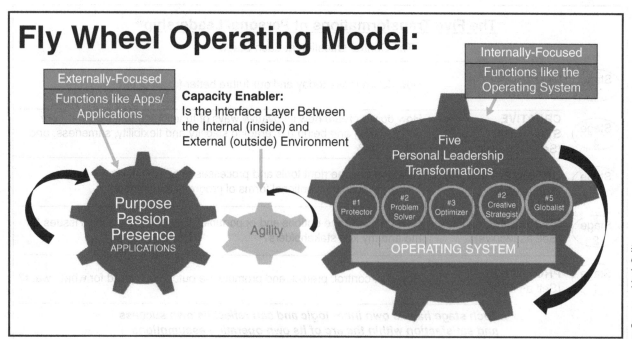

© Courtesy Mark Sullivan

Figure 5.14: A way of looking at the interdependent nature of personal leadership and its relevant supporting contributors

Overall, it is important to keep in mind that the leadership styles are an organizing framework reflecting a dynamic organism, the self. It is constantly in 'work-in-progress mode.' Whether we are in college, retirement or in-between, we seek to bring relevance and functionality to our moments and methods of living life. In the process, a few pointers about the model[10]:

- **Growth occurs in a sequential order,** from *protector* to *globalist*, yet is organic and free floating within each stage of development.
- **Developmental Platforms** (i.e. PLS: *protector*-to-*globalist*) staged from one level of capacity to the next, describes an ever increasing potential and capability of understanding, skill, wisdom and impact. However, preceding stages can be no less successful and satisfied should there be a goodness-of-fit between intent, effort and outcome at that given stage.
- **World views or big picture operating frames,** evolve within each PLS *protector* to *globalist* stage: from simpler to more complex, from somewhat concrete to more conceptual, from more of a me-we view to a more of a we-us view. See figure 5.15.

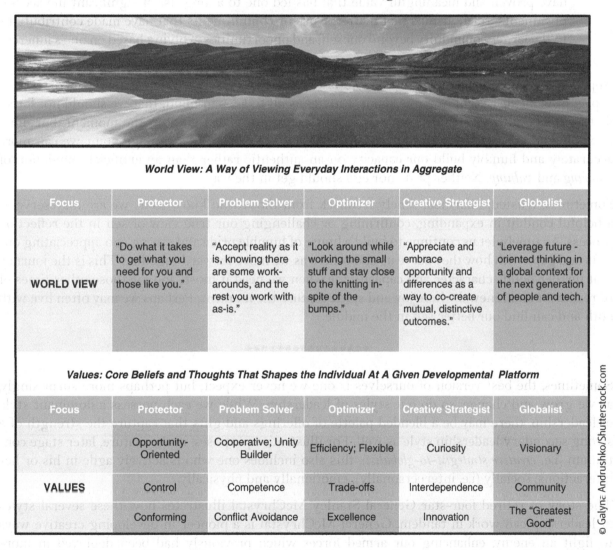

World View: A Way of Viewing Everyday Interactions in Aggregate

Focus	Protector	Problem Solver	Optimizer	Creative Strategist	Globalist
WORLD VIEW	"Do what it takes to get what you need for you and those like you."	"Accept reality as it is, knowing there are some work-arounds, and the rest you work with as-is."	"Look around while working the small stuff and stay close to the knitting in-spite of the bumps."	"Appreciate and embrace opportunity and differences as a way to co-create mutual, distinctive outcomes."	"Leverage future - oriented thinking in a global context for the next generation of people and tech."

Values: Core Beliefs and Thoughts That Shapes the Individual At A Given Developmental Platform

Focus	Protector	Problem Solver	Optimizer	Creative Strategist	Globalist
VALUES	Opportunity-Oriented	Cooperative; Unity Builder	Efficiency; Flexible	Curiosity	Visionary
	Control	Competence	Trade-offs	Interdependence	Community
	Conforming	Conflict Avoidance	Excellence	Innovation	The "Greatest Good"

Figure 5.15: A view of the Personal Leadership Styles from a perspective of what is important at each stage

© Galyna Andrushko/Shutterstock.com

10 Note: Some-to-many of these five personal leadership model principles are somewhat related in spirit to the pioneer research on ego development done by Susanne Cooke-Grueter's seven stage model in the same area.

- **Later stages** are based on growing through developmental platforms and gaining insights, experience and skills from preceding ones. Earlier stages do not grasp the insights and capabilities of later stages; but later stages understand and leverage the inherent value of earlier stages.
- Each later stage is simultaneously **more differentiated and integrated**, flexible and durable, complex but efficient in addressing challenging goals, decisions, issues, feelings and actions in what is discovered or realized as an increasingly more dynamic (ambiguous) environment.
- **Each stage has value unto itself**. They have their own inner logic based on a series of in-the-moment choices or preferences (conscious and unconscious) that have provided its own level of comfort, security and functionality.
- **Stage gazing or comparing one set of style capabilities** against another often leads to something less than an appreciative stance of oneself in-the-moment. It is important to remember that fully functioning, empowered personal leaders in any style, at any stage, have proven and meaningful value that has led one to a long list of significant life accomplishments: relationships that matter; work or commitments that have made contributions to the larger community beyond oneself; and opportunities evolving based on one's inherent presence in the world.

Appreciating and affirming oneself as one is today, while acknowledging growth opportunities, is part of what successful living is about. I invite us all to keep in mind, that we should not force-fit that image into an artificial self-construct that makes us feel good in the moment; but more honestly and appreciatively recognize where we are now. From this vantage point we can more accurately and humbly build our capacity on an authentic rather than an artificial foundation of *knowing* and *valuing*. Neither pride nor ego should get in the way.

Sometimes, trusted, informed, timely feedback from those who know us as we are may serve as a helpful conduit in expanding, confirming or challenging our true view of self in the reflection process. As timely, let us continue to build a house of humble pride and strong ego appreciating our gifts and gaps with how they serve us and others as we move forward together. This is the journey that further builds character and capacity for when we need it most; and for those other times of refreshment and renewal where joy and spirit capture the moment. Perhaps we may often live with both and can find our better self in the middle.

****

Sometimes, the best version of ourselves is one we never expect; but perhaps more surprisingly, as we grow and change, so do our styles of leadership. While we each possess a dominant style of leadership, there may be a blended palette of offerings and gifts that capture the strength of a strong secondary leadership style as well. For illustrative purposes, in the mature, later stage continuum (i.e. *creative strategist-to-globalist*), this also includes one who is actively agile in his or her interactions: socially (i.e. interpersonally), emotionally and physically.

The story of retired four-star General Stanley McChrystal illustrates how these several styles of leadership can work in tandem. General McChrystal is a pioneer in developing creative ways to fight an enemy, enhancing our armed forces which previously had been deployed in more traditional ways. When, in the global war on terror, our forces were being undermined by smaller, less equipped, but nonetheless deadly adversaries, McChrystal's inclusive, adaptive, global and imaginative approach helped to change the tide.

General Stanley McChrystal Interview

General Stanley McChrystal comes from a tradition of commitment; both his father and grandfather served in the U.S. military. Like his father before him, McChrystal graduated with a B.S. from West Point Academy in 1976, and in his long career of military service, became the general in command of the American and international forces in Afghanistan.

Rising through the ranks, McChrystal lived with military discipline and gained insight while serving around the world in high-stakes assignments. Like all successful military leaders, he learned to think systemically. However, he is also known for advancing more creative approaches to new forms of warfare in the later years of his career, especially as he gained experience and responsibility.

McChrystal was appointed to serve as Commanding General to the Joint Special Operations Command (JSOC), the military's premier counterterrorism force, in September of 2003. When he took that job, the group was operating under traditional systems that were effective in quickly destroying hierarchical terrorist networks, but not as adaptable as the new insurgencies emerging in the Middle East. McChrystal could see that JSOC needed to change; instead of asking his soldiers to operate in carefully delineated silos , he began to integrate intelligence, combat, and strategy communications within the JSOC community. The new structure made his troops more agile and effective resulting in the high-profile capture of Iraqi dictator Saddam Hussein and killing of Abu Musab al-Zarqawi, the terrorist leader of Al-Qaeda in Iraq.

In June of 2009, McChrystal was appointed to lead American troops in Afghanistan, and shortly thereafter assumed command of NATO operations. Again, he thought about the war in a new way. He was a leading proponent of the "surge" strategy in Iraq which would require additional troops be sent in to wipe out enemy combatants. More simply, the strategy was to add more troops with the goal of ending the conflict faster.

In 2010 though, after an off-the-record quote appeared in *Rolling Stone Magazine* which was critical of the administration, McChrystal began to think systemically again. The story appeared online at about 2 a.m. in Afghanistan. He remembers, "my military assistant woke me up and told me about it. I went down and read the article and said, 'Okay, this is a nuclear bomb.' I made some calls back, went out running right there in the compound at three in the morning, I actually thought I was dreaming and that I was going to wake up because this is just not possible. This was not something I thought I could ever be accused of. Immediately you think, okay, I can connect the dots where this is going to end, not everybody could but I felt that I could then. I started to think about my son in college, my 86-year-old father, my wife and all this stuff takes place on the front page and on TV at every moment. First thing in the morning we're working and that afternoon I'm told to fly back to the States to see the President." A few days later, President Obama accepted McChrystal's resignation.

McChrystal said he then had decided how to command the rest of his life. "I started making decisions sort of on an hourly, daily basis but they start to weave together as sort of a thesis for the rest my life. I think it probably took about a month where I made enough decisions that the direction I was going to take was clear." For example, he initially did not want an official Army Retirement Ceremony (commonly called a parade). He thought the pomp and circumstance would make him feel embarrassed by the circumstances of his retirement. But after an assistant suggested the parade was more for those who would be attending, he "started making those decisions and interestingly enough, the more you do that, and the more you take the high road, the more the high road becomes the only option."

In line with this view, McChrystal has another take on the hero's journey. In his mind, "there is this narrative construct on the hero's journey where the hero has a big climax or crisis and then the hero wins in the end. There is always a danger for the kind of work that you're doing when you end up talking to those kinds of people who have a happy ending. That's skewed," McChrystal said. "Not everybody has a happy ending because the crisis can end at different points. You can have the ability to rebound, you can have the time. My story to date, it's not completely over, has been one that is pretty lucky."

After retiring from the army, McChrystal founded a consulting firm to help guide companies through the kind of organizational transformation he led in the military. He published his autobiography, *My Share of the Task,* and is now working on a book that, in just its premise, serves as an example of creative strategy. The book analyzes accomplished individuals, often in surprising pairings, to drive home McChrystal's points about what makes a leader "good" or "bad." For example, one chapter contrasts the leadership of the still-iconic fashion icon, Coco Chanel, and the eccentric and colorful Walt Disney. McChrystal explained both were incredible entrepreneurs, but the way we have come to view their success does not always reflect their nuanced roles as leaders of their respective industries.

McChrystal's new work also navigates the contours of zealots, like Abu Musab al-Zarqawi, and heroes like Harriet Tubman, the abolitionist who ushered slaves to freedom on the underground railroad. Both of these leaders, he said, became larger in death than in life. McChrystal said viewing each of these individuals as humans and as leaders, helped his team to "reach a general thesis that leadership has never been what we thought it was. It's never been the great person theory, list of traits, behaviors. In this complex interaction of factors, the leader is only one part."

****

Similar to McChrystal, another story is of a governor shaping a new, socially transformative environment when all stakeholders had significantly differing starting positions. Former Kentucky Governor Steven Beshear's capacity to knit together very diverse and competing interests in an imaginative manner provided the energy to travel over a rocky road to a hoped-for better destination.

Also, like General McChrystal's creative and global leadership style, Governor Beshear offers a similar rich mix of the same. While his life's work is in a different field, he too illustrates the agility of moving with facile, flexible ways to engage with a diverse group of people, also in socially challenging, complex environments. Governor Beshear, noted formerly as the "Health Care Governor," has a story of turning around a state that largely had serious health care coverage issues. His eight-year effort to pull together very divergent and sometimes adversarial political and community groups helped to transform Kentucky into one of the leading health care states in the country. I met him in Massachusetts where he was busy teaching at Harvard University's Graduate School of Public Health. His personal leadership style of blending *creative strategy* and *globalist* practices particularly featured an agile manner of building a genuine consensus in a sometimes hostile environment.

Governor Steven Beshear Interview

Steve Beshear, former governor of Kentucky, put a strong emphasis on healthcare during his time in office which spanned the introduction of the Affordable Care Act, known as Obamacare, in a state where President Obama and his healthcare plan had low approval ratings.

Beshear, a Democrat who served as governor from 2007 to 2015, said he campaigned on a simple message. "I said I don't care if it's a Democratic idea or a Republican idea, if it's a good idea, we are grabbing a hold of it and implementing it," said Beshear. "I went around our state saying that and I would get a standing ovation whether it was in a Republican stronghold or a Democratic stronghold because people, regardless of their party, are really looking for that kind of leadership. Leadership that would rise above partisan politics and put the people first."

As governor, Beshear had to deal with the challenge of working with two legislative bodies dominated by the different parties: A Republican Senate and Democratic House. "I said the elections are over and now the people of Kentucky expect us to be Kentuckians first and Democrats or Republicans second," he said. "It didn't work every time, but as I continued to talk and communicate with both sides of the aisle, pretty soon people would start responding to that message."

Meanwhile, Beshear said, "And I learned that you have to listen as well as talk. As a matter of fact, if people would listen twice as much as they talk we would all be better off," Beshear said. "Everyone looks at the issues differently, and that's human nature. And so, you have to have a conversation—both parties and individuals – in order to work through differences and find the common ground on which we can agree and move forward."

Beshear pointed to an example. He wanted to raise the age at which a student could drop out of school from 16 to 18. He said he had no trouble convincing his fellow Democrats, but for years Republicans resisted. His wife, Jane, also supported the change and lobbied for it in the statehouse. "My wife is really persistent. She kept smiling and saying, 'I will be back.' And we kept having those conversations and finally found a way." The Republicans would allow the change statewide if 70 percent of the individual school districts approved. Beshear said he negotiated that down to 55 percent. When the Senate agreed he then began a campaign to get the districts to vote for the change and within a few weeks he had reached the threshold. The entire effort took five years.

"We felt it was worth an eight-year effort if necessary," said Beshear. "It's frustrating and irritating at times," he said. "But you have to keep coming back to the realization that people have different opinions and you just have to keep the conversation going. Be persistent but be understanding and listen and see if you can find a way to work through. And we found a way to work through."

Beshear said he had to understand the importance of respect rather than anger when a difference came up. "There are times we are mad as hell. But we don't win over people by going over and throwing gasoline and a match at them. You have to show you respect the difference of opinion. That doesn't mean you agree with it. But you can disagree without being disagreeable," said Beshear. "When you do it in that way, it always leads you to the opportunity to find another way. "If you go and burn the house down the first time that you lose," he continued, "you are never going to have the opportunity to move into that house. So, you've got to respect other people's opinions and you've got to leave room for the difference and find the way forward."

While in office, Beshear said his focus was on people, and what he could do to better their lives. The controversial new federal health care law provided a dramatic opportunity for the state government to help people receive health care. While many surrounding states rejected the Obama program, Beshear initiated both key components, a statewide healthcare exchange and expansion of the Medicaid program subsidizing premiums for low-income residents.

"The main reason that it worked in Kentucky was because we turned it from a political issue to a people issue," said Beshear. He noted that Kentucky's health statistics had been among the worst in the nation for years. "I knew coming into office that healthcare was one of those areas where we might be able to make a little difference, but it is so complicated and so expensive we wouldn't be able to make a lot of inroads there," he said. "Never in my wildest dreams did I think that when I went out of office I would be known as the healthcare governor."

"The Affordable Care Act was a tool to use to change the course of history in Kentucky in terms of health care," he said, even though he noted it was as unpopular as President Obama in a staunchly red state. "But I also knew that I would not be doing our people justice if I did not try to grab ahold of this opportunity to make a huge difference in the future of our peoples' lives."

Beshear used federal planning money to help develop a sustainable state insurance exchange. He also had to decide whether to expand Medicaid in the state in order to extend access to care to more low-income residents. "That was a tougher decision to make because I knew it was the right thing to do, but I had to decide whether Kentucky could afford to do it from an economic standpoint. Or, would this be a budget buster, that would basically bankrupt the state."

"So, I asked PriceWaterhouseCoopers to come in to do an actuarial study and give me, to their best knowledge and ability, predictions about what the expanded program would do for Kentucky or to Kentucky," said Beshear. He said that six months later, "They came in, sat down and looked me in the eye, and said 'Governor, you cannot afford not to do this.' So, I knew that was the right thing to do, and now I knew as much as I could, that we could afford to do it."

Politically, the expansion plan was a huge risk. But Beshear said, "We just needed to figure out how we sell it. So, we went out across the state to campaign. On the campaign, I said, 'You don't have to like the president. You don't even have to like me. Because it's not about him, or me. This is about you, your family and your kids. So just do me a favor and it won't cost you a dime. Just go on the Website, look and see what you might be able to get. And I guarantee you, you are going to like what you see,'" said Beshear. "We also sent out various people in all the communities to talk to our people. We call them connectors. They were connecting people with health care, and we went into every library, every community and every festival that summer. That was my goal. I figured that if they saw what they could get, they were going to like it by what whatever name it's called. And that's what happened."

Beshear said people who had never had medical attention were able to go to the doctor for a check-up and to the dentist. "All at once, these families couldn't believe that they can not only go but take their kids to get health care. They were thrilled," he said. Beshear explained that when people have increased access to medical treatment they are able to find out about problems and chronic conditions sooner. "Because they are learning how to manage it, they are going to have a much better life and a longer life."

Beshear said he began to be recognized for his work in healthcare reform in the state. He recalled being at a bowling alley with his grandchildren when a worker there said, "'You were the governor, weren't you?' And I said, 'Yes, I was.' He said 'All of my family have health care because of you. Thank you.' The very next day, I went in a coffee shop to get some coffee, and the young girl behind the counter handed me a cup and said 'Governor, I want to thank you for my health care,'"

Beshear's wife, Jane, has played an important role in his professional work. "Quite honestly, I couldn't have been as successful as I was without her," he said. "She's my chief advisor, my best friend, and my confidant. To have support like that makes a huge difference." Through his life, Jane has given Beshear unconditional support. "We've now made 48 years in our marriage. Sometimes, you have to compromise and negotiate and consent to different opinions to have a successful marriage. And that applies to how you deal with other people. Jane obviously would be supportively understanding, but more importantly, she could train me to debate, add ideas about issues and how we can all get things done."

His career in politics had early ups and one major down. In 1974 when he was 29, Beshear was elected to the state House of Representatives. In 1979, he became the state attorney general, and four years later was elected lieutenant governor. He then ran for governor when he was 43. "I was really a rising star and I ran for governor and I lost. Quite honestly, I was devastated."

Beshear took the loss hard. At that time, he ran across a quote from a 1910 speech by a Republican president, Teddy Roosevelt that had an impact on him. The speech is titled *The Man in the Arena*. "He wrote: 'It is not the critic who counts; not the man who points out how the strong man stumbles, or where the doer of deeds could have done them better. The credit belongs to the man who is actually in the arena, whose face is marred by dust and sweat and blood; who strives valiantly; who errs, who comes short again and again, because there is no effort without error and shortcoming; but who does actually strive to do the deeds; who knows great enthusiasms, the great devotions; who spends himself in a worthy cause; who at the best knows in the end the triumph of high achievement, and who at the worst, if he fails, at least fails while daring greatly, so that his place shall never be with those cold and timid souls who neither know victory nor defeat.' It consoled me a little bit. I had lost, and I lost something I really wanted. But at least I had tried, and I'd been in the arena."

Twenty years later, while working to get a credible Democratic candidate to run in the 2007 Kentucky governor's election, every candidate that Beshear and his group suggested turned down the opportunity. "One of the fellows in this small group of people with me, came to me and said, 'Well, Steve, I guess you are going to have to run.' I literally laughed at it and said 'Right, I have been there done that. That's not going to happen,' He said 'No, I am serious. I want you to seriously think about it,'" said Beshear. Later the man handed Beshear a card that had the Roosevelt quote on the back. "He had no idea what that quote meant to me," said Beshear. "But that made the case."

Beshear's second, successful campaign for governor illustrates his most important piece of advice. "Never give up. You need to be persistent. You never know what opportunity is your last. You are not always going to win, but you will learn a lot no matter if you win or lose. You take a step further in the effort you made. You are going to learn something somewhere along the way," he urged. "I am not saying to be reckless in decision-making. Obviously, you calculate your opportunities and chances for success. But the risk is there. There are no sure gains. You've got to be willing to take the chance of losing in order to win."

Chapter 6

A Way of THRIVING

Personal Leadership Style: The PROTECTOR

PLS Characteristics: Speed, Decisive, Resourceful, Attentive to Interests, Creates Loyalty, Family and Clan Cultures, Examples of Working Against the Odds – Making Things Happen

"Universe is frightening; we need a protector, and a meticulous mind is the best protector; it is like a watchful dog which guards us all the time!"

Mehmet Murat ildan

"Those who are skilled in combat do not become angered; those who are skilled at winning do not become afraid. Thus, the wise win before the fight, while the ignorant fight to win."

Morihei Ueshiba

"When a protector leaves you, it looks like the end of the world. But you gradually learn to walk by your own feet."

Bangambiki Habyarimana

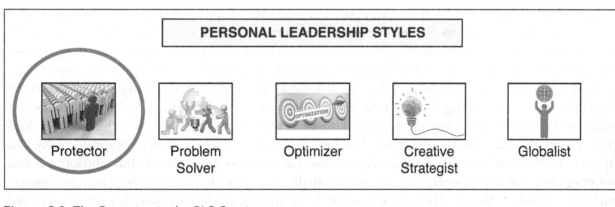

Figure 6.1: The Protector in the PLS Continuum

Featuring

■ **Shin Dong-hyuk**, North Korean Prison Camp Defector

■ **Weston Smith**, HealthSouth CFO Whistleblower

Santa Claus has a bit of the *protector* in him. Inherently good, *protectors* focus on interests and actions. They want to deliver. They are keenly aware of life's balance sheet from a trading and transactional perspective. They work hard and can be very focused within chunks of time. *Protectors* deliver incredible amounts of meaningful value in many ways. They are extremely loyal to people and causes that reflect what they are about. At the same time, like Santa, they keep score of who is on the naughty and nice list. If you cross the Protector, however, your name gets scratched off permanently. They expect you to be "all-in."

Protectors have their own form of a loyalty pact that must be re-upped continuously through action and words. This is linked to ground-foreground issues[1], or how I see myself showing up in the midst of competing interests or a high density, rivalrous social context. This underlying tension between *who I am* and *who I want others to think I am* influences one's presence in the moment. The loyalty pact helps to ameliorate or reduce such tension between the two. Being real and relevant for *protectors* is about helping them get their way on their terms. This allows *protectors* to focus and reinforce the agenda, their agenda, at hand. However, there is also a tender side that reflects deep appreciation and kindness toward those "like me" that have excelled at demonstrating loyalty and support. To those who are deemed loyal, *protectors* can be most generous of spirit, hospitable and less on-guard. An early developing *protector* actually does not differentiate between 'self-as-me' and 'others like-me.' We are all one-in-the-same. They are also all the more deeply pained, surprised or upset if 'other's like-me' violate *protector's* norms or expectations. In some regard, it is me letting me down.

Later stage *protectors* go out of their way to meaningfully assist and enable others who are part of the in-group. They demonstrate true leadership in helping others like them to have a better life or a better way in the near term. They can be deeply committed to a cause and will fight to the end to ensure things turn out the way they want them too.

---

1 *Ground-Foreground* issue is a classic Gestalt principle that contrasts the difference between what is in-front, or up-close, in relative comparison to what is behind, or in the background. In an everyday context, one could say that in a sales pitch the ground is the attractive set of benefits offered and the foreground is the service, warranty of other related promises supporting the benefits and proposed near term felt-value.

While agility is not their strong suit, *protectors* will defer to outside authority structures or more imposing, powerful others if they believe they would lose some of the incumbent advantages they now hold. They pivot to deference or to subservient compliance as a means of holding sway with higher authority. This is not to take away from their inherent strengths as a 'strong-man' coalition builder – it is their way of surviving and thriving in tough times. When pressed, they do deals in the moment with themselves, trading off their normal ways, complying to powerful others for approval, stature and safety. This transactional approach is a means-ends orientation of bargaining with "the Man" not always taken seriously as life-changing, but rather morally expedient to get through the moment.

From the outside, other leadership styles appear to do the same. Yet *non-protectors*, particularly those in the later stages of the continuum, are different in that on a conscious-level they may wrestle with their behavioral trade-offs in association with a different set of values and principles. (i.e. compliance for safety and approval versus authenticity at a price). Also, later stage protectors sit with questions like *What am I becoming by joining in; Who am I by ignoring the inner better self.* They are wrestling with "me against the not-me." *Protectors* are wrestling with "me as me" or "me as no more." They sit with *how do I win—so that I and the others 'like me' will get a relational payout that I or we deserve? Protectors* focus on supporting self by standing internally as a unitary whole preserving the interior self from the imposing differing other outside of self. Sometimes the external force is experienced as not only more powerful but also more threatening.

However, *protector's* outward compliance is not taken seriously as the "real me," rather a necessity of relational give-and-take. Later stage non-protectors may end up with the same outward behavioral trajectory—compliance in the face of overwhelming power—but their inner reflective path has a different blueprint. Their energy is focused internally on attempting to maintain / calibrate integrity or integration of "what I believe in" with "what I am doing and being now." This give-and-take mediation for later stage non-Protectors may yield an awareness of an unsettling inner presence often tugging at options for a better me if there is one.

Protectors often rise through organizations where structure and concrete value is appreciated. The rule book is both literal and figurative. The military, law enforcement, accounting and audit organizations are but a few examples where *protectors* can thrive and where they contribute greatly. These environments are honorable and notable in their own right, yet for *protectors* they can also be opportunistic. In industry, Albert S. Dunlap, a classic *protector*, made a reputation as a CEO turnaround artist transforming balance sheets into high value, highly leveraged assets before he would sell the company or parts of it off, at great personal gain[2]. For some he was a hero. He delivered results if you were on the right side of the investor cliff.

In 1996, on the outside appointment of Dunlap to CEO of Sunbeam Corporation, the company share price leaped nearly 50 percent on the announcement. He was viewed as a rock star on Wall Street. The share price rose even further after the company reported another 'Dunlap turnaround' a year later in 1997. Sunbeam's board responded by agreeing to double Dunlap's base salary to $2 million a year. These stunning results did not happen without a cost on multiple fronts. Interestingly, he embraced the nick-name "Chainsaw Al" after laying off thousands of jobs at his previous employer, Scott Paper. He claimed the large-scale reductions in force were necessary to cut operating costs at Scott. He justified his $100 million pay out when he engineered a Scott and Kimberly-Clark merger claiming they were now more competitive and leaner than before. Perhaps

---

2 Floyd Norris. (September 5, 2002). *Former Sunbeam Chief Agrees to Ban and a Fine of $500,000.00*, NYC: New York Times newspaper.

they were, but the emotional and institutional cost as deemed by former employees, suppliers, and other stakeholders claimed it was at a price.

Protectors are decisive, resourceful and results-driven. They appreciate both means and ends and will often use both in service of the other. At Sunbeam, Dunlap drove the share value up to $53 when it peaked before the Securities Exchange Commission investigated his questionable accounting practices. Upon SEC review, Sunbeam's stock tumbled to nine cents per share value prior to liquidation. To be fair, Dunlap claimed previous management had overstated earnings which appeared in his first and subsequent year by classic "cookie jar reserve" tactics. The SEC contested his view and noted one such possible Dunlap tactic was his "buy and hold" sales approach, ironically a cookie jar tactic in itself. Sunbeam would sell barbecue grills to retailers in the winter at deep discounts even though the grills would not be delivered and paid for until the spring. As such, that pumped the incumbent year of sales and profits at the expense of the following year.

No matter who was responsible for what appeared by some to be fraudulent practices, Dunlap had a history of making things happen in demonstrative ways. *Protectors* are like that. They are anywhere but in the mushy-middle. Life is clear and concrete. They often have limited tolerance for ambiguity. They are less about ideas and more about people and results. They look at circumstances from a standpoint of winning or losing. Who is calling the shots, who is out of line, who is on my side, who is against me. This may create an abrasive edge. However, the orientation enables one to quickly take corrective action in protecting or preserving interests that matter and hypervigilant to underlying intentions of others – perceived or otherwise. *Protectors'* interest are served by knowing if they are in trouble—or should create some—if the system is not playing to their side. For *protectors*, thriving under duress requires road blocks for offenders while attentively pushing ahead with their agenda, seeking opportunity or advantage in the moment wherever possible.

Their way of thriving under duress is to create road blocks or deals (i.e. behavioral trade-offs such as compliance for acceptance and affirmation) with the offenders; while attentively pushing ahead with their agenda seeking opportunity or advantage in the moment wherever possible. *Protectors* may use raw, banal, free-floating energy to assertively power through resistance. Under perceived threat or intense challenge, they may use either or both ends of the engagement polarity: from some form of withdrawal (i.e. silence, masking, sarcasm, distorting) to more assertive energy (i.e. stereotyping, demonizing, bullying). The speed in which all of this happens is in nano-time, instantly.

In general, idea-driven, cognitive-based arguments are *electrical* in nature, calling on the quick neuronal signaling and transmission of the brain and related hardware. Emotion-driven, or affective-based reactions are *chemical* calling on a different process dynamic that is also lightning fast yet can become gooey or stuck in the emotional process terrain. Regardless, bottom-line, in the eye of the storm, Protectors double-down in preserving and protecting their core interests for self and for their constituents – those 'like me.' As suggested, it may take the form of defiance or compliance. From their standpoint, either or both serve the greater good of their eco-system. *Protectors* are ever true to their nature of delivering speed, decisive actions when possible, results and reinforced safety for the enterprise – self and 'others like me.'

****

The following story further illustrates how the world view of a *protector* can play out in simply trying to stay alive in a more dramatic and difficult environment than what most of us could ever imagine. *Protectors* are often durable, persistent and strong-willed. *Protectors* can survive where others may not. Shin Dong-hyuk, a North Korean prisoner, raised in Camp 14 for 24 years from birth, is one of the very few who escaped from horrific conditions deep in the back-country of this primitive, hostile communist state. His beloved wife, an American friend turned soul-mate, was our translator. Now, both living in Denver, CO, Dong-huk and his wife are committed to running an active human rights campaign, in part, to free his father and others from the same prison in which he was raised.

Shin Dong-hyuk Interview

Shin Dong-hyuk escaped from the infamous North Korean Camp 14 in 2005, when he was 24 and became a human rights advocate and critic of the North Korean regime.

Dong-hyuk's upbringing can only be described as traumatic, growing up in Camp 14 and similar camps. "The moment I opened my eyes and could really think for myself, I already considered myself just as an animal who needed to live my life as a slave. I had no other concept around me. I literally didn't know if I was living in a good place or a bad place. I didn't know that it was wrong, I knew nothing but my life as a prisoner," Shin explained.

While in Camp 14, Shin had to endure beatings, starvation, and psychological torture. Even his biological parents did not serve in a parental role. "At the end of the day, they were just fellow inmates. It's not like they had a chance to sit down and guide me or give me any kind of advice.

"I can't think of them, that I necessarily really learned from them," Dong-hyuk continued. "We were not even allowed to share emotions or use expressions that were caring or loving. We didn't have this concept of family, there was really no notion of my parents at that time inside of that kind of circumstance. You don't have a sense of family because you were born in a circumstance where they are fellow inmates. They didn't even have the opportunity to share any type of emotions towards me. So, unfortunately, at that time I didn't have a whole lot of emotion."

As laborers, Dong-hyuk said, "All of us prisoners had a quota to meet during work hours. There would be certain requirements on how much work we were supposed to do. We would have to think of something to say that I should've done better or think of something to say that I could have improved on. The guards always want to hear you calling out your peers, whether it be your mother, brother, or fellow prisoners. So, you would try really hard to come up with something to snitch on the other person even if it didn't exist. You really want to try and make it seem like you were paying attention because, you're required to report on people if they are lacking in some area. You basically say what they want to hear and ultimately, they'll say, 'Okay, so-and-so gets another scoop' of whatever distasteful thing that they're serving or, 'We're satisfied with what we heard, here's another slap of mush for you.' It's pretty unfortunate, but literally our whole purpose was to do anything we could to get on their good side. Any chance we got to tell on somebody else, we would, just to make ourselves look a little bit better."

Dong-hyuk has told journalists that he unknowingly gave information to guards that led to the public execution of his mother and brother. After watching them die, Dong-hyuk plotted to escape Camp 14 with a fellow prisoner. "A really smart person wouldn't even attempt to escape. Someone who had common sense wouldn't even think to attempt it, because all you're trying to do is survive day-to-day, under the continued watchful eye of prison guards. You already know better than to even let that cross your mind. So, in a way, it was because I was so dumb that I thought

© ChadwickWrites/Shutterstock.com

I could try," he said. "But I did have the desire to just go across this fence, to just get across and see what it's like over the fence and maybe I can have a full stomach for once in my life. Maybe, just thoughts like that were a part of the reason. Obviously, there was a higher probability of dying crossing that electric fence successfully. All my life, my 24 years, I had seen and witnessed countless executions in front of me from the moment I was a little boy. I know very well that a lot of those executions were due to individuals who either attempted, talked about, thought about, or tried escaping."

"There was one other person who was trying to escape with me," Dong-hyuk recalled. "As we approached the electric fence, he either got to it faster or fell on it, but he got electrocuted first and his body kind of made an opening. I was just lucky to get through. I still had gotten a little electrocuted on my shins, but it was luck, really. Although the other man fell on the wires before me, I still got the electrocution on both of legs and they were bleeding, but I went through, and I kept running."

Dong-hyuk had focused on freedom his entire life. "There was something I really envied for 24 years of my life living there—I really used to envy the birds that could just fly in and out of the camp. They were just so free to fly anywhere." The birds were the first hint at the possibility of freedom for Dong-hyuk.

When he finally was free, however, he had trouble adjusting to new thoughts. "When I lived in the prison camp, I never considered myself to have any type of potential or gifts. After ten years of living in freedom, little by little, I started to realize that I do have potential and abilities," he said. "I had so many years of my life without love or happiness, or the notion of love and happiness. I had so many years where I thought it was hard to really wrap my head around these feelings I was feeling and comprehend these emotions I was dealing with. Even right now, I am struggling to find myself, day-to-day still learning how to cope with these emotions good or bad."

Now that Dong-hyuk is married and settled in a free and safe nation-state, he has had the opportunity to meet many other people, from different cultures and upbringings. These experiences have made him realize the resilience of the human spirit and see potential in himself and in others. "As I lived in South Korea and traveled the U.S., I noticed that there were quite a few young individuals with potential who would give up so easily or just didn't have the resilience that I felt like they should really have, as humans all have resilience. I felt like sometimes they lacked that kind of resilience." But, sometimes they need something more. "I can truly say without a doubt that I believe in miracles. My life is a miracle," Shin said. "If I could do anything to improve somebody's life or give hope then, I will be content with that alone."

Protectors are not all one way or another. They are a unique combination of strength, resourcefulness, self-absorption, resilience and fallibility. They often get things done under incredible conditions that others can't. In the story about Dong-hyuk, his *protector* personal leadership style, in-part, helped to keep him alive and find an advantage that worked in his favor. He became the first home-grown, fully raised North Korean internment detainee to ever escape. Jumping over his dead, electrocuted camp-mate to get to the other side of the live fence, and then running while partially electrocuted himself through a mountain pass to China beyond to freedom was an amazing accomplishment. It was also pure *protector*: Fast action, decisive, results-driven, self-serving–to save his own life.

★★★★★★★★★★★★★★★

This leads us to another fascinating and far different setting than Shin Dong-hyuk's that shows how a *protector* can play out in a multi-faceted manner within an organization. Weston Smith was a bright, talented controller and CFO of HealthSouth in the 2000s. His healthcare company had nearly $4.5 billion in revenue in 2003, dominated the rehabilitation, surgery and diagnostic services market and employed more than 60,000 people at 2,000 facilities in every state of the U.S. It also had facilities in the United Kingdom, Canada, Australia, Puerto Rico and Saudi Arabia. It owned and operated a number of acute care hospitals that specialized in orthopedics. At the time Smith was CFO, the company was the largest publicly listed healthcare company in the United States, based on the number of locations, and the third based on revenue[3].

Weston Smith, raised by a "wonderful family with good values," as described by Smith, worked hard to provide for his family and to climb the corporate career ladder in a competitive financial services environment. Fast forward a number of years and he became the CFO of HealthSouth, a high growth health care company, working for a tough, charming, "take-no-prisoners" kind of CEO boss. It was for a publicly held company, demanding the typically ever-increasing numbers for the boss and for the stockholders. The pressure to produce was relentless and the boundary between what was legal and not continued to blur. This is a story of redemption and renewal for Smith: One that started with good intentions, then led to greed, then fear, then an active and conscious state of trying to do what was right, regardless of the consequences.

I met Smith while he was a guest lecturer on business ethics to some MBA students at *The Ohio State University*. His personal story was so compelling that it caused many of the business students to question in a more serious manner what they would do if they were in Smith's place. Smith now spends all of his time working to get future business professionals to function in the way he did in his early career and not to be enticed by the trappings of big money acquired in a less than honorable manner. In terms of leadership, as later stage *protector*, Smith sought to come clean on his terms and that of the government. Then through a personal transformation, in part due to

---

3 Interesting on-line source for *CFO Newsletter*: McCann, David. (March 27, 2017). *Two CFO's Tell a Tale of Fraud at HealthSouth*. CFO.com.

the shock, pain, depression and fear of prison life, he has grown beyond the protector style as he seeks to help others to have a better life than what he experienced.

Weston Smith Interview

Whistleblower Weston Smith was in deep after participating in widespread financial fraud at HealthSouth Corporation, a fast-growing Birmingham, AL, healthcare provider through the 1990s. Ultimately, he became an FBI informant and served 14 months in prison.

Smith joined HealthSouth in 1987 and soon became aware that company executives were routinely overstating financial results. At first the deception seemed small, possibly within the discretion of the company. He told himself that they could be resolved in audit adjustments later. But as the years went by the pressure to maintain and expand earnings growth eventually became a fraud estimated at $3 billion.

© Soiroview Inc/Shutterstock.com

Smith said the clear objective was to pump up the earnings to meet, or exceed, Wall Street expectations and drive up the company's share price. A higher stock price gave the company more cash to finance acquisitions and fuel more growth. "Any company is going to have certain judgment gray areas or whatever you want to call it that the numbers can go in any direction. It felt like a lot of judgment type calls at that point. At least, that's what we were saying to one another. The fact of the matter is that these judgment calls are being driven by the need to hit the Wall Street number. "

The tone of the company was set by its hard-charging CEO Richard Scrushy. "He was the bigger than life CEO. He wasn't just in the business world, he was a major power figure within the state of Alabama," said Smith. "I've had people tell me this that obviously they didn't like that I had participated in this fraud. At the same time, I got a lot of credit because I finally stood up to Richard and blew the whistle on him."

Smith knew about the overstated earnings from the start. "I just saw it as a very aggressive place with very aggressive goals and financials. It was getting slippery at that point, but Richard's a pretty tough guy to work with, very demanding. At the same time, I kind of viewed it as what a great career opportunity I had in front of me. I'm with a start-up company that had gone public. If we can truly grow this company and make something out of it, wow I'll retire by the time I'm 50 years old."

"Richard always wanted to exceed whatever internal growth we could possibly budget," continued Smith. "Part of that is management, setting tough goals, making people work harder. I understand a part of that but the other part of it was that he knew that the existing numbers were being fraudulently met." Each quarter the earnings inflation grew. "It began as kind of a small number and it had this snowball effect."

In all, Smith estimated that 25 people were directly involved in the fraud and another 200 probably knew it was going on. By 2000 he became controller of the company with more responsibility over the HealthSouth audits. "That is when things became elevated as far as getting some real personal accountability. That is when I became very serious about how are we truly going to fix this problem? We have to take ownership to this problem. How are we going to decrease the earnings and expectations or how are we going to improve our internal operations enough to bridge the gap?"

Meanwhile, the company began to face new competition and unfavorable changes in the industry. "Our own internal numbers were becoming worse. However, Richard would have nothing to do with it as far as guiding Wall Street. He continued to announce that we were going to grow at certain levels which we knew internally weren't possible," said Smith. "At that point, we had blood on our hands. The numbers were way off base. If we just suddenly say, 'Richard, we're not going to cook the books anymore and we're going to report the truth,' the falloff would have been so great that somebody would have recognized that we had been cooking the books for a long, long time at that point. Just stopping the fraud at that point, didn't feel like a viable option because that would have revealed the fraud itself."

Smith and other executives began to try to come up with strategies to structure the business so that the fraud would not be detectable. One executive used the word "fraud." "Richard said, 'Don't ever use that word in this office again. Your plan sounds good, go do those things, but we're not going to use that word.'"

Scrushy justified the financial lies because many thousands of employees and their patients were depending on the firm. "There were all these rationalizations of why it was okay to play with the numbers because of some kind of noble cause that was there. Richard was the kind of guy that if you wanted to have a hard conversation with, it had to be one-on-one because he liked to be the bully. Group settings are no place to challenge the guy because you got hammered pretty hard," recalled Smith. "He was also very paranoid the entire time. If anyone ever handed him a piece of paper with fraudulent information on it, he would kind of slide it around with his pencil, look at it and then, slide it back. It was to the point of not getting his literal fingerprints on a damaging piece of paper."

In 2001 Smith was named chief financial officer and the following year was subject to the new Sarbanes-Oxley Act, also known as the "Public Company Accounting Reform and Investor Protection Act." The law carried tough penalties for corporate executives who submit misstated financial results and was prompted by financial scandals at Enron and WorldCom. Smith said: "That was the slap in the face of, 'Weston, you have been living this lie for so long it's time to put it to an end.' I started making noise with Richard and some of the execs at that point and basically said, 'Count me out, I'm not going to be here.'" He said he would not sign off on the next financial statements.

Scrushy leaned on him to stay. "As he put it, you may be willing to fall on your sword, but think about all of the other people that are going to get hurt when you do. He started naming names of the other people that are involved in the fraud. He was saying things like, 'Angela just had a baby. She's going to go to prison and who is going to raise her child when she goes off to prison?' There was this emotional pulling of heartstrings. This went on for quite some time."

Smith said Scrushy promised he would restructure the company and put Smith in a division untainted by fraud. Smith stayed on and signed another set of statements, but then Smith said Scrushy reneged. "At that point, I said, "Enough. Enough.""

He called a lawyer and met with a team of federal agents in hotel attached to a Birmingham mall on a Saturday night. Smith's instructions were to walk through the mall first to make sure he was not being followed. "It was like something out of a John Grisham novel," he said. Smith spoke with the agents for three hours and said that the expression in the agents' eyes indicated the fraud was much larger than they had expected. "I was obviously scared to death. I knew my life was about to change in a number of very unpleasant ways," said Smith. "I didn't have a promise of immunity, or a plea deal or anything like that. I knew I was in trouble. What I do remember well is when I left that hotel room that night, I felt the biggest sense of relief. I was thinking, Thank God, the lie is over.'" He slept well that night for the first time in years. "I knew I was in trouble, but my attitude was, Okay, I'm in trouble, but it's also over at the same time. This is the past and I'm going to accept the consequences of what I've been involved in, but the lies are over."

Before federal agents raided HealthSouth and the scandal became known, Smith felt he was in danger. He said the company had a well-armed security force. "The weeks leading up to it becoming public, I watched my back," he said. "I think they would have had me whacked. I really do. I'm not exaggerating. I think one way or the other, they would have had me killed." Soon, though, he was less concerned. "It became less of an issue because everybody would have had to be whacked once it became public."

Smith said his decision to come clean was rooted in strong values passed on from his parents. "When I did start crossing the line with what I got involved with I was still blessed with good parents. I knew right from wrong. Later on, when I was distracted and all of the other temptations that came along, at the end of the day, I think that foundation that my parents provided was what kept me awake at night." He said that background led him to think, "'This isn't right. What are you doing Weston? Why are you going down this trail?' Ultimately, that is what led to my final decision to blow up the fraud at the company. It was just the fact that I wasn't going to live my life like that anymore. I was living a lie. It was a terrible internal conflict as far as who I was."

He recalled that during HealthSouth's boom times he bought a big house in Birmingham. When his parents came to see it for the first time he said his mother told him, "'Oh Weston, we're so proud of you.'" Smith said that felt like a punch in the gut. "So much of that was based on lies, this so-called success in life. At that point, I felt like I denied their trust. This wasn't real in so many ways. Of course, I hid that from them. I wasn't going to confide in what I was in the middle of. She meant it as a compliment which really stood out at the time because I knew who I really was."

Smith received a 27-month sentence for his part in the HealthSouth fraud, but was not prepared for prison. "I felt like I was trapped in time and in somebody else's body. The first night I was there lying in a top bunk bed and thinking, 'Oh my gosh, this is my life for the next two years.' It literally felt I was suffocating. I literally felt like I couldn't breathe," said Smith. "It just didn't seem real. The whole time I was thinking, 'How am I going to get through this.'

He relied on a schedule and staying very busy with chores, reading and anticipating Sunday visits with his children. "On Sunday, late afternoon, once visitation was over Sunday nights were by far, the worst time as far as, 'Okay another week of this place,' just kind of getting through the whole humility, depression, and in dignity of the whole thing," said Smith "I learned a lot about humility during that time. Just all of the material things stripped away really not so much that as just being in federal prison. Being an inmate is it was suffocating in many ways. It took a lot of soul searching during that time of, 'Weston, how did you let your life become so messed up that you're now in prison?'

Scrushy was tried but acquitted on charges related to the HealthSouth fraud. He did serve five years in prison on unrelated bribery charges. Smith said Scrushy takes no ownership of the HealthSouth fraud. "To me, let's just say for the sake of argument that he didn't know about the fraud, he still owed a lot of people an apology. He could have at least said, 'This happened on my watch.' For many years as this was all going down, he never even did that. He just continued to hold himself out as a victim from a bunch of folks."

After his release from prison after serving 14 months, Smith found it awkward to run into some acquaintances, "They looked at me like I had leprosy or something like that. They were afraid of what they could talk about," said Smith. "There was almost a fear of carrying on a conversation. That was just extremely humbling to not want to see people I used to know." More often, though, he was surprised to be met with warmth and acceptance. "The reaction was a thousand times better than I expected. People were good. People were kind and forgiving more than anything. Even leading up to that, there were a lot of times when I was between coming forward and actually going to prison that people were much better than I really deserved or expected."

As mentioned earlier, Smith now works as a speaker lecturing on business ethics. He was struck by a plaque on a wall at Dartmouth University that read 'Who does not answer to the rudder will answer to the rocks.' "I saw that plaque and thought that's me right there. I was living an undisciplined life without the rudder and keeping everything under control and look at where I wound up. I wound up on the rocks but more important than that, look at who was on my ship. My family, friends, parents. All of those people were on my ship when I crashed that thing into the rocks," he said. "Of course, there is the wind that can blow a ship way off of course. The wind in our life can be the distractions and the temptations that can blow us off course. There I was trying to build the super career and make all of this money and all of the so-called riches that go along with it. That was nothing more than distraction. That was just blowing me off course with who I really knew I was."

Courage. The courage for Smith to do what he did was perhaps more salient and significant while sitting in his jail cell in re-considering his life purpose-his identity of who he was and what he wanted to do about it. Prior to jail, his actions to come clean appeared to be perhaps more about pain reduction – coming clean to have more of an emotional baggage-free life. This is not to minimize his attentiveness to right and wrong. Going public would knowingly be at a tremendous personal cost on multiple fronts. Tough to do but not surprising for a Protector taking inventory on the emotional and familial costs of self-deception.

Also, with years of mounting, weighty, conflict-laden pressure his decision to go to the FBI was a strategic early step toward transitioning to a later stage of functioning on the personal leadership continuum. He could begin to view the world from something less than me versus 'not me' transactional calculus. He could begin to think of himself in relation to his family, friends, neighbors and colleagues with new eyes and more malleable relational values under construction. It was also a return to his roots where life was good. But perhaps in his return, it was now as a road-tested life warrior with new and deeper sensibilities affecting his knowing and valuing life orientation. It has been said in the popular culture, that life is about growth or decay. For Smith, he chose growth. He chose a better way.

****

See Book Web-Site For More Detail On Engaging The (Protector) Storm Chart!

STORM CHART		
storm Intensity		
Developmental Strategy Focus To Assist in Turning Tough Times into Better Times (See THRIVE book web-site for detail on how to use THRIVE Capacity Enablers)		
Personal Leadership Style	**Category 1-3** Strong Winds (Revive-Thrive Strategy)	**Category 4-5** Intense Hurricane Force (Survive-Revive Strategy)
	THRIVE Capacity Enablers	**THRIVE Capacity Enablers**
Protector	Care & Awareness	Courage, Effort, Affirmation
Problem Solver		
Optimizer		
Creative Strategist		
Globalist		

Courtesy Mark Sullivan

Chapter 7

A Way of THRIVING

Personal Leadership Style: The PROBLEM SOLVER

Focus on Getting Things Done; Achieving Unity, Community and Collaboration in a High-Change Environment

"When something bad happens, you have three choices: You can either let it define you; Let it destroy you; or you can let it strengthen you.

Dr. Seuss

"Too many problem-solving sessions become battlegrounds where decisions are made based on power rather than intelligence."

Margaret J. Wheatley

"The direct use of force is such a poor solution to any problem, it is generally employed only by small children and large nations."

David Friedman

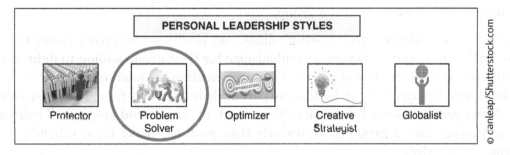

© canleap/Shutterstock.com

Figure 7.1: The Problem Solver in the PLS Continuum

Featuring

John Foley: FBI Street Field Commander of the Boston Marathon bombing

Photo © John Foley

Bart Decker: First 9/11 Special Forces Horse Soldier Team in Afghanistan

Problem Solver

Problem Solvers are the core of any organization. Whether a family business, or a commercial, faith-based, military, special interest or government entity, *problem solvers* bring the capacity to get things done. When trouble arises, as it inevitably does, the *problem solver* is there to help figure things out. Unlike the protector, they can assess what's happening from a broader view, beyond the me versus the 'not-me.' The landscape is less me-against-you and more about how to work with others to do the right thing for the right group. In some ways, being the 'company man' or 'company woman' may seem less than glitzy, but *problem solvers* are critical in transmitting necessary norms, roles and rules that make the culture and operations work. Without them, things can fall apart pretty quick.

Problem solvers have reached a level of confidence that allows them to go out beyond the self in acknowledging how others view the world, at least somewhat different than themselves. Unlike protectors, others who are different are not perceived as a threat or an attack on one's own identity. Such differences are seen more as an oddity that needs to be dealt with. This recognition of a more expansive collection of interests is not one of fully understanding or appreciating such differences. *Problem solvers* completely owe their allegiance to their in-group, yet seek to make peace or be a neutral arbitrator to those outside the group.

Their efforts to sometimes get-along-to-go-along can cloak an underlying intent to win others over, if possible. Other times, they are an ombudsman for their group willing to fight or clash with others but ever so respectfully and gently. They are sensitive to violating boundaries and are also keenly committed to supporting those that are part of their in-group. Equally, they are community-minded. Many *problem solvers* have a vibrant network of friends and contacts. Their capacity to nurture a broader, mixed group of individuals than *protectors* make them valuable, particularly when support is needed.

All the while, *problem solvers* may focus not on what they personally think is best, but rather on what others and the organization think is best. Without always thinking for themselves, or in an original manner, *problem solvers* are more dependent on leveraging the ideas and actions of their high-status in-group with which they strongly identify. This does not diminish their capacity to observe and engage with what the *protector* cannot see. In challenging contexts, *problem solvers* can come up with many more options than *protectors* and have the social repertoire to more deeply connect with others over a broader set of complex issues and opportunities. They can be resourceful and, like the *protector*, very determined.

Problem solvers also enjoy providing advice and counsel which makes them additionally valuable, particularly as tension mounts in high-demand environments. They build credibility and trust-worthiness as they seek solutions for better times. *Problem solvers* build a reputation as 'can do' players in organizations as they are motivated in pleasing or satisfying leadership for the very nature of their efforts. They can particularly address challenges in high-demand situations that are concrete, structured and involve a social ecosystem respectful of the incumbent authority or hierarchy. Six sigma, military, and technical cultures that focus on efficient methods and practices, particularly more structured environments such as manufacturing, combat and information technology units, are well-suited for and often have many problem solvers.

Conversely, organic, innovative more abstract challenges such as creating and piloting new business models in a start-up company or trouble shooting goodness-of-fit issues between large contrasting organizations in a post-merger integration would typically not be comfortable areas for the more concrete-thinking problem solvers. Nor, on an individual level, would diagnosing multi-layered relational issues creating conflict between two very different types of people. However, ever-practical problem solvers will often seek the support of institutionally sanctioned others such as advisors or external consultants who can do more of the abstract, critical-thinking or work requiring a third person perspective or deep empathic or analytical powers. Once the plan evolves they are exceptionally strong in executing or implementing clearly stated objectives.

While *problem solvers* enjoy providing advice where they can, they do not necessarily reciprocate. *Problem solvers* will tend to only be most attentive to taking advice from specific high-status individuals. The notion that good ideas and insights can come from anywhere is not necessarily recognized by problem solvers. Rather, good ideas come from officially approved or trusted sources. Certain dogma, rituals, methods, practices and positions can be swallowed whole which is a means of showing loyalty and dedication to the revered or respected members of the in-group. Their appreciation for the right way of seeing things as expressed by their key source leaders, helps them to respond quickly to problems that are unfolding. Often problem solvers express little doubt or questioning of the narrative, key messages or content in terms of implications, interaction effects, synergies or root causes. Questions are more about what, when and how versus why. This confidence in the in-group or its leadership also means they trust from a truth and accountability perspective. *Problem solvers* may be accountable for some of what they do, but the overall decision, direction and destination is often outsourced to others.

When things heat up, the *protector* and *problem solver* function very differently. The intent of the protector is to get what they see fit. They are more oppositional in a full-throated way to protect interests at-large. That is to protect the self and those like-me without regard to the cost on others. Bottom-line, life is good if the *protector* has control. Part of the effort is to claim power, or in the face of an overwhelming force defer, distract or conflate. However, this does not diminish *protector's* capacity to care deeply about those in their "family." *Protectors* can be as generous and even charming as much as they are forceful and assertive, if they have the opportunity. Likewise, those in the 'family' would do anything for the protector.

For *problem solvers*, being loyal and dedicated versus being in control is the primary thrust. The look and feel of conflict appears differently for a problem solver than the knife fight of a *protector*. *Problem solvers* engage seeking common ground but are still very intent on shape-shifting the ground to get the opposition to follow their in-group's agenda. The *protector* attacks, or charges ahead pushing; the *problem solver* affirms, ingratiates or entices as their opening salvo. Similar to *protectors*, *problem solvers* will follow-on with transactional ways to pay-off or trade favors, but for very different purposes.

Protectors seek to protect the interests of those like them with somewhat limited regard to others. It is not that protectors are cold or callous. They are often just not genuinely in touch with their own feelings or that of others, in the moment. Intellectually, they want good things for everyone.

And they will claim it boldly. Experientially, everyone must fit in their box as defined by them or they simply don't exist in any meaningful manner. Empathy is not their strong suit. *Problem solvers*, from a Gestalt perspective, are more stable on unbalanced terrain. You can lean on them more without fear of temperamental waywardness. They can deliver when the chips are down with less drama and more focused energy. It is always directed in a way that confirms their loyalty to their in-group, their source for meaning and value.

****

John Foley had a notable career with the FBI with more than two decades of distinguished service solving some of the biggest challenges on the streets of Boston. His capacity to fight crime was particularly accelerated with an adroit ability to develop informants. Dealing with the underworld was not easy. But he addressed dangerous, sometimes life-and-death problems by building high trust relationships with key street informants who felt respected and appreciated in his straightforward manner of dealing with them. He never abused or turned on any informant so he built a reputation of being a credible law enforcement official to work with if the incentives were right.

As a seasoned *problem solver*, Foley knew the rules and roles required to get the job done. As a later stage *problem solver-optimizer*, he was efficient and flexible enough to bend in multiple directions to get and manage street resources, skills and assets to always stay one step ahead of the bad guys. This proved invaluable when the biggest challenge of his career came along, the 2013 Boston Marathon bombing at the marathon finish line. Here is his story of a talented professional and *problem solver* able to hunt down and secure an out-of-control threat and put a big city at rest after almost five torturous days of terror and anguish.

Mr. John Foley Interview

© Marcio Jose Bastos Silva/Shutterstock.com

Former FBI Asst. Special Agent in Charge (ASAC): Field Commander; Investigative Lead in the 2013 Boston Marathon Explosions. Featured in the movie, "Patriots Day"; featured in the National Geographic documentary "Inside The Hunt for the Boston Bombers."

John Foley had a long and high-impact career with the FBI, spending more than 22 years with the agency. He worked his way up through the ranks and then just three days after turning in his resignation, the biggest challenge of his career surfaced, the Boston Marathon bombing.

"I was far out West. My family and I were on vacation. We were taking a trip of a lifetime," Foley said. "Next thing you know, Monday, the marathon." He and his family were exploring canyons in Arizona without cellphone service when the bombings took place. When they got back to their hotel, he said, "My phone is on fire. My wife's phone is on fire." He returned a call to his office. "'What's going on?'" The response was, "'We've got a bombing. It's bad. It's big. I need you back here right away.'"

"I am there. I will get the next flight out," said Foley. He arrived in Boston the next day at 5 a.m. "Things were not good. People were at their wit's end. I was a source of comfort for them," said Foley who had experience with the agency working through shootings, hostage situations, abductions, gang feuds, drug wars and mafia hits. I had been in charge when the Boston field office had been in crisis events like agent involved shootings, etc. and people were looking to me to help them make it better like in the past.

Foley's performance and ability to lead the fevered search for the bombers, was rooted in years of problem solving on the street. He had become particularly adept at developing informants, the key to solving crime.

When Foley arrived back in Boston his problem was to give everyone involved, including officers from partnering law enforcement agencies, the confidence to do the jobs they were trained to do. During his time at the agency Foley had been through other high-stakes cases. Now, he said, he needed to reassure the many teams working to capture the bombing suspects to solve their own bits of the case. "We had good training. We had good people," he said. He wanted them to understand "' You know what to do. You just need to trust yourself and do it. And that's what they were looking for from me."

"I've got no secret recipe for this," said Foley recalling the early part of the investigation. "We were going to make it right. I know our world is upside down. I know it's not what we want. But you all have the skills to make this right," Foley said he told officers working the case. "In some sense, I gave them that confidence walking through the door," he continued. "They were looking up to me to make it right." When there were past problems and kidnappings and shootings we solved the case, saved the victims, or stopped the violence and got through the crisis. It's like you just kind of help them and encourage them to get through it." At that time the people working the crisis, the investigation, needed to know we were going to get through this and we were going to figure this out.

After the bombings Boston remained under siege for days. By Thursday, Foley and others involved in the hunt for the bombers had little or no sleep. He planned to get some rest that night, but those plans changed after the bombers killed a college police officer, car-jacked a driver, and threw bombs at pursuing police officers in nearby Watertown, MA.

When Foley arrived on the scene in Watertown he said there was smoke in the air. "Cops were yelling with high pitched stressed voices like schoolgirls 'Watch out they're throwing bombs,'" said Foley. He initially responded as a pure problem solver and began a foot chase after one of the suspects with others. Then he stepped back and told himself, "I have to be a boss. I can't be running through the streets and the backyards of Watertown."

"It was surreal," he continued. "People were yelling and screaming. It felt like a war zone." While the crime fell under federal jurisdiction, Foley stressed the importance of federal, state and local law enforcement working together. "It was a team effort. No ego," he said. Foley added that if people are given the chance to develop belief in themselves, they are easier to lead in a time of crisis. "If you are the boss, you are going to have to make a call. And no one has a problem with you making that call. They want you to make the call. But not if you are dominating people and regularly saying, 'I'm the boss. I am in charge." Moreover, he said, "My experience is if I have to tell someone I am in charge, then I've already lost."

The Boston Marathon bombing came at the end of Foley's FBI career, but two decades in the bureau provided him with plenty of opportunities to solve problems. For more than a decade Foley had worked long hours in an inner-city drug squad. Agents were expected to work six days a week. They started their days banging down doors and making arrests while suspects were asleep and easier to safely bring into custody. In the afternoon he wrote affidavits and did other investigative work. At night he went out on the street. "The bad guys were rolling out of bed in the late morning or afternoon, so you wanted to be out there when they were kicking around making moves." The days and nights were long, but the positive effect we had on the community made it all worth it.

Foley said that while he was on that squad he worked too much, but felt he was making an impact. "There are certain squads within every field office. They are the go-to men and women. They are the Clydesdales. They are all in, they are committed, they're razor sharp, they are focused. And if things go bad, you want them." The members of that squad were tough, he said. "Tough not in the sense of rough and cruel, in a sense that we worked hard. The bar is very high. We took our job real serious. And there were serious consequences for doing anything that is less than the best. Because someone could die, someone could get hurt," he said. "People would not raise their hand to be on that squad."

Even after a friend who was operating undercover was killed, Foley was not ready to leave that assignment. His partner asked whether Foley thought it was time for them to be done with the long hours and dangerous work. But Foley said he was still "all in." To cope with the stress and demanding schedule, Foley said he stayed disciplined and worked out to maintain his physical condition. Working out was good to relieve stress and was necessary to stay in shape to do the work, which involved crashing through doors, weighed down by firearms, ammunition, protective vest and helmet. "You need a level of fitness in order to be spry. To move," he said. "You had to be an all-around athlete to perform physically and mentally. You had to be on your game."

Foley said that he also relied on strong people skills. Foley is dyslexic and had "rough edges" growing up, but his father told him he had many abilities and urged him to continue to develop them. At the FBI, Foley said, good people skills tend to give an agent an edge. "The FBI's bread and butter is informants. Human intelligence. I excelled at that. I had a good cadre of really strong informants," said Foley.

He recalled an informant once let him know that a well-known mobster had been killed and was lying dead in a car. Foley called the organized crime office to let them know. The agent who picked up the phone said, "'What are you talking about?'" Foley replied, "'He just got assassinated.'"

Foley said the exchange continued, "'Why do you know this?' 'I got a call.' 'Oh, my God. Is anyone there?' 'No, there's no officer on the scene. No, nothing.' 'So, you are just calling me to tell me you have someone on the street, calling and saying he's here in a car, dead. 'Yep. They just killed him.' 'Incredible. OK. We will roll the cars.'"

Foley said informants have any number of reasons for offering tips, especially if an agent has developed trust. "People who live in the underworld were willing to talk about things. I didn't judge them. And we created a relationship," he said. "I would always look to find a common ground. And there is some good in everyone. I try to look for that. To work with them on that and create a relationship. I had people who had done some horrible things in life, but they would talk to me. That was incredible."

He stressed, however, that he did not exploit his informants. He looked for people who had a specific reason to talk. "Whether it was they felt they were making good on their past sins, getting revenge, financial, or respect from someone in your position. Whatever it is, you had to find it and you had to go there," Foley said. In some cases, he said, he helped informants out of a life they wanted to leave.

Now director of law enforcement at the Federal Reserve, police force Foley said he urges his officers to take on an open and engaging posture toward the building's 3,000 employees rather than a stern, unapproachable look. "If the employees or public see something that's not right or looks suspicious and your police officers are playing tough guy role and are unapproachable, then guess what the public is not going to do? Talk to you about it," he said " if you are engaging everyone who comes in the building then, right away it will be obvious to you when there's something not right with this person here and then you approach them to determine if there is something wrong. It's all people skills.

Foley recalled an FBI recruiter told him early on that he would have good and bad jobs at the agency. The recruiter advised him to work harder at the bad jobs in order to get the good ones. You live it every day. Foley said, "You apply for your next promotion or your next job every day you come to work. You work hard every day. You bring it every day. And if you do bring it every day, then when the crisis happens, when the big things happen, you are there you are ready!"

****

Similar to John Foley, Bart Decker focuses on getting things done when others pass or find it difficult to do so. Both Foley and Decker worked for different employers but have a similar approach to life and work. Decker, as an elite soldier in combat, proved the value of a *problem solver* as he executed against hostile Taliban forces, always attentive to in-the-moment warrior solutions needed, based on a unique skill set he developed in training. Decker with a premier special forces team were inserted into Afghanistan only days after 9/11.

Both before and after his days in the military he has continuously demonstrated a *problem solver* theme of identifying ways to meet challenge by assessing what the reality is, figuring out best options and approaches and then executing with focused attention. Here is Decker's story.

Bart Decker Interview

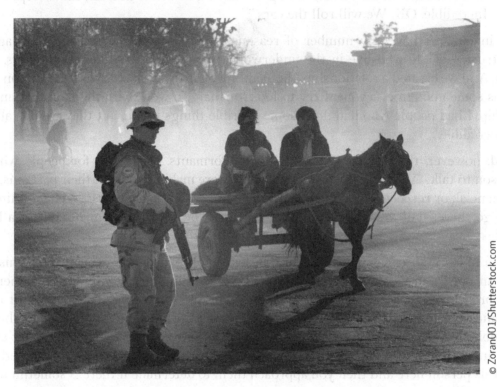

USAF Combat Controller as member of the first post 9/11 special forces horse soldiers attacking the Taliban in Afghanistan.

Source: ThadForester.com and WeAreTheMighty.com

© Zoran001/Shutterstock.com

In the movie "**12 Strong**", Bart Decker as an Air Force Combat Controller and his Special Operations team were portrayed as some of the first men inserted into Afghanistan soon after 9/11. They arrived by helicopter and then realized horseback was the only way to move to their target location since many of the ledges were 2'-3' wide. These men were covert operators named Task Force Dagger that joined up with the Northern Alliance to defeat the Taliban. As a radicalized Islamic military movement, the Taliban ravaged the Afghanistan country-side beheading and torturing the locals into submission.

Decker's team, the first American soldiers post 9/11, rode with the Northern Alliance on horseback to capture the Taliban-controlled military base at the city of Mazar-i-Sharif. The commandos' horses were trained by the Northern Alliance warriors to run toward gunfire. Charges pitting Alliance forces against the Taliban were much like those centuries ago, but the fighters used AK-47s instead of sabers.

After the successful advance at the Mazar-i-Sharif battle, the Taliban retreated and his team were welcomed as liberators. Decker and his team are forever honored at One World Trade center with a 13' bronze statue of an American Commando on a horse.

Bart Decker was born and raised in a small community in Northern, Illinois and after high school he struggled to make ends meet and to find a definitive purpose moving forward. But at 22 he joined the U.S. Air Force and became a combat controller. He was among the first airmen to enter Afghanistan to fight the Taliban after the September 11 attacks.

At one point, Decker had to ride a horse, atop a wooden saddle that slipped from side to side, to join with friendly local forces in Northern Afghanistan. "Looking back on it in hindsight, it's pretty remarkable when you get off a multi-million-dollar machine, a helicopter, and then jump on a horse back. You kind of go back in time," Decker explained. "What wows me was just the whole battle plan. It was basically just special forces teams with our guys attached to the teams, joining up with a faction, the host nation faction. I guess you could call it that because the Taliban took over and ruled that country by iron fists, in fear, intimidation, and murder. That's the remarkable thing when you look at that, moving in with indigenous forces."

Decker and his eight-man special operations team rode in a long horse trail for 10 days, sometimes moving at night, sometimes in the day. "When we went into the unknown, our job was to hook up with the Northern Alliance. That was the fighting force, ten-man, twelve-man teams, hooking up with different factions to oppose the Taliban. So, when you're with that group, that's kind of an unknown. You have to trust them somewhat because you're there and that's your objective," said Decker. "Once we got in the country, you know that the reason we are successful is because of the training that we did prior. When we got on the battlefield, to me, that just looked like the bombing range out in Arizona. It looked just like it except there were live targets out there. All of the procedures we were doing, were all based on what we trained with. You really saw it all come together. In the end, looking back, you go, 'That's why we did all those things. That's why training was just as tough as going to war,' it was identical."

His path wasn't always smooth. "I wasn't really interested in college, plus I didn't want to waste my parents' money. I bopped around a little bit. I remember going to Houston with a buddy of mine and I was there for a total of about 13 months—twenty years old at the time. My parents had retired down to Florida and I went with them initially, before going onto Houston.

Decker said he was living paycheck to paycheck. "I was too proud at that time to call back home and ask for money. That was definitely a struggle. I guess I just had that realization. I saw where I wasn't going and decided to make a change." After some failed business ventures, Decker was stuck. He didn't have the right clothes to land a job interview, he didn't have his own car which kept him from getting a bartending position.

"My buddy got an apartment and I needed to pay my share of the rent. So, at that point I realized that I had to do something to contribute so, I was working at a car wash for about six months. Another friend later moved in who was a cable tv guy and cable tv was really taking off at that time in 1981 and '82. So, I got on doing that and made more money. We moved to a nicer apartment, but in the end, I still did not have any of my own transportation and I remember sitting in the parking lot eating a baloney sandwich and drinking a Lone Star beer and I just said to myself, 'I'm not going anywhere.'"

He was a couple hundred dollars in debt when he called his father and said, "'Hey, I need to come home and reload.' He never asked me or gave me the, 'I told you so,' or anything. It was like, 'How much do you need?' and, 'Obviously, come on back home.' That was the kind of guy he was,"

Decker said. "I came back and I made the best choice of my life months later and I enlisted into the air force. It was a great run but living in Houston at the age of twenty-years-old, it makes you grow up fast when you are on your own. "

Moved back to Florida with his parents Decker was working in construction, primarily, masonry. "It is a young man's job, no doubt. You're hauling blocks across a concrete slab in 98 degrees heat every day. I was looking at being a mason because it is a next step up from the laborers. I was laboring half the day learning how to lay block and brick the second half of the day. But, I looked at the masons and was like, 'Wow, you guys look rough.'"

He met with and Air Force recruiter the following week. "I always had aspirations to be a cop. I thought I would go into the air force for four years, become a cop and then get out and try and do some law enforcement in the civilian sector," said Decker. At the recruiter's office he opened a copy of *AIRMAN* magazine. "There was an article about combat control—jumping, diving, rappelling, helicopters. I said, 'That's for me.' I talked to the recruiter and he said, 'Yeah, that's a pretty difficult career, not a lot of people make it.' I guess there is an 80% fail-out rate. I wanted to give it a shot and my recruiter was actually really good. He told me exactly what was going to happen, 'On day four or five you will go down to career field day and pick out these careers, make sure you put that as number one.' So, I did, I joined and went in late '83 at 22 years old. It's kind of weird, you look at a 22-year-old and an 18-year-old and it's kind of a big maturity difference. You really see it when you're in those environments like military training."

Decker credited the military with turning his life around. "I joined the service and got married young at age 24," he said. "When you're 23 or 24 in the enlisted ranks back in the '80s, you're not making a lot of money. We struggled a little bit financially, living paycheck to paycheck. We just kept at it and I made rank and the kids got older," Decker continued. "You just keep trucking and working forward."

He also had mentors along the way. Most notably, Mark Scholl. He was a staff sergeant and guided Decker through his earliest days in the Air Force. Decker described him as his "mentor before that word was even being used." Decker said Scholl, "just seemed to have all the right answers. I could sum it up with him. He was the guy that on a Friday night he could be putting on an exhibition at the bar with the best of them. On Saturday morning, he would be walking into the mall with his kids. On Sunday morning, he would be in church with his family. On Monday morning, he is writing the entire aircraft movement plan on the ground for the invasion of Panama. That was the kind of guy this guy was. He could get under any hat and be that guy. He was probably one of the most beloved guys in the career field, definitely on our team."

Scholl was killed in 1992 during a military exercise, but Decker remains humbled by the way Scholl approached his job. "He was the guy always leading the way. Like I said, he wasn't the fastest runner, couldn't do the most pull ups, but he would never quit in a situation. He was so good at everything and anything else. He was the guy that we looked up to."

Decker, now retired from the military, lives a quiet life in northern Florida, with his wife of more than three decades. His experiences in the Air Force gave him the discipline for the next phase of his life when he entered the civilian workforce. "When you look in the civilian world, usually what is different is when you're in the Department of Defense and you jump to a civilian job it's for profit out there in the civilian world. It's not-for-profit in the DOD world. Those type of roles and guidance kind of follow you, but you can definitely bring your skills in leadership from the military over," said Decker. "I'm telling you that most of these companies like to hire former military, probably because of the discipline that was instilled in them when they were in the military. Most of the time, you're going to get a guy on time that never shows up late, he's going to be a hard worker, he's going to see it through—those type of qualities."

He found his purpose in the military, and Decker encourages young people who have a "love of country" to use that initiative for good. "Be a productive member of society and everything else will fall into place after that. That is number one," he said. "You are already halfway there because you were fortunate enough to be born into this great country. Make a difference in a positive way."

A key point in his life, Decker said, was when he knew he would have the support of his family after he decided he wasn't getting anywhere in Texas and moved back in with them in Florida. "I just had that realization. I saw I wasn't going anywhere and decided to make a change," Decker said. "I just can't pinpoint what made me make that phone call back home. But I knew that was my opportunity to reload and go back home to family. That might not mean that somebody can't call and rely on a friend for something like that too, whatever situation it may be. Everybody might fall and stumble and all they need is that helping hand up. Not a hand out, but a hand up. I'm a firm believer in that type of philosophy"

****

Below is a Storm Chart that assists in choices helpful for problem solvers in high-demand environments. More details on how best to use it can be found in the book web-site.

See Book Web-Site For More Detail On Engaging The (Problem Solver) Storm Chart!		
STORM CHART storm Intensity		
Developmental Strategy Focus To Assist in Turning Tough Times into Better Times (See THRIVE book web-site for detail on how to use THRIVE Capacity Enablers)		
Personal Leadership Style	**Category 1-3** Strong Winds (Revive-Thrive Strategy)	**Category 4-5** Intense Hurricane Force (Survive-Revive Strategy)
	THRIVE Capacity Enablers	**THRIVE Capacity Enablers**
Protector		
Problem Solver	Competence, Excellence & Awareness	Community, Effort & Affirmation
Optimizer		
Creative Strategist		
Globalist		

© Courtesy Mark Sullivan

guidance kind of fellow you, but you can definitely bring your skills in leadership from the military over," said Decker. "I'm telling you that most of these companies like to hire former military, probably because of the discipline that was instilled in them when they were in the military. Most of the time you're going to get a guy on time that never shows up late, he's going to be a hard worker, he's going to see it through—those type of qualities."

He found his purpose in the military, and Decker encourages young people who have a "love of country" to use that initiative for good. "Be a productive member of society and everything else will fall into place after that. That is number one," he said. "You are already halfway there because you were fortunate enough to be born into this great country. Make a difference in a positive way."

A key point in his life, Decker said, was when he knew he would have the support of his family after he decided he wasn't staying overseas in Texas and moved back to with them in Florida. "I just had that realization I saw I wasn't going anywhere and decided to make a change," Decker said. "I just said, pinpoint what made me make that phone call back home that I knew that it was my opportunity to reload and go back home to family. That might not queen that... both... call and refer... friend for something like that too, whatever situation it may be. Everyone might fall back that... and all they need is that helping hand up. Not a hand out, but a hand up. I'm a firm believer in that type of philosophy."

* * * * * * * * * * *

Below is a Storm Chart that assists in choosing... helpful for problem solvers in high-demand environments. More details on how best to use it can be found in the book's web-site.

See Book Web-Site For More Detail On Applying The Problem Solver Storm Chart

Developing Leadership Focus to Assist in Turning Tough Times into Better Times

Personal Leadership Style	Category 1–3	Category 4–5
	THRIVE Capacity Enablers	THRIVE Capacity Enablers
Protector		
Problem Solver		
Optimizer		
Creative Strategist		
Globalist		

Chapter 8

A Way of THRIVING

Personal Leadership Style: The OPTIMIZER

Focused, Magnetic, Responsive, Excellence, Attentive-to-Details, Accelerated Performance

"Genius is making complex ideas simple, not making simple ideas complex."

Albert Einstein

"Insanity: doing the same thing over and over again expecting different results."

Albert Einstein

"Today you are YOU, that is TRUER than true. There is no one alive, that is YOUER than you."

Dr. Seuss

Figure 8.1: Optimizer in the PLS Continuum.

Featuring

Harold Donahue: Congressman (1947-1974), House Judiciary Committee during Congressional Watergate hearings

Mr. Ben Lesser: One of the very few to have survived the Buchenwald-Dachau Death Train and to be liberated from the WWII Nazi Prison Camp Dachau, in 1945

Optimizer's take everybody up a notch. They know how to support, fight, advocate, and solve problems. But most notably, they know how to inspire excellence and action in a purposeful manner. *Optimizers* build brands or become one themselves. They create a tangible difference in how people experience or participate in the broader organization or community. They  bring high standards and will often create a buzz as things are different with an *optimizer* in the room. They know how to translate intention into outcome, sometimes in a larger-than-life sort of way. They can be the celebrity coach, specialist, technologist wonder-kind, troubleshooter, executive consultant, etc.

Similar to *problem solvers*, for *optimizers*, the culture and operating mantra of the enterprise still holds sway in terms of their allegiance and action. They still follow conventional forms and routines that earn them respect and provide support for self and embedded groups. Knowing and doing the right way is still important. Standardization, rules, and order provide fair and expedient outcomes. They leverage a mature, structured analysis approach to address efficient ways to understand and embrace issues. And they are disciplined in using root cause analysis, process excellence and gap-closure strategies.

However, external dictums are softening. *Optimizers* are not quite so robotic or symbiotic with their organizations. They are less apt to follow blindly as their key embedded groups are not as much of an all-defining means with which to identify. Self-fulfillment is not principally or purely fed externally by the all-powerful high status other. The self is not as attached or as tightly wound to the embedded group. There is an internal awakening and awareness of knowing and being beyond the grasp of the more concrete-driven *problem solver* and *protector*. They are beginning to question authority in an ever so gentle manner. *Optimizers* are accepting of answers that may be a bit off script from traditional answers, or ways of doing things. They are more tolerant, flexing and adapting toward both efficient and more diverse practices. They are aware of possible options beyond the fence line.

Interestingly, *optimizers* are a transition style between earlier more concrete me-and-we style of knowing and valuing and later stages that are more conceptual, we and us style of knowing and valuing. Early signs of pattern recognition, theming and guided imagery begin to blend elements of abstract thought with concrete reasoning. They can anticipate conditions and consider interaction with the tone and texture of differing people and circumstances. The emerging abstract capacity allows optimizers to question what was taken for granted and to begin exploring people and interactions from third-person perspectives. This offers optimizers more power as they can personally reach and touch others with more sensitivity, awareness and attentiveness, in an under-the-skin, salient way. Such is the making of what can be the public face of institutions and organizations as *optimizers* can present an interpersonal magnetic quality that attracts others with their engagement or contact style.

Part of the distinguishing character of *optimizers* is how they bring both rigor and a malleable posture to what is expected. They both support and hold people accountable in a more discerning, less black-and-white fashion that brings fairness and respect in a more nuanced and appreciative manner. As such, *optimizers* begin to see others in a different light. *Protectors* are comparing others as like-me or not-like-me; problem solvers look at others in slightly expanded fashion as like-me or me-we.

Whereas optimizers recognize differences in others with more clarity and context. For the first time, there is an emerging, deeper appreciation for how others not like themselves make sense of things. Their 'knowing' has more of an early conceptually oriented perspective where they can begin to recognize or anticipate others' differing motives and intentions from different angles, sometimes even without others awareness of themselves.

Optimizers are more open to both giving and getting feedback. In fact, they are comfortable in inviting critique or soliciting feedback from others that deepen their awareness to underlying issues and root causes. They are not as quick to be lulled by artifice, symptomatic noise or canned positions offered by the larger community in which they are a part of. They do not fully let go of the 'institutional mind' but are ever so aware of some of the discrepancies in the organizational mindset and are willing to acknowledge contradictions and attendant tensions that come with it. The inner, psychic tension between being bound to their embedded group and objectively seeing holes in the terrain is part of their dynamic ying-and-yang challenge. *Optimizers* can engage from a second- and third-person perspective. This enables them to differentiate between self and group interests and goals in a more expansive, intentional, confident and, even occasionally, curious manner.

In earlier stage thinking, doing and being is based more on the concrete and present 'me' that I see and experience in carefully constructed, safe ways. Now, as an *optimizer*, it is more than a steady, stately, sturdy posture. At times, with broader awareness and attunement, there is intermittent recognition of new, uneven, prickly realities from both self and other. It can be messy, but there is an appreciation of what is there. With this new expansive lens on life there is no going back. It is a different vantage point, for getting information, sorting and sensing, valuing and discerning that blends multiple streams of self and other in a more dynamic environment.

Think New York City Mayor Edward Koch (January 1, 1978– December 31, 1989) and his signature phrase, "How am I doing?" He used that as more than a line, as he solicited feedback from a broad and diverse contrasting set of constituents citywide. His informal intelligence-gathering allowed him to validate, challenge or calibrate his positions and interactions to varied degrees. Koch often laughed in his large, gregarious in-your-face manner that he had his own focus groups as he questioned bus drivers, pedestrians, train commuters, restaurant wait-staff or whomever else he would run into in the course of his daily schedule. It was always the same question: "How am I doing?"

Mayor Ed Koch

© Barbara Alper/Archive Photos/ Getty Images

Koch interestingly maintained high public approval ratings for many years with his intensive close monitoring of his performance. Koch was first elected mayor of New York City in 1977, and he won reelection in 1981 with 75% of the vote. In 1985, Koch was elected to a third term with 78% of the vote. As a life-long Democrat, he was the first New York City mayor to win endorsement on both the Democratic and Republican party tickets.

He regularly got a pulse of varied ethnic, political, religious and socio-economic indicators that led him to support both major conservative and liberal causes. He was author of an ambitious public housing renewal program in his later years as mayor, he began by cutting spending and taxes and cutting 7,000 employees from the city payroll. As a congressman and after his terms as mayor,

Koch was a fervent supporter of Israel. He crossed party lines to endorse Republican Rudy Guiliani for mayor of New York City in 1993, Michael Bloomberg for mayor of New York City in 2001, and George W. Bush for president in 2004[1]. *Optimizers* regularly have a close and intimate understanding of trends and practices and able to do something with them that often create stronger capacity for individuals and their organizations.

Related to intelligence gathering and partnering with others of different stripes, when scandal arises optimizers, unlike the preceding personal leadership styles, are interested in determining facts, confirmed intentions and relative underlying factors that help to determine the truth as the truth. They are less absolute and forceful in their conclusion, more accepting of relative dimensions and how they support or challenge their own personal principles and values. In the end, however, they are still strongly biased by the opinion and positions of their embedded groups. *Protectors* will dictate the truth. *Problem solvers* will follow or support the pronounced truth as spoken by respected others in their in-group. *Optimizers* will respect, but question, the truth painfully and selectively accepting some of the realities that violate the in-groups strongly held norms.

When confronted with situations that challenge their natural approach, the protector's defensive measures are usually denial and distraction; for the problem solver it is absorption, or introjection. They tend to swallow the prescribed story. For the *optimizer*, it is rationalizing or explaining with a weighted bias that favors the institution. For example, when revealed that a cleric has had an inappropriate sexual relationship, style defenses vary in substance and form. *Protectors* will challenge the authority of the messenger. In spite of missing facts, the *protector* in defensive mode rushes to support the cleric forcefully questioning the motives of others. Or perhaps in addition, changes the focus to messenger versus the cleric. "What does the messenger gain from these lies? Look at all the shortcomings of the messenger – that is what we really need to be paying attention to?" This conflation or substitution of focus from one shiny object to another is a way of distracting attention from the original claim.

A *problem solver* in defensive mode would tend to recirculate the *protector's* moves, not offering new thinking but rather louder and more frequent claims of the *protector.* They are primary participants in the echo chamber. Their energy in being loyal and deferential to the in-group further supports their way of making sense of their world. Self-inquiry into their personal values and how they line up with the contradictory or questionable behavior of the valued other in question is often too painful or threatening at this stage. Integrity or integration of values and practice are shaped to fit a prescribed externally approved picture. The defense is to duck and dodge, to mask the truth with an alternative narrative with great volume and veracity so as not to deal with it directly. Questioning such actions would often lead to denial or a re-statement of their recirculated position. *Problem solvers* go circular while the *protector* clamps down or fabricates alternative truths.

Optimizers in defensive mode would recast the context to explain, but not refute, the violation. They might say, "The cleric is human like the rest of us and is deserving of mercy and forgiveness. Let us not walk away in the cleric's hour of need. Perhaps, out of exhaustion and sacrifice of so much on one's end the cleric deserves to be cut some slack." *Optimizers* are less willing to twist the truth as they have a lot of energy in holding themselves and others accountable. Defensive routines are more open-ended and adaptive. In general, they also have more perspective and bring an emerging sense of empathy given their capacity to now be able to see things from multiple vantage points.

---

1 Smith, Benjamin (February 1, 2013). *"Mayor Koch, Self-Proclaimed 'Liberal With Sanity' Who Led New York From Fiscal Crisis, Is Dead at 88". New York Sun.*

More confident in self as strong, but fallible, *optimizers* have the ego strength to accept contrasting behavior in others, not as a threat but simply as different. They are less rule-bound by categories, labels or stereotypes. For the first time in the leadership styles continuum, some ambiguity is tolerated. *Optimizers* can suspend judgment and not jump to conclusions over unknown motives. Unlike *protectors* and *problem solvers*, *optimizers* are more rigorous in confirming facts and intentions prior to placing judgement or attribution. Difference among others are viewed by the *optimizer* as a work-in-progress based on observation and interaction over time. Interest is beginning to shift from quick answers to deep answers; from being first or being right to getting there when needed by taking the right path.

Optimizers demonstrate a broader sense of responsibility and obligation to others while still honoring their own agendas. Some growing interest in social consensus is emerging. There are early formulations of what community is all about. They know community is not merely a collection of people going through the motions of the same thing the same way. Unlike the other styles this sense of community allows *optimizers* to have a world view that is more interconnected, more relational.

Value orientation is shifting in a more external global perspective: less about me, more about we and us. There is less judgment driving quick answers and more perspective taking that is shaping options and conditions for tentative conclusions. However, institutionalized form and function still matter and there is still very much a concreteness in delivering actions and efforts that align with embedded groups to varied degrees. Experience, expertise and judgment softens earlier stage ways of regimented response and approach with some flexing, custom-shaped, in-the-moment alignment as needed or allowed. The *optimizer* self is more cognizant of an ever-emerging, differentiated world of interests and more accepting of them unto their own right.

****

Enter the World of Government and Public Service

In government settings, *optimizers* leverage protocol and procedure with relative fluidity and can re-shape effort and action to align for legislative approval and impact. This effort to make rules and laws work within pre-determined boundaries may create gridlock, yet *optimizers* are undeterred in their efforts to find progress in the fog of competing interests. My cousin, Harold Donahue[2] from Worcester, MA., was an *optimizer* and the Democratic Congressman from Massachusetts' Third and Fourth Congressional Districts from 1947 to 1974.

Rep. Donahue served 14 terms in the House of Representatives. Like Mayor Koch, he understood his constituencies well. Every Friday afternoon, he would catch the Washington D.C. Amtrak bound for Boston. His weekend schedule consisted of in-district Friday night dinners, school sporting events and community activities. Saturday's consisted of public, open-door, walk-in office hours from 10 a.m.-2 pm. Sometimes he would get an early morning quick haircut at the local barbershop where he picked up on timely local concerns at a street level; preceded by a local

---

2   Congressman Harold Donahue, a somewhat quiet but outgoing gentleman, was my much older cousin who would regularly participate in our family gatherings.

© Steve Northup/the LIFE Images Collection/Getty Images

ham-and-egg breakfast at a lively diner near Main Street, Worcester. He then would have scheduled appointments from 2-5 pm and more dinners from 6-10 p.m., on Saturday evening. Sunday morning consisted of a brunch at a popular public restaurant and attendance at a local Catholic Church. He then took the return Amtrak shuttle to Washington D.C., and repeated the same routine for some 25 years. Rarely did he miss a weekend in his home district.

He eventually served as the second-ranking member on the House Judiciary Committee. He offered the formal motion and the articles of impeachment against President Nixon for his role in covering up the Watergate scandal[3]. Before the hearings, Donahue said the Watergate scandals were the "crest of a long and steady erosion of the nation's moral fiber," and he promised that the inquiry would be "done in an absolutely thorough and impartial manner, because it is a blemish upon the face of our country that all of us must try to remove."

As an *optimizer*, Donahue, like a number of his peers was motivated by a clear sense of Congressional norms, rule of law, institutional heritage and views on historical precedence. He also sought to reach across the aisle to help build an emerging consensus for solving what at the time was seen as an intractable problem. Given those were different times, his efforts may have yielded different results in the current climate. However, modern day *optimizers* are still inclined to do the same to varying degrees, regardless of party or ideology. They are still very attentive to party, institutional and broader stakeholder norms, but also seek to sort out practical solutions, if at all possible.

Donahue was fortunate that in his day there was a broader tolerance for embracing a range of partisan dialogue. This led to a unique coalescing of interests that yielded an institutional and national community of thought around impeachment, not necessarily as readily available in today's more rigid, hyper-sensitive, polarized setting. *Optimizers*, in all walks of life, continue to embrace force and social tension in a more indirect manner by getting around or behind more powerful others. This is somewhat of a jujitsu-like move, often involving quieter, softer, private and public

---

3 AP Archives. (1984). *Harold Donahue Dies; Was Member of House.* NYC: New York Times.

engagement and acknowledgement of differences while also recognizing and leveraging hierarchy and leadership. If the leadership is fragmented, *optimizers* look for strength from the in-group they are most closely aligned with, or seek timely, soft, less-hardened positions or openings, as they carry on as a mouthpiece for their agenda. When there is resistance in or around the edges with respect to policy and practice, *optimizers* seek to incentify, befriend, or soften the differences in multiple ways.

This approach contrasts with the more black and white *protectors* who either directly challenge or directly withdraw from battle, in a face-saving manner. Today in Congress it appears the *protectors* stake out clear boundaries that cannot be violated without quick punitive measures considered. This of course leads to a push-pull energy force that yields little progress across fractionalized, competing coalitions – some *non-protectors* who are more willing than others to have dialogue.

****

Rising above political discourse and legislative affairs is the actual execution and implementation of government policy and position. Taken to its extreme, we enter into the inhumane, totalitarian regimes of dictators and their brutal repressive and sometimes unconscionable acts. Ben Lesser, who is believed is the last living Holocaust survivor from Camp Dachau, was one such victim of Hitler's World War II effort to exterminate the Jews. Listening to Lesser talk was painful as he described the human terror, torture and tragedy he and his family endured as a Jew[4]. Under Adolph Hitler's Nazi party (NSDAP, 1933-1945), all aspects of life were controlled as reflected in his philosophy and book, *Mein Kampf*, a deeply anti-Semitic creed espousing genocide in efforts to create a "master-race."[5]

Lessers' *optimizer* personal leadership style assisted his being able to stay alive during a frightening time, and then to live a worthwhile life as described in his memoir, *"Living A Life That Matters: from Nazi Nightmare to American Dream"* (see footnote 4). After the war, he resettled in California where he raised a family, worked for the United Parcel Service, and later as an accomplished realtor. Through it all, his many awards and notable citations as a citizen, employee and Holocaust survivor, reflect the continued focus, standards of excellence and performance so typical of an optimizer.

Ben Lesser Interview

Ben Lesser is a Holocaust survivor, author, and the founder of the Zachor Foundation, which provides pins or mementos for holocaust speakers to give to audience members as a tangible remembrance of their experience.

In May 1944, Lesser and his family were brought to the Auschwitz concentration camp. Later, he and his cousin, Isaac, survived the Death March to Buchenwald and the Death Train to Dachau, where they were later liberated. Lesser said this is where his story begins. "In most holocaust

---

4 The conversation with Ben Lesser also included his daughter Gail Gerber, who manages the *Zachor Holocaust Remembrance Foundation* founded by Lesser, as an educational institution on all aspects of the Holocaust. His book is, *Living A Life That Matters: from Nazi Nightmare to American Dream.* (2012). Abbot Press. It is both a memoir and history lesson on "how the world turned mad" and what Lesser suggests we need to remember today.

5 Rabinbach, Anson; Gilman, Sander, eds. (2013) *The Third Reich Sourcebook*. Berkeley, CA: California University Press. P4.

books, they end with liberation and that's the end of the book. I felt that it has to go to the present," Lesser said.

"I was still able to make a beautiful life for myself and family. It's so important for kids, especially those that come from broken families and they feel that they have a deprived childhood, and after listening to me or reading my book and seeing what I went through and still able to come up," he said. "I point out that there is no such thing as a deprived childhood because it's just another excuse. It is all a matter of choices. I feel that individuals can't always choose what happens to them, but whether it's a crisis or calamity, people can always choose to let it ruin their life or learn from it and move forward. So, it's important to understand the consequences of personal choices. It's possible to let tragedy or trauma become a reason to stop living, but it's also possible to live through extreme circumstances and commit to a life that has meaning and that matters."

After coming to America, Lesser took a job making deliveries. "I used to work as a driver for UPS and they had a system where you can make more money doing the same hours by pushing yourself and doing the right things that right way, instead of goofing off. You can actually make much more money and be a producer—they had a great incentive system—they gave me an idea about business. They didn't have to go out and watch the people they employed to see if they were goofing off or doing something they weren't supposed to be doing because everyone drove themselves."

He learned extra skills the company needed. "I found out how to drive a truck and a trailer. In the middle of the night, if they needed someone to take the truck load to a lot or something, they called on me. I wanted to know how to route packages, which is a profession in itself, and I learned how to do it. Then, they needed a reporter, someone to write an article, which didn't pay anything, and no one would do it. I did it and I hardly spoke English. For ten years in a row, I was the number one reporter for the entire company and I hardly spoke English so I was asking, 'How. Why?'"

Lesser said he won trophies at the company banquet each year. "They wanted me so much as a company executive, but because I couldn't pass that rigorous test they had me take, I didn't have enough schooling at that point to pass it. They couldn't take me in, but 25 years working for them without a single accident, every year being rewarded safe driving was very unusual—even a scratch or broken mirror counts. When I came back from work, I wouldn't go with my buddies and get a six-pack or something. Instead, I asked my boss, 'Is anyone in trouble, can I help?' 'Oh yeah, John is running late, please see if you can help him.' I was the highest paid driver in Southern California for many years, but Why? Because I did it full-heartedly, I loved what I was doing."

This mindset was nothing new for Lesser. "I am a strong believer that whatever you do, you have to be the best at it and whatever it is, try and find out what you can do to make your job successful. Forget about the clock, you find out what you can do to help your job if they need any help and what more can you do. Do it with your full heart. Be helpful and see how you can make the company prosper. Your boss will eventually realize that you are part of this and you will be rewarded. Don't do it just for that reason, just whatever you do, try to be the best at that profession. I always tell people, 'Not just good or very good, but the absolute best.'"

Interestingly, this mentality came from the darkness of the Holocaust. "The way I survived the Holocaust was because I did whatever I was asked to do, but I didn't just do it because they asked me. I made sure I did it the best possible way so that there is no repercussion and no one and come back to me later and single me out because during the Holocaust, you didn't want to be remembered, you just wanted to be a shadow that they would forget about," Lesser explained. "I knew

I had to be the best and do things the right way. There are no mistakes, you make one mistake and it's over. It made me what I am today."

After 25 years of working with UPS, Lesser made a career change and became a real estate broker. "I had to be the best realtor. I thought, 'How am I going to compete against all of these big offices?' I'm from Europe, I barely spoke English and was going to be competing with them, but I would only go in if I was the best so, I started to go to night school and I became competent in real estate law. I had unbelievable brains and I did it for many years and I felt finally that I was knowledgeable enough to try real estate. I dared to go into it and I was very successful," Lesser recalled. "This showed me what you can achieve in this country. There is no end if you really want it and you work hard. This is what I'm telling the kids; you are so fortunate to be born in America. You can reach anything you want, who is going to stop you? Who is holding a gun against your head that you can't do it? No one. It's strictly a matter of choices and you can choose it."

In 1995, Lesser decided to retire and move with his wife to Las Vegas. Around this time, his grandson learned from his teacher that Lesser was a Holocaust survivor. Only then did Lesser begin to speak publicly about his experiences and what they had taught him.

"I'll never forget that here in Las Vegas, there is one section in town that has a lot of gang members and I spoke in this high school. On the stage, they had the teachers surround me because they didn't know how the kids would behave—if they were going to start throwing things at me, they didn't know. They were all gang members and you could tell by the different color kerchiefs that they wore. Afterwards, when I speak, I always give out this little pin and it says 'Zachor.' Zachor means to remember the Holocaust. While I was speaking to them, within two hours, teachers chased the kids out because at three the buses came to pick them up and they all lined up to shake my hands and get a pin. I felt that the pin is very important and one girl, as she received the pin, she saw the pin and she said, 'Mr. Lesser, we'll cherish this pin for the rest of our lives and when we have children of our own and they find this pin, they'll ask what the pin is and I'll tell them it means to remember the Holocaust.' When I heard this from this young girl, that was when I decided I had to do this and I started to manufacture the pins and I give them out to every listener. I don't expect them to wear it, but it's important for the future to show their kids," Lesser said.

"Afterward, the teacher called me and asked me for my address and they sent me a bundle of letters. The kids had all written a letter about what they took from my talk. By the way, I have about 10,000 letters and my great-grandchildren are going to have a good time going through them. One day, I received a phone call from a parent saying, 'Mr. Lesser, what did you do to my son? When he came home after listening to you, he came home and gave me a hug and a kiss. He never did that in his life.' Started to cry, 'You can't imagine how you changed him, he quit the gangs and stopped failing school. I will never forget what you did to my son.' When I heard that—it makes it all worthwhile. You can't imagine what a good feeling that gave me. It changes the youngsters. They realize, 'Here is a man who had nothing coming to America and had no one and no education and look how he turned his life around.' They have the schooling, and family, and education and are so far ahead so, they cannot use the excuse that they had a deprived childhood. No matter how bad their life is, it is still a wonderful life compared to mine so, it makes a big difference and turns them around."

Sometimes, he said, he gets letters from adults who are out of work: "After hearing you, there is no excuse, I'm going out tomorrow and finding a new job. I'll do anything to make a good life for myself.' I feel that is my purpose in life. People ask me, 'Ben, how do you feel? You survived and some other members didn't.' My answer is always: God needed a witness. Because not all survivors can talk about it, it hurts too much. Those of us who talk about it, is so important because, we are running out of time, and we know it's going to end soon."

"When I speak to these kids, I point out the fact that the Nazis and Hitler didn't start with killing, it all started with hate propaganda which is how it came to be killing," Lesser explained. "You have to learn to appreciate each other. Education is very important because when you're educated, you should know the difference between right and wrong, but I point that out to the youngsters especially. Right now, there is a bullying epidemic going on in schools, especially middle school and high schools. I point out the fact that Hitler was a big bully along with the Nazis and when you bully someone, you make an enemy for life. That person who was bullied will never forget you if you bullied them. Is this what you want to do, to grow up to become sadists and maybe even murderers when one thing leads to another? Why would you want to create enemies?

Usually, I'm re-invited next year and so on and I ask the teacher to tell me if any of the kids that listened to me or read my book ever go around and bully anyone else. The answer is always the same, 'Mr. Lesser, are you kidding me? They are the best-behaved children in this school, not only don't they bully, but they go around to see how they can help or what they can do.' It's nice to hear that you are making a difference and doing something. One middle-school, I went there and actually had a hard time at first because what do you tell kids in the fifth grade? But I found the right subjects to talk about and the following year I came and they showed me a bench in the hallway, and on the bench, is my picture and it says, 'Ben's Bench.' I asked the teacher what it meant and she said, 'Mr. Lesser, any child that feels like they're bullied or depressed for any reason, they go to that bench and sit down and the very first teacher that goes by has to counsel that child and make them feel better.' I asked them if it really worked and she said, 'Mr. Lesser, they're the best-behaved children and you can see after the teacher counsels a child how they come back with a smile on their faces and they feel stronger and better.' So, the following year, they had two benches. It worked apparently."

Lesser emphasized the need to tamp down hate. "Anything we can do to make our kids grow up more humane and stop with the hatred, whether it's anti-Semitism or anti-this-or-that, there is no difference. Usually, sometimes when the kids are asking me questions, many times, they would ask, 'Mr. Lesser, what can I do to make this a better world?' I point out to them that during World War II, the whole world was silent. Yes, you can do something, you can shout out and let your voices be heard. It will Go viral."

Lesser noted that the Nazis not only destroyed Jews. "There were all the people that Hitler deemed had no right to exist in this world whether you were gay or Jehovah's Witness, or any kind of religion. It's strange to believe that men like Hitler—now Hitler, probably was a very educated man and was able to transform a lot of good people into monsters. It's hard to believe how far words can transform the human body because they were not born monsters, they were human beings like you and I, yet they were able to do something like that."

In 2009, Lesser founded the Zachor Holocaust Remembrance Foundation. "We're doing an awful lot of good for the future to keep this world from forgetting. Someone has to speak up for those millions who were slaughtered. 'We were here in this world. Don't forget us.' This world would love to forget. We are doing everything humanly possible to keep the world from acquiring amnesia. We want them to continue to remember the Holocaust because it could happen again. It's going on right now in many parts of this world. People have not learned from the past. If we didn't have the Zachor Foundation, you can say, 'Well, there are museums.' But the person has to go to that museum in order to find out what went on. We are going to the public on the website and all over, and I'm doing what I can to have them listen to me. We want them to hear us. We will not allow this to be forgotten.

Lesser made the choice long ago to rise above the hatred, to not only survive, but thrive. "A lot of people in the camps gave up. It was easier to die than to live through some of those circumstances. My cousin went with me on the death march. He begged me to sit down and have them walk past and shoot him so that it would be over with. I said, 'As long as I'm alive, we will survive.' I kept dragging him to another week. I was dragging him in the snow without shoes. In the end, he didn't survive. He survived long enough to be liberated, but that night after liberation, he died in my arms, and maybe he couldn't help but think, 'Now I can die.' He got me to liberation and I will survive. Sometimes it just took the will power to survive and get through all these punishments," Lesser said.

"I made a decision as a young man—'Ben, this is the first day of your life, you came to America.' That was when I was 18 years old and I came to this wonderful country and took a look at the New York skyline and the ship that came in. But it had such an influence on me, and I said, 'Ben, this is day one of your life, never forget the past, but from this day on, you're going to make a success out of yourself and if you have a family, it's going to be a successful family.' Well, to me, what I do have is a success. I have never asked anyone to help me my whole life. I never collected a dime of unemployment. I just knew I had to do it and whatever I did, I knew I had to be the best."

Lesser said he wanted his own children to grow up without fear. "I wanted them to feel like an American child. This is America, a free country," Lesser said. "I wanted their friends to be American friends. I wanted them to mingle with all kinds of different nationalities. I didn't want what the other Holocaust survivors wanted, to keep them safe and secluded. My kids knew I was a Holocaust survivor, but I never told them, and they never asked. I didn't want to put that burden on them."

He has very few memories of his life before the Holocaust. "My parents were wonderful people and unfortunately, I don't remember much from my home as a child. Somehow, my memories were erased by the bad things that happened to me," he explained and then continued, "There are some memories coming back to me so, I know I must have had a very good upbringing." Then quietly, ever so painfully, yet poignantly he looked upwards and whispered, "out of a wonderful family of seven only my sister Lota and I survived. The rest of the family was slaughtered."

★★★★★★★★★★★★★★★★

> Lesser's non-profit Zachor Holocaust Remembrance Foundation is seeking 6 million "shout outs" or postings on their web-site to honor the 6 million voices silenced during the Holocaust (https://www.i-shout-out.org).

I SHOUT OUT! I-SHOUT-OUT.org

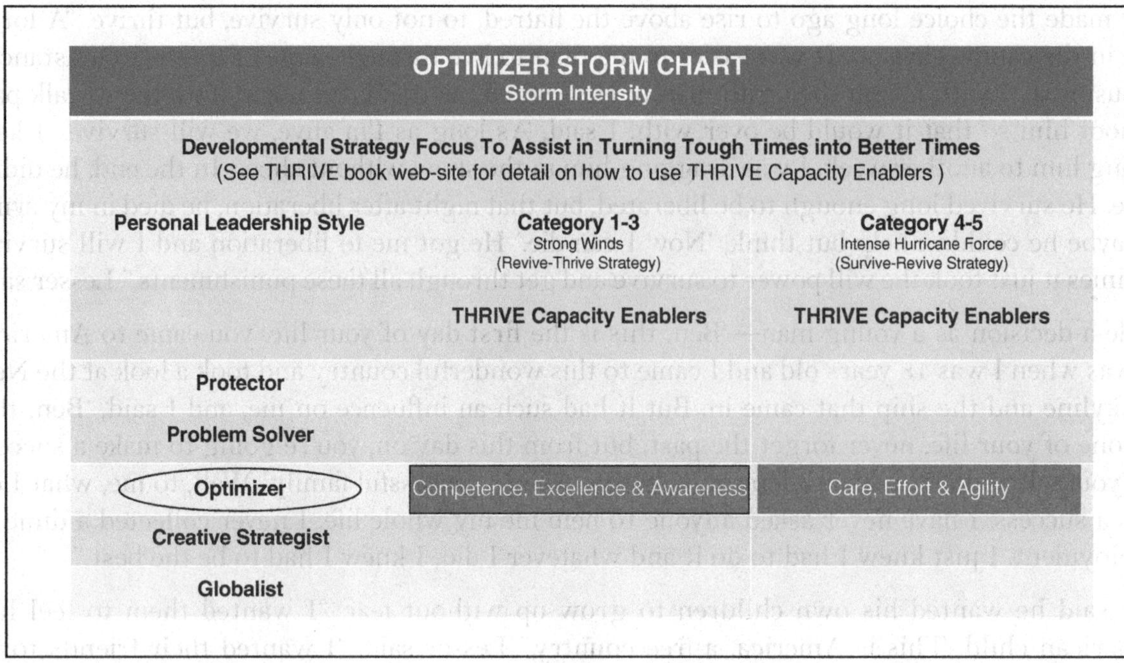

OPTIMIZER STORM CHART		
Storm Intensity		
Developmental Strategy Focus To Assist in Turning Tough Times into Better Times		
(See THRIVE book web-site for detail on how to use THRIVE Capacity Enablers)		
Personal Leadership Style	**Category 1-3** Strong Winds (Revive-Thrive Strategy)	**Category 4-5** Intense Hurricane Force (Survive-Revive Strategy)
	THRIVE Capacity Enablers	THRIVE Capacity Enablers
Protector		
Problem Solver		
Optimizer	Competence, Excellence & Awareness	Care, Effort & Agility
Creative Strategist		
Globalist		

© Courtesy Mark Sullivan

Figure 8.2: can be further reviewed and considered in the book web-site for developmental exercises.

A Way of THRIVING

Personal Leadership Style: The CREATIVE STRATEGIST

Curious, Insightful, Systemic Thinker, Disciplined, Keenly Aware, Inclusive, Imaginative

"Life is the art of drawing without an eraser."

John W. Gardner

"Every man must decide whether he will walk in the light of creative altruism or in the darkness of destructive selfishness."

Martin Luther King, Jr.

"Life can only be understood backwards; but it must be lived forwards."

Soren Kierkegaard

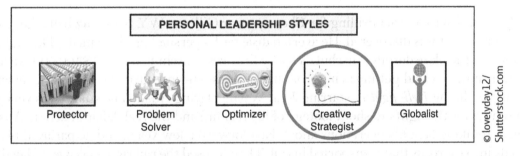

Figure 9.1: The Creative Strategist in the PLS Continuum

Featuring

Dr. Story Musgrave, A physician and astronaut credited as being the only one to have flown on all five space shuttles

Dr. Raphael Pollock, Director, The Ohio State University Comprehensive Cancer Center

The *Creative Strategist* looks at life's puzzles and finds ways to extract image and order out of a meaningless mess. When confusion and complexity have arrived, they bring insights into ways of making life meaningful or manageable. They are sometimes seen as an organization's magicians or wizards. Their questions are different. *Creative strategists* embrace metaphors and patterns. They challenge the underlying assumptions, often not seen but felt. They are comfortable, and even excited at the full wonder of paradox and contradiction. They can often see around corners making the invisible visible. They ask more why and how questions and entertain what-if scenarios with creative jaunts into futuring or trending, and worst-best case analysis. *Creative strategists* are bored with repetition, especially more of the same pat answers. Uniformity is less interesting to them. Ambiguity is to be expected and anticipated.

© lovelyday12 /Shutterstock.com

I remember doing research into the life of a publicity shy, talented Denver billionaire, Philip Anschutz[1] regarding a business opportunity development effort with Accenture Consulting LLP. Anschutz was known to be a creative business genius and pioneer in multiple industries. This achievement is very difficult to do. Most of us develop interests, skill, competency and contacts in one area, not multiple ones. Not so with Anschutz. He was the son of an oil driller, bought out his dad, went broke and then struck oil in Utah and Wyoming. This was his start in becoming one of the very few multi-industry superstars like John D. Rockefeller, Andrew Carnegie, Cornelius Vanderbilt and Warren Buffet.

© Jamel Toppin/The Forbes Collection/ Contour by Getty Images

Philip Anschutz

In his early days, while contract drilling for Chevron near Gillette, WY, Anschutz had a huge oil field catch fire soon after it was discovered. He averted disaster by persuading the famed oil firefighter Red Adair to take on the blaze despite Anschutz's shaky finances. Anschutz secured $100,000—enough to tide him over until he could get financing from his bankers—from Universal Studios[2]. Universal just happened to be filming *Hell–fighters*, starring John Wayne playing Adair. The studio was very pleased to pay Anschutz for the rights to shoot footage of his real fire and the real Adair in action. Anschutz's fast, creative thinking kept his operations afloat. Fast forward a few years, and he parlayed his oil and gas proceeds into railroads that transported his oil. Then he used the rail rights-of-way to lay fiber-optic cable along his train tracks as his entre into telecommunications. Anschutz later repositioned his investment into what became Quest Communications.

Later he imagined there was a way to leverage his telecommunications assets to replace the manual distribution of movies from studios to theaters by digitizing films and sending them out over his over his telecom lines. This put him solidly into the entertainment and media space buying up and owning controlling interest in Regal Entertainment Group, the largest movie theater chain in the United States. From there he got into producing concerts and events which led him to acquiring

1 Fortune Magazine places Philip Anschutz #35 on their *2017 Fortune 400 List of the Wealthiest In America*. His 2018 net worth is $14.1 billion. He has built fortunes in oil, railroads, telecom, real estate and entertainment. He owns the NHL's Kings and a third of the Lakers, plus the building they play in, the Staples Center. His Anschutz Entertainment Group operates more than 100 arenas and concert venues worldwide. On 300,000 acres he owns in Wyoming, Anschutz aims to build the world's biggest wind farm.

2 Brian O'Reilly and Reporter Associate Ann Harrington. (September 6, 1999). A story of the "*Billionaire Next Door, Phil Anschutz may be the richest American you've never heard of,*" appears in Fortune Magazine, archive.fortune.com.

arenas and sports facilities including the Staples Center in Los Angeles and London's O2 Arena. He filled them with entertainment content from sports teams and purchased the Los Angeles Lakers basketball team, the Los Angeles Kings ice hockey team and five major league soccer teams. In his concert division Anschutz started underwriting tours of musicians including Jon Bon Jovi, Cher, and Justin Bieber. His creative 'imagineering' led to many dozens of huge vertically and horizontally integrated offerings across multiple industrial sectors including energy, entertainment, transportation, commercial real estate, construction and financial services. This is a *creative strategist* that has built multiple industry empires over a five decade period.

Preceding personal leadership styles, *protectors, problem solvers* and *optimizers* are more linear and logical and reflects varying degrees of concreteness. Their focus is on who needs what, when and where. *Creative strategists* use more systemic, holistic thinking and abstract analysis of what is unlikely and impossible, possible, or probable and the predictable. Rules and perspectives are no longer absolute. The answer is not always 'yes or no.' Perhaps the answer is 'it depends.' Relativism is more central to their way of being. Creative strategists recognize multiple realities and understand things are rarely as they initially seem to be.

Consider the blockbuster stories of Harry Potter. J.K. Rowling[3], another *creative strategist*, has said the major theme in her books is death, but not in any singular or solitary manner. Rather how death links to life, fear of the unknown, and acceptance of death's opposite – living life on the edge, full-throttled, embracing the adventure of the next big and scary threat. Rowling's creative talent, of course, is spinning the abstract and conceptual themes of death, life and acceptance to make you sweat and cheer. Her stories become a part of us in a most real and concrete manner.

Further, *creative strategists* can debate issues and convincingly argue both sides of a point. They may in fact suspend judgment and not necessarily have a need for closure or resolution on contrasting opinion or positions. They can live with the drama and its contrast, the mundane, and be curious about both. This is a different place and platform in which to conduct the business of living.

Creative strategists can be in every field, including as members of the creative class such as: comedians, talk show hosts, consultants, writers, politicians, preachers, performers, professors, and so on. They connect and integrate common, and disparate ideas, issues, feelings and actions in a crisp, cohesive, compelling fashion. They bring fresh, imaginative, original thinking. With a broader lens, they view and appreciate competing values, interests and obligations.

Creative strategists can be found in a team and can embrace diversity of all kinds which, in itself, can become a creative tool or practice. Beyond appreciating typical racial and ethnic lifestyles, they can create or cultivate diverse experiential offerings. A few years back, Hallmark Corporation developed a new line of specialty cards for 'seniors' and had a unique mix of contractors and employees representing octogenarians, boomers and millennials on the product team[4]. A *creative strategist* as team facilitator reported there were more than wheel chairs and walkers in the room.

3 Joanne Rowling writes under the pen name of JK Rowling and her books, the Harry Potter series, have won multiple awards and sold more than 500 million copies. They are noted as being the best-selling book series in history. Rowling was working as a researcher and bilingual secretary for Amnesty International when she conceived of the idea for the Harry Potter series while on a delayed train from Manchester to London in 1990. The seven-year period that followed, saw the death of her mother, birth of her first child, divorce from her first husband, and relative poverty until the first novel in the series, *Harry Potter and the Philosopher's Stone*, was published in 1997. Source: Shapiro, Marc (2000). J.K. Rowling: *The Wizard Behind Harry Potter*. New York: St. Martin's Press.

4 The Hallmark product team story was personally relayed to the author while sitting next to a passenger associated with Hallmark, on a Kansas City outbound flight. This is a second-hand source, not verified to date.

The diversity of thought, experience, and history led to an extraordinarily popular line of cards for that season.

The product team's capacity to create original, fresh thinking for their new line of offerings had much to do with how *creative strategists* works with a diverse mix of talent. As a boundary-spanner who can connect, sort and engage with very different feelings, ideas and images, *creative strategists* tacitly use a conceptual process of *framing, flexing and fitting* to shape and bring order and meaning from a disparate field of stimuli (see figure 9.2). Simply, they know how to "connect the dots," where others may just experience a confusing jumble of conversational mish-mash. This conceptual capacity of pattern recognition, theming or analysis is helpful in sorting out the core, adjacent and outlier issues and effects. This is particularly helpful when you have a cross-functional team mix of very different disciplines and business languages (i.e. finance, marketing, human resources, operations, sales, etc.), different skill mix (i.e. quantitative, graphic artists, writers, analysts, product experts, technologists, etc.), different experience levels (i.e. new hires, seasoned individual contributors, middle managers, executives). Very quickly, such diversity can create confusion or frustration as the non-conceptuals (i.e. concrete thinkers) will not appreciate what they see as an overload of irrelevant, unclear competing stimuli. The concrete practitioners have a very different skill set and value contribution that is often amplified with a speed and execution focus.

Creative strategists may not be linear in their thinking but they are both disciplined and organic/creative in thought. This means that instead of jumping to conclusions or rushing to a solution, they will spend the majority of their time on defining the problem. Their curiosity and rigor will cause them to ask many questions about the environment of the problem; experiment with ways of *reframing* the question; determine what can be rearranged, re-sorted, or *flexed* for a broad range of advantages; and finally, how such options may align or *fit* creating a more unique and valued offering.

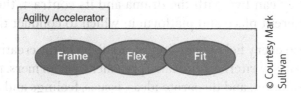

Figure 9.2:

While doing some executive coaching for a national sales vice president, a *creative strategist* in an airline-travel supplier environment, I was treated to how the sales executive was skillfully able to diagnose a set of issues with a key customer. The client was a president of a major cruise line and was complaining how the airline reservation system was to slow and costly for what they needed in their call centers. Instead of talking about speed or price, the *creative strategist* (i.e. sales executive) spent much time learning about the nature of the in-bound customer calls in the call center, the skill level of the employees, the kind of training they received, the culture of the call center work environment, the type of incentives and bonuses employees got on the line, and the nature of their supervision. Very little focus was on the technology of the reservation system itself.

As the conversation progressed, the client began to see the productivity decline had less to do with the functionality of the system and more to do with poor supervision and lack of training for new hires. To improve his operating costs, the president had cut training budgets and almost doubled the number of front-line employees the supervisors had to manage. This created low morale and high turnover with supervisors. The *creative strategist* was quickly able to help the cruise line president re-focus efforts that would accelerate productivity and revenue based on workforce management changes and less on the technology itself.

Moving from a *knowing* perspective, that highlighted the sales executive's conceptual capacity on diagnosing and analyzing issues, *creative strategists* are also different from a *valuing* perspective. They are empathic and accepting of changing conditions and threats while working from contrasting vantage points. The national sales executive while assessing what was going on with his client, also was recognizing the pain, frustration and embarrassment the president was experiencing as well. Through conversation, he realized that the president would need to report to the board in an upcoming quarterly meeting that under the president's watch numbers would be posted that were declining for the first time in a long time. It was in the midst of a healthy economy where the competition was claiming banner results. The president was not use to self-disclosing his fears and anxieties with others, but the sales executive had created a genuine, high-trust, high-care environment. In this context, the president shared more than facts and figures and found in the process the sales executive had become a trusted advisor and friend. As mentioned, *creative strategists* are emotionally, intellectually, and socially agile. They can comfortably create supportive environments where vulnerability and tender moments can unfold in a constructive, respectful manner.

Also, interesting, their humor can be self-effacing and spirited, causing even deeper levels of self-disclosure and authenticity. This contrasts with some of the earlier staged personal leadership styles where humor may sometimes be at the expense of others–targeted in a personal and sometimes painful manner.

Not that all is perfect with *creative strategists. Protectors* and *problem solvers* can make speedy decisions and move forward with concrete, decisive actions, but that is not necessarily the case with *creative strategists.* They can sometimes struggle with implementation. Non-creatives may say they are full of talk but can't get the job done. Or that *creatives strategists* are too theoretical or detached at times. Their blind side can be their affinity for ideas and imagery at the expense of action. More talking than doing. Not that the talking is irrelevant, but at times it may serve as an excuse for avoiding much needed behavioral engagement in an overt manner.

Sometimes, they may also be viewed as artificial or insincere. Their extraordinary intellectual, social and emotive powers may unwittingly create distance from those with fewer internal resources. Some creatives may express intentionally, or not, an air of entitlement. They can be cursed and/ or blessed with a way of functioning that stands out as unique or demonstrative and opportunistic. Other defensive routines for creatives include stubbornness despite their agility. They may be so invested in and admiring of their own ideas that it is hard for them to let go if need be. Vanity would be a related characteristic. *Creative strategists* may tend to believe they are deserving of special adulation above and beyond what may be due.

Yet, the creatives, bring distinctive value unparalleled by other styles. They not only bring flavoring to life's interactions, they often co-create the very structure of it as well. Take something as simple as bar soap. The story of how soap evolved highlights the unfolding journey of a creative in the tradition-bound commerce of home products and consumables. For over a century, bar soap was the only option for mass domestic consumption.[5] While William Sheppard patented liquid soap in 1865, it was not until 1980 that it was mass produced.

---

5 Botanie Soap Blog. (September 14, 2015). *"From the History of Liquid Soap: Invention and Cornering of the Domestic Market."* BotanieSoap.com.

Robert Taylor[6], visionary marketer and former Johnson & Johnson Services Inc. salesman, acting in the true spirit of a creative strategist was driving to work one day pondering the messy bar of soap sitting in a soap dish at his home. His company, Village Bath LLC, later Minnetonka Corporation of Minnesota, first marketed what eventually was a hugely successful new product category – liquid soap. It was no small feat for Taylor to outmaneuver the much larger Colgate-Palmolive Company, makers of *Irish Spring*, and Proctor & Gamble Company (P&G), makers of *Ivory*. Both Colgate and P&G were positioned to release their own version of liquid soap in roughly the same period to take advantage of a wide-open market opportunity.

Taylor's strategy was to do an end-run on the more dominant competitors. He realized early on that the key differentiator for liquid soap would be the pump in which the liquid soap was packaged, not the soap. At the time there was no way to dispense the solution without a suitable pump. Interestingly, such pumps were only manufactured by two factories under special intellectual property protection in the United States. Knowing larger rival companies would quickly produce a competing product knocking him out of the market, he leveraged every cent he had to buy a year's worth of pump orders from both manufacturers, the only ones available. This move essentially restricted his well-heeled competition from being able to order from the same two manufacturers for more than a year. Taylor had time to get established in the marketplace. Seven years later, Colgate bought Taylor's company to gain ready access and to scale what has now become a $100 million a year business.

Moving from the strategy to the creative side, manufacturers later came up with new, alternative ways to fabricate soap such as sprays, foam, and paper-based leaf pads. Creatives have a ready handle, awareness and attunement to the experience and needs of others. Their view of others from different vantage points is not only useful in the creative process, but also in the broader social arena. They think market-back or world-back versus product-forward or issue-forward. For them, the trajectory or line of sight is more broad and global in their more conceptual 'knowing and valuing' constellation of context and content.

Creative strategists are like Henry Ford,[7] who was not trying to replace the horse-and-buggy with a motorized engine. He wanted to realize a larger vision of creating a more attractive, economically accessible means to transport a nation at scale. *Protectors* would frame the issue as one of beating out the horse-and-buggy. *Problem solvers* would focus on product features, particularly solving the power and transmission issues. *Optimizers* would gravitate toward manufacturing processes, efficiency and building scale. Unlike the non-creatives who would

Henry Ford

© aradaphotography/ Shutterstock.com

---

6   Schwartz, John. (September 11, 2013). *"Robert Taylor Who Puts Hand Soap in a Bottle, Dies at 77."* NYC: New York Times Publisher.

7   The Model T was Ford's first automobile mass produced mass-produced on moving assembly lines with completely interchangeable parts, marketed to the middle class. Henry Ford said of the vehicle:
   "I will build a car for the great multitude. It will be large enough for the family, but small enough for the individual to run and care for. It will be constructed of the best materials, by the best men to be hired, after the simplest designs that modern engineering can devise. But it will be so low in price that no man making a good salary will be unable to own one – and enjoy with his family the blessing of hours of pleasure in God's great open spaces."
   Source: Hounshell, David A. (1984), *From the American System to Mass Production, 1800-1932: The Development of Manufacturing Technology in the United States*, Baltimore, Maryland: Johns Hopkins University Press.

legitimately look at the opportunity from a more narrowly focused, but necessary and requisite manner, the creatives would start with a broader aperture looking at the market-to-be. Obviously, all styles and perspectives are needed as they bring very different value and contributions to the mix. Together the collection of personal leadership styles offers a range in capacity and power across the continuum.

One last thought on *creative strategists*. They bring energy toward the big ideas and causes of the day. They seek to benefit others even if it runs counter to incumbent rules or ways of doing things. This is what makes them both creative and strategic. They cultivate new innovative ways of functioning that transform our way of doing and being.

****

This is particularly represented in the following conversation with Dr. Story Musgrave. During his life, he overcame great childhood hardships and then sought advantages under constrained resources. He grew up physically and verbally abused as a child, regularly tormented and put down by parents who were struggling themselves. Out of this grew an ambition to experiment and create new opportunity that eventually led to becoming both an astronaut and physician. Musgrave continuously found creative and strategic ways to make nothing into something, and then something substantial out of that. His daily operating model and philosophy included "just putting one foot in front of another" while unpacking the textured layer of life—"looking at challenges as a nested set of systems, embedded in systems." This demonstrates the life of a creative strategist. One that leverages a conceptual head-set *thinking-through* a problem in a disciplined, systemic fashion. Clearly this helped Musgrave in the complex work of medicine and astrophysics, as both physician and astronaut.

Dr. Story Musgrave Interview

Though he never finished high school, Story Musgrave went on to earn seven graduate degrees, including a medical degree. He served as a U. S. Marine pilot, a trauma surgeon, and a scientist-astronaut for NASA. He made six space flights and now operates a palm farm in Florida and works as a conceptual artist and speaker.

Raised on a dairy farm in Massachusetts, Musgrave dropped out of high school his senior year after a car accident and then joined the marines. Growing up, he had few strong, positive influences. "All the way through childhood, I had nothing but discouragement," said Musgrave who said his family was marked by alcohol and physical abuse. "The discouragement I had was also powerful, 'You're not going anywhere.' It was not only lack of mentor, it was discouragement. 'You're a loser and you're not going anywhere.' That is the only thing I got from family and school. I plowed on not knowing."

Musgrave said he looked to the outside world for guidance. I had an amazing inspiration from the people who perform on the playing field—the Dorothy Hamills, the great artists, the gymnasts, the great musicians. Maybe I didn't know them, but they served as a massive inspiration, remote mentors to me. When I see people on that playing field, it's a playing field for performance, of living up to the world's expectations. It's the people who are the best and keep raising the bar.

"You cannot believe how bad and how sick my life was. Somehow, not even having the intellect to understand it, and not being conscious of it, somehow, I continued to take one little step after another at just plodding along," said Musgrave. "I am who I am starting at the age of three. I have not changed one bit since the age of three. My operating mode has not changed. I came into an amazingly bad, sick world and at the age of three, I said, 'I'm going to make it and go forward.'"

To Musgrave, passion is a key element to success. "No matter how bad, just take the next step. Find something that you're in love with. Find somewhere your heart wants to go. There is tomorrow, and you can get a whole new start," he said.

"Spirit is number one," Musgrave continued. "If you have spirit, you never lose the possibility of optimism and a positive view of things. It's a sense of tomorrow. Dog gonnit, I've got tomorrow, and this is what I'm going to do with it. I've got opportunities and I don't care who I am. I'll make opportunities and going forth, it's a new playing field and I'm going to do what I've got to do."

"It's a love for life. It's a love for the playing field. That is the way I like to do it. I like the world to put their expectations on me, where I've got to live up to something. If the expectations are not internally driven, then I've got to live up to what *they* want. I can redefine my own objectives if the expectations are things that I create," said Musgrave. "I'm on a playing field having fun. But when you've got, purpose, passion, and presence then, you've already got it there. My purpose in life isn't to meet people's expectations. My fun in life is to get on the playing field and kick to the finish line. I find that fun."

Perseverance through tough times is important to Musgrave, even the brutality he faced as a child. "When I look at how bad things were. I mean, I got beat up so bad, I had to have neurosurgery to stop the hemorrhages and seizures," he said. "How do I feel about all that? I feel just great because I'm here today. Every one of those seconds in the past, I needed to get here. The whole thing about going forward is that there is a future and there is hope and I don't give a damn what happened back then. I am me and we're going forward."

"What you're going to do next in life, you must identify and control and take hold of the factors that are going to help you get to the finish line, the ones that are going to get in the way, the ones that are going to stop you. It is essential to getting to places," said Musgrave. "Nothing in life is simple. What you're doing is a system within a whole bunch of other systems especially, nowadays life is a networked, social solution."

Musgrave reflected on the importance of being mindful of your purpose. "If you run into a situation that you don't fit into and you're trying to leverage everything you ever did in life and you're not getting there, walk away," he said. "You've got a dozen opportunities or infinite number of possibilities—if you're running into a brick wall, in particular a human brick wall, say, 'Adios. I don't need you.' I've got 10 other things I can do. You've got to be careful about determination, perseverance, stubbornness."

"A lot of times, it is one step at a time. It is doing things that are working for me in the moment. I'm going forward and am able to master this discipline, this domain at this time," said Musgrave. "I've walked away from so many false starts, but they're not even in my emotions or mentality. If I don't get a high school diploma, is that a failure? Most people would think that's a failure. Well, I don't know if that's a failure or not."

A pilot Musgrave knew said he liked Syracuse University, so Musgrave decided to apply there after service in the marines where he had learned to fly planes. "I went there. They didn't take me. That was fine because I showed up anyway," said Musgrave. "I knocked on the dean's door and, 'Sir, I'm getting out of child labor, I've never finished school, and I'm coming back from the marines ready to go to work, sir.' He didn't hesitate one second. He walked me out front and said, 'Matriculate this gentleman.'"

When Musgrave wanted to pursue a medical degree, he ended up at Columbia University. "I liked this place, so I did it. I went through this place and was going to pick up the pieces later and see how it is going to fit," said Musgrave. "The heart is unbelievably important in where you're going tomorrow. It's not just intellectual analysis or, 'Is this college going to get me where I need to get?' No," he said the question to ask is, "Do you love it?"

In addition to the medical degree, he has advanced degrees in math, computers, chemistry, literature, psychology, and physiology. "Throughout life, I was pursuing things and I didn't know where I was going. It's one step at a time. I got my first PC at 48 years old. It's a brand-new life and a new opportunity that was never there earlier," said Musgrave. "You just keep moving down the line and don't know where it's going. All of a sudden, it's a push and a pull. My life is pushing me out of that world, but I see another huge pull, so that is where we go. It's not a failure anymore," said Musgrave. "You just bend that into something else because it's not going well and it's miserable. You take it somewhere else. I never leave anything behind. I take it all with me. I take my medicine with me, I take my physiology, I take my marines, my flying, I take it all with me. So, I end up with a multiple domain synergy and skill set."

"If you sit around drowning in your own pessimism, there is a lack of hope and it's not going to work. You've got to do something," said Musgrave. "The winners, the losers, everybody do something, and then make that thing matter. Once you've done that thing—it's another playing field, another opportunity."

"Something I learned is to take it with you and don't ever forget that you did that thing because the synergies and relationships you will be able to apply that wherever you go next. Do something, learn it, and you've got to do it to the best of your abilities. The more you put into it, the more you're going to learn," said Musgrave. "You cannot sit around and dream about the failures. I look at myself and it's like hope springs eternal. I don't care about the past."

"There is luck in life, unfortunately. It isn't where you go and how well you do, it's not just that you've made the right choices and did the right things," said Musgrave. "At times, life is not going to be good to you. I don't like luck. I like people to get where they got. I like a merit-based system."

To Musgrave, your product is your purpose. "You have to build a storyline unique to your experience. I don't care what your product is. If you're not customer-oriented, you ain't goin' nowhere. If you ain't got the investment behind you, you ain't goin' nowhere," he said. "I had it all, what it took to get the job done. You've got content, but how do you get it to the world? It can be public speaking, it can be mathematical equations, you have to be able to get yourself out of there."

"I appear to be competitive, but I am not. I do my thing, one little step at a time and became a differentiated person. So, I'm not competing," said Musgrave. "I'm able to leverage every possible thing that I did in the past to my current endeavors, and *that* is unbelievably powerful. I'm able to use everything that I ever did. I'm a differentiated person that follows my own passions and my heart and I do what I do for better or for worse."

"I will fail in certain areas and I will excel in others and I pick the places where I will do well. I don't work on my weaknesses," Musgrave said. "You don't go through life saying, 'I'm not so good at this, I need to improve.' No sir, you raise what you're good at to a higher level and differentiate yourself. That is the way you go forward. This is my brand, it's what I do, it's my handle."

****

Similar to Dr. Musgrave, Dr. Raphael Pollock has an equally inspiring story as a *creative strategist*. As a surgeon and cancer center director with a beloved reputation as a doctor's doctor[8] he balances his own personal illness, a potentially aggressive form of leukemia, with a thriving clinical practice, leadership of a laboratory research team, and service as a medical executive of a high-growth health-care function. This capacity to create, cure and care for self and others, in dire need, with positive, disciplined and creative energy is the hallmark of a *creative strategist*. Pollock retells how his family heritage is one of humble means. He learned early from his father and immigrant grandfather, who in spite of their own struggles, made the family transition from being a carpenter (grandfather) to a physician (father) in one generation through sacrifice, grit and hard work and taught Pollock the value of street wisdom as well as book knowledge. *Creative strategists* learn to dissect the complexity of the moment into an actionable, coherent whole. They also move significantly on the value continuum to focus more on *we* and *us* and less on the *me or me-we*. This attitude is encapsulated in one of Pollock's favorite quotes from Gandhi: 'To find yourself lose yourself in the service to others.'

Dr. Raphael Pollack Interview

Dr. Raphael Pollock has several distinct roles at The Ohio State University Wexner Medical Center: First, he is the Director of the Ohio State University Comprehensive Cancer Unit. Second, he is a cancer patient, afflicted with chronic leukemia.

Pollock was a precocious, intelligent child who learned to read at a very early age. He remembers reading the newspaper to his grandfather, an immigrant from Poland who was a carpenter in Chicago, who would explain the meaning of the news articles to his grandson.

"What I remember is there was some guy, typical Chicago story," Pollock said. "Some mafia member crossed another mafia member, so they chopped him up into several hundred pieces which were stuffed into a sewer. That was the headline. So, I read this to him and after I was done reading, he said 'So, you know what the moral of the story is?' He said, 'If you play with shit, you will get your hands dirty.' His whole life was punctuated by these little gems of wisdom."

Pollock grew up in Chicago, where his father was a doctor, having earned his MD from the University of Illinois medical school at age 21 and a PhD two years later. But Pollock's father came from poverty. Pollock's grandfather, Hershel Pollock, an immigrant from eastern Europe, was very poor. He was one of the only child of his 12 siblings to have escaped being murdered by the Nazis during World War II. He came to America alone at the age of 16.

Pollock looks at his father and grandfather and sees the meager means from which they started and the achievements they were able to accomplish. Perhaps the most important lesson that Pollock felt his father taught him was that not all knowledge can be learned in school. "He showed me the difference between learning and wisdom," Pollock said. "The wisdom of what you live is not necessarily acquired from books or from schooling. And there's a different code by which you approach other people or circumstances. Street wisdom. But I also think a measure of empathy for people who don't have it as good as you. My father didn't have it so good."

---

8 As a faculty member of the same University that oversees Dr. Pollack's medical practice at the OSU Wexner Medical Center, I hear selectively from some of my students who affectionately and/or reverently speak of Dr. Pollack based on family members who are his patients, in dire need. It is quite apparent they are grateful of both his extraordinary clinical skills and his presence (i.e. bed-side manner).

Not everyone starts life under equal circumstances, which Pollock saw from both his grandfather and his father. "You must be a pragmatic realist," Pollock said. "No one said it was fair. You basically can either get into the loop and do nothing, or accept that, and make a decision about how you are going to position yourself, and what you are going to do."

Pollock learned lessons of grit and determination from his mother's side of the family as well. His mother's father was a Ukrainian immigrant who moved to the United States, taught himself pharmacy and passed the certification test. He opened a drug store in a Polish neighborhood, so he taught himself Polish. Later, as the neighborhood became Puerto Rican, he taught himself Spanish. "That's the American way," Pollock said. "They didn't look at it as an obstacle, they looked at it as a land of opportunity."

Initially, Pollock was not interested in following his father's footsteps to become a doctor. His true interests were in studying history, which is how he began his college career. However, his father always wanted him to be thinking about a contingency plan, a backup in case he couldn't make a career out of his passion for studying history.

So, Pollock compromised and took chemistry and biology and began fulfilling the pre-med requirements as well as continuing to take history classes. Pollock's father bought him a student membership to the American Historical Association, where Pollock was able to attend a conference in Chicago and got a better feel for the job opportunities in the field of teaching history. Pollock said his father told him, "Go to the meeting, listen to some of the papers, but make sure you go and take a look at the job registry.' There were 3,000 PhD historians applying for two jobs that were available for teaching history. "There, I learned the fact that just because you are interested in it, that is not necessarily enough to make that your life path."

Pollock applied to 15 medical schools and was accepted only by Saint Louis University, a school that historically accepted Jewish and black students at an earlier time when there were quotas for admission at many medical schools. "I came to feel a strong sense of discipline and family there," Pollock said. He came to love and respect the professors he had in medical school and his passion for medicine grew. "The man who taught us neuroanatomy was Father Sullivan," Pollock said. "This man has a PhD in anatomy, a PhD equivalent in theology, and a PhD in physics, all earned because he was simply interested in these subjects. His lectures were amazing," Pollock recalled. "I was absolutely blown away. I spent as much time in his lectures as I possibly could."

However, Pollock's experience in medical school was not a breeze. The coursework was grueling, the time spent outside of the classroom that was necessary to learn the material was demanding, and the tests were exhausting and constant. "What ended up happening is I would study to pass one set of exams as well as I could, and I ignored the other subjects because there simply wasn't enough time in a day to go to the lectures, go to the labs, and study at night," Pollock said. "So, I was constantly trying to catch up."

Originally, Pollock wanted to become an endocrinologist based on the courses he was enjoying during his first few semesters of medical school. However, that changed when he began rotations at the chronically understaffed Saint Louis City Hospital, where students on rotation experienced all kinds of patients.

On his first night on rotation, one of Pollock's first patients permanently altered the course of where he wanted to take his medical career. "I remember the first night I was on a call," Pollock said. "Here I am. I just spent two years in all these lectures, collecting splinters in my butt, and the intercom says, 'Dr. Pollock, Dr. Pollock come to the emergency room.' My first reaction was, 'Gee, what's my father doing here?' And then I realized it's me."

"It was something I've never seen before," Pollock continued. "This man was actually sitting up on a gurney in the ER. He was literally missing his face. He had told his wife about an affair he was having with this woman down the block, and they got into a fight. He laid down on the sofa to sleep and she went down and got a bottle of lye, boiled it and poured it all over his face. You could see his cheekbones exposed and his ears were missing. This is the first patient I'd ever seen. I was just like, 'Ah—what am I supposed to do?' How do you actually handle this?" Pollock recalled. "I was in total shock. What is a history student doing here? How am I going to manage this literally burnt off face? How am I supposed to process this? How you pivot on that one?"

Pollock called the plastic surgery resident doctor, who sprung into action and showed Pollock how to graft the skin and start to heal the patient, instructing Pollock how to help along the way. "What he said was, 'You are interested in this, I can tell.' I didn't actually know that. 'I am going to show you how to graft the skin. And I will teach you all about burns.' It was fantastic, because I had just spent two years of my life passively absorbing and regurgitating so much information that I didn't care deeply about. Now, I actually care about this, because I could see that I was critical to helping this man. There was a road for me. And the additional benefit, that I talked with this man daily, and we became very close. This first patient made a tremendous impression on me."

From this experience onward, Pollock decided he was going to become a surgeon. He returned to his studies with a zeal he had not previously felt. "People in this type of work who are really successful bring their personality to the healing process, which is something that I learned from my father as a psychiatrist," Pollock said. "It's a sense of hope. This is a person, maybe very different than you, but nonetheless as a patient this is a human being worthy of your time, energy, and learned skills as an investment."

Pollock's career received a jolt when he was diagnosed as having chronic lymphocytic leukemia two years ago. This can be an aggressive form of leukemia in many patients, and forced him to confront his own mortality in a very concrete way.

"I just sort of stepped back for a moment," Pollock said. "And I focused on the contribution I had made in my professional activities and that my kids have all developed into really good people. I may not live long enough to see how exactly it turns out for them, but I have watched them with pride and an awareness, taking stock of my situation, that I've provided for them. There's enough finances. Even if I am not around, they will take care of themselves and each other; I am relieved."

"I recognize the randomness of these things," Pollock continued. "You know that as fear of the unknown and the uncontrollable. You either embrace the new reality and respond or you let it unwind you. I'm not interested in having it unwind me, because there are too many things that I am interested in or curious about and I want to keep going. I think this is my grandfather and father coming back in spirit. I've had that thought for a while, and I have consciously chosen to continue trying to make my contributions on behalf of others."

Pollock was thrilled with his daughter's acceptance into medical school, and her decision to follow him and her grandfather in practicing medicine. "It was also very gratifying, becoming more and more of a hero to her, and a whole new dimension of sharing has opened up" Pollock said. "She's almost 30 right now. Caring about other people, the professionalism, the altruistic dedication of your life in the service to others is inspiring and has become deeply meaningful to her. She's embracing that herself, for which I am so very grateful. I know she will be a really, really, good doctor. She is caring, compassionate, and goes the extra mile. She gets that. And I actually got her a copy of her grandfather's PhD dissertation. There's a sense of continuity."

There are a few ideals that Pollock has carried with him, first during his career as a doctor and are now guiding him during his journey as a patient. "There was a poster on a wall in the OSU Cancer Center offices. On it is a quotation from Gandhi: 'To find yourself lose yourself in the service to others.' That's one thing I often think about. The other is a quotation from Saint Francis of Assisi, 'Seek ye to listen rather than to be listened to.' These are so profound precepts, and it resonates with what I have really tried to do."

"There are also a number of quotations from Benjamin Franklin and Mark Twain that I love. I've gotten very interested in these pithy packets of wisdom as I grow older. One of Franklin's comments is "A man wrapped up in himself makes for a very small package." He also pointed to a saying often attributed to Mark Twain, "When you finish changing, you are finished." When you see this, it closes the loop. These people are no longer alive, but the wisdom and concepts are immortalized, in some much smaller way in my own life. Although I am certainly not their caliber, can I nonetheless pass some of their wisdom and insights around? Are there extractable lessons? I'm going to keep going. And I am not obsessed with my own mortality. I've taken care of too many people who ultimately die from disease to recognize that indeed it's not fair, it's very fragile. Bad things happen to good people, but we have to keep going!" In-spite of this, Pollock's effort to cure and care for his patients is his own way of bringing goodness in the midst of what could be seen as bad times. Pollock shares his own illness with his patients. Invariably, they express appreciation for this level of trust. "It is a powerful combination to be both a cancer care provider as well as a cancer survivor and patient. It helps you empathize even more profoundly with those who trust you with their care while helping me to see myself in the perspective as simply another human being passing through time, trying to make this a better place to be."

****

Figure 9.3 can be further reviewed and considered in the book web-site for developmental exercises

A Way of THRIVING

Personal Leadership Style: The Globalist

Visionary, Inspiring, Open to the Unknown,
Community-Minded, Multi-Faceted Wealth and Wisdom

"I have long believed that the true worth of a person is measured by how faithfully we serve a cause greater than our self-interest that encompasses us but is not defined by our existence alone.
U. S. Senator John McCain, 2005 University of Arizona Commencement Speech

"The world has a very serious problem, my friend' Shiva went on. 'Poor children still die by their millions. Westerners and the global rich—like me—live in post-scarcity society, while a billion people struggle to get enough to eat. And we're pushing the planet towards a tipping point, where the corals die and the forests burn and life becomes much, much harder. We have the resources to solve those problems, even now, but politics and economics and nationalism all get in the way. If we could access all those minds, though…"
Ramez Naam, Crux (Nexus, #2)

"In those meetings, I learned that even economic diagrams needn't be linear. Ours was a nest of concentric circles, and an enterprise was measured by its value to each circle, from the individual and family to the community and environment. I realized that Rebecca and her colleagues were trying to do nothing less than transform the System of National Accounts, the statistical framework here and in most countries for measuring economic activity. For instance, the value of a tree depends on its estimated value or sale price, but if it is sold and cut down, there is no accounting on the debit side of the ledger for loss of oxygen, seeding of other trees, or value to the community or the environment. This group was inventing a new way of measuring profit and loss. By the end of our days together, I understood economics in a whole new way. A balance sheet really could be about balance."
Gloria Steinem, My Life on the Road

PERSONAL LEADERSHIP STYLES

Protector

Problem Solver

Optimizer

Creative Strategist

Globalist

Featuring

Mr. David Gergen: Advisor to four U.S. Presidents (i.e. Nixon, Ford, Reagan, Clinton), Harvard Kennedy School Professor of Public Service and CNN Senior Political Analyst

Photo © Gregory Heisler

Photo © Thomas J. Fitzsimmons

Mr. Les Wexner: Founder and CEO of L Brands (i.e. Victoria's Secret, Pink, Bath & Body Works)

The *Globalist* focuses on the greatest good for the greatest number. They often act as a catalyst in shaping others' lives and organizations. This is serious and important to them, yet they can be spontaneous and spirited as well. *Globalists* are curious, respectfully confrontational, tough, caring, candid, and visionary. They are the big thinkers who can take in the landscape or create it. On an individual and deeply personal level they have heart and can make others feel worthy and whole with dignity and deep respect. *Globalists* foster a sense of community or communitarian ethic and inspire others to be their better self. They are humble and proud, service-minded, spiritual in a practi-

Globalist

© Aha-Soft/Shutterstock.com

cal way, yet seek opportunity and wealth on many levels for themselves and others. They are truly their brother's keeper but can seek advantage for good and nefarious reasons. They are not perfect, but globalists elevate the tone and temperament of public discourse, institutional strategy and ethos, community and country as honest brokers for lived aspirational values.

Globalists in History

From a historical perspective, Abraham Lincoln, as a *globalist*, was the 16th President of the United States (1861-1865) "led the United States through its Civil War—its bloodiest war and its greatest moral, constitutional and political crisis. In doing so, Lincoln preserved the Union, abolished slavery, strengthened the federal government, and modernized the economy.[1]" Perhaps one of Lincoln's greatest speeches beyond the Gettysburg Address, was his second inaugural address[2] delivered during the final months of the war and just six weeks before his assassination.

In the speech, Lincoln expressed little in the way of blame for the war or triumph in the impending Union victory. He reminded the citizenry to equally recognize the distinct feelings of loss and sadness throughout the nation. He went on to say that any jubilation should be tempered by the knowledge that God, "gives to both North and South this terrible war." This realization he said must somehow guide a reunited nation forward. The speech highlights Lincoln's humble, humanitarian, aspirational tones, mixed with the clarion call for better ways and days of a globalist. It is timely and timeless in both message and mantra.

---

1 William A. Pencak. (2009). Encyclopedia of the Veteran of America. ABC-CLIO. P222.
2 Ronald C. White. (February 10, 2002). *Lincoln's Greatest Speech.* NYC: New York Times Publishers.

Closing days of the Civil War at Lincoln's Second Inaugural Address

March 4, 1865; Washington, D.C.
(Abridged)

"Neither party expected for the war the magnitude or the duration which it has already attained. Neither anticipated that the cause of the conflict might cease with or even before the conflict itself should cease. Each looked for an easier triumph, and a result less fundamental and astounding. Both read the same Bible and pray to the same God, and each invokes His aid against the other. It may seem strange that any men should dare to ask a just God's assistance in wringing their bread from the sweat of other men's faces, but let us judge not, that we be not judged. The prayers of both could not be answered. That of neither has been answered fully..."

"...With malice toward none, with charity for all, with firmness in the right as God gives us to see the right, let us strive on to finish the work we are in, to bind up the nation's wounds, to care for him who shall have borne the battle and for his widow and his orphan, to do all which may achieve and cherish a just and lasting peace among ourselves and with all nations."

Globalists wrestle with moral implications and broad, differing communities of thought. They care about justice, benevolence, and riches for the greater good. They seek truth and relevance, but *globalists* do not "wear their values on their sleeve" as if to judge others. Simultaneously candid and caring in crucial moments, they listen deeply and share the concerns of others, allowing them to have hard conversations and share difficult messages. Due to their sensitive and attentive manner, others will hear them in a way that allows understanding as opposed to conflict. *Globalists* may not always agree with others, but they have a deep and genuine respect for them.

Because *globalists* are often generous in nature, others can feel globalist colleagues have their best interests at heart. And this underlying intent affects the content.[3] *Globalists* can say the most difficult things in a most straight-forward manner and because they are seen as supportive in an appreciative[4] and fundamental way, others with differing views will trust, respect and accept what might ordinarily be seen as a threatening message. In many ways this is the essence of Lincoln. He had anguished and sometimes challenging messages to give to both the North and the South. Like Lincoln, the *globalist* can be persuasive and not abrasive and create the conditions for deeper shared meaning.

Creating a collaborative context for understanding is what is often most needed when the temptation may be to stand in judgement or to attack under threat. The *globalist* may be firm, tough and principled yet under threat will also be supportive, attentive and respectful of adversaries. This often creates a disarming quality to the conversation and allows both sides to stay open to each other's contrarian interests, positions and needs. This is not easy to do and is why *globalists* often have a reputation as being gifted in knitting together communities of conflict to one of cooperation and respect.

---

3 The message that intent influences content reflects the importance of attitude conveying in an actionable manner what the speaker hopes to be the outcome to some intended target. It is highlighted in several ways and places within the following NYT best-selling source material: Kerry Patterson, Joseph Grenny, Ron McMillan, and Al Switzler. (2002 and second edition, 2012). *Crucial Conversations: Tools for Talking When Stakes Are High.* McGraw-Hill Publishers.

4 Appreciative inquiry is a methodology that reflects the intent to focus in a positive manner while seeking outcomes with different parties. David Cooperrider is the author of multiple books by the same name.

In another time and place, British Prime Minister Winston Churchill offered an equally majestic and consequential sentiment as Lincoln. A politician, army officer, and writer, who served as Prime Minister from 1940 to 1945 and again from 1951 to 1955, Churchill led Britain to victory in World War II.

■ Of course, this did not come easily as illustrated in Churchill's *"Finest Hour"* speech[5] on the cusp of Britain's entry into the war. France had capitulated to Hitler's overbearing, ruthless Nazi invasion. Churchill had to explain the dire nature of a Nazi-occupied France while remaining optimistic and hopeful with a willingness to stand up to what many considered to be invincible Nazi forces. Hitler's evil reach was dominating Europe and appeared to be accelerating to a troubling point of no return. At this moment of great danger, Churchill spoke in the face of overwhelming odds not only of national survival but urged his countrymen to think of grand causes: freedom, civilization, national sovereignty. He called for a safe and better future for Britain's neighbors across the English Channel and for a reluctant, but friendly partner, the United States which he predicted would join the fight in time. The 1940 address to the British House of Commons and his countrymen[6] is one of Churchill's most powerful and stirring speeches:

Winston Churchill's Finest Hour Speech

June 18, 1940; House of Commons
(Abridged)

"However matters may go in France or with the French Government or with another French Government, we in this island and in the British Empire will never lose our sense of comradeship with the French people. If we are now called upon to endure what they have suffered we shall emulate their courage, and if final victory rewards our toils they shall share the gains, aye. And freedom shall be restored to all. We abate nothing of our just demands—Czechs, Poles, Norwegians, Dutch, Belgians, all who have joined their causes to our own shall be restored.

What General Weygand[7] has called the Battle of France is over ... the Battle of Britain is about to begin. Upon this battle depends the survival of Christian civilization. Upon it depends our own British life, and the long continuity of our institutions and our Empire. The whole fury and might of the enemy must very soon be turned on us. Hitler knows that he will have to break us in this island or lose the war. If we can stand up to him, all Europe may be freed and the life of the world may move forward into broad, sunlit uplands.

But if we fail, then the whole world, including the United States, including all that we have known and cared for, will sink into the abyss of a new dark age made more sinister, and perhaps more protracted, by the lights of perverted science. Let us therefore brace ourselves to our duties, and so bear ourselves, that if the British Empire and its Commonwealth last for a thousand years, men will still say, "This was their finest hour."

---

5 BBC Written Archives quoted in Gilbert, Martin (June 27, 1983). *Finest Hour: Winston S. Churchill*. 1939-1941. Heinemann. P566.

6 'Countrymen', citizens of the British empire, was an important constituency amongst many, as he was aware of needing their full support in quickly building an army of size and consequence with what some thought were against overwhelming odds.

7 General Maxime Weygand was the Supreme Commander of the French military forces in World War II when the Nazi's over-ran the French in pursuit of total dominance of the European Continent.

His words offered needed inspiration, vision, national unity and wisdom. Churchill translated an array of troubling, disparate issues and events into a broader, global context for meaning, purpose and action. He was willing to face the unconventional, or impossible, with the power of community, faith and purpose.

As communitarians, *globalists* leverage diverse strengths in a focused, collective manner often surprising the resistance with creative resilience and strategic action that sustains and empowers. They span boundaries and scan, conceptualize, align, and assess energy and action on an individual, group and organizational level for adoption and effectiveness. *Globalists* are comfortable or at least agile enough to lean, learn and leverage a variety of relationships, whether adversarial, cooperative, or collaborative.

Churchill did not know where or how he was going to get the help he needed. But he knew why. This is what mattered to him and his people. And in scanning and assessing the moment, he still imagined victory despite long odds and low resources. Enduring months of nightly bomb assaults, unchecked attacks by land and sea, and allied forces still less than present, Churchill had faith, wits, will and wisdom to direct expertise and effort to the maximum. A *globalist* in action, this was the difference-maker.

Equally important as their talent and vision, *globalists* recognize their shortcomings. Like creative strategists, globalists may express—intentionally or not—an air of entitlement. They can be cursed and blessed with a way of functioning that stands out as unique or demonstrative and opportunistic. As with some creatives, defensive routines for globalists include stubbornness, despite their agility. They, too, may be so invested and admiring of their own ideas that it is hard for them to let go if need be. Vanity is also an issue with *globalists* on occasion when they believe that they are deserving of special adulation above and beyond what may be due.

Also, on occasion, some *globalists* may abandon individuals and/or their cause. This abandonment from the perspective of the non-globalist may have the feeling of betrayal given their high hopes and expectations of the *globalist*. On a very deep and personal level, the globalist does not want to hurt or abandon most anyone. Yet when their values and priorities clash, *globalist* may freeze and detach themselves from their environment in a cold-blooded or cold-hearted manner. They go from their heart to their head and over-intellectualize turning people and issues into objects, as being out there in some distant place that one does not need to deal with (i.e. objectifying). They arc out of sight and hopefully out of mind, for at least the moment. This may often happen when there is a lack of an inner compass.

From a historical perspective, one could look at US Presidents like Richard Nixon and Bill Clinton. Regardless of your politics, a number of presidential advisors and historians have referred to them as having a questionable inner compass, and in the process, have abandoned key advisors and supporters at certain points along the way[8]. Of course, this does not necessarily diminish their

---

8   Assessment and commentary on Bill Clinton: George C. Edwards has pointed out: George C. Edwards, "Frustration and Folly: Bill Clinton and the Public Presidency," in Colin Campbell and Bert A. Rockman, eds., *The Clinton Presidency:* First Appraisals (New York: Chatham House, 1996), p 235.
    Assessment and commentary on Richard Nixon: Arthur Schlesinger, Jr. asked; Arthur M. Schlesinger, Jr., "The Ultimate Approval Rating," New York Times Magazine, December 12, 1996, p. 46.

accomplishments, intelligence and skills. As mentioned below, here is a brief commentary on Clinton's possible lack of compass in earlier days, as articulated by David Gergen (2001).[9]

Biographer David Maraniss reports that in 1981, Clinton gave a lecture at the University of Arkansas, analyzing key figures in politics from Willie Stark to Lincoln, Hitler, and Churchill: "In all political leaders, he told the class, there was a struggle between darkness and light. He mentioned the darkness of insecurity, depression, and family disorder. In great leaders, he said, the light overcame the darkness, but it was always a struggle." Clinton was touching upon his own internal struggle, Maraniss believes, especially with lying and philandering, two traits that had been part of his family life since he was young.

Perhaps we should think of Clinton locked in a titanic struggle between light and dark. But my sense is that description better fits Richard Nixon. Clinton has never shown the darkness of a Nixon. He isn't harboring interior demons the way Nixon was. Clinton is a sunny figure who doesn't want to hurt anybody and feels bad when he does. He can certainly be paranoid and lose his temper, but he isn't a hater. What he hates is other people hating him. He desperately wants other people to like him.

Instead of a struggle between light and dark, my sense is that Clinton's central problem has been the lack of an inner compass. He has 360-degree vision but no true north. He isn't fully grounded within. Explaining the success of an earlier president, historian David McCullough once wrote of Harry Truman that "He knew who he was, and liked who he was. He liked being Harry Truman. He enjoyed being Harry Truman." Bill Clinton isn't exactly sure who he is yet and tries to define himself by how well others like him. That leads him into all sorts of contradictions, and the view by others that he seems a constant mixture of strengths and weaknesses.

Whether growing up as the stepchild of an alcoholic and without his real father left Clinton without the kind of disciplining force in his life that he needed, as others have suggested, I am not qualified to say. It is relatively clear that by shaping his entire life since childhood to winning public office and then catapulting into the governorship of Arkansas at age 32, Clinton never had the chance most people have of making their mistakes in private. He was under such intense public scrutiny from early on that when his sexual energy got the best of him, as it did frequently, he learned to lie with gusto in order to cover his tracks. Nor did Clinton ever have time in his early adulthood for quiet reflection and internal growth. He started running grueling, time-consuming political campaigns when he was 27 years old and he has been running non-stop ever since.

Contemporary Globalists

Beyond the precipice of history, there are many contemporary globalists from all walks of life. A few of many good representatives of the *globalist* leadership style – arguably and selectively – appear on the *Fortune 50 Top Best Leader's List*[10] including:

---

9   Gergen, David. (2001). *Eyewitness To Power: The Essence of Leadership Nixon To Clinton.* New York City: Touchstone; Simon & Schuster, Inc, p. 327-328.

10 2014-2018 Fortune Top 50 Best Leaders List or alternatively referred as the WGL/World's Greatest Leaders List.

- **Christine Lagarde, Managing Director, International Monetary Fund (IMF):** Juggling the European debt crisis and concerns of 188 country members she mediated the bailout of Greece, Ireland, Portugal, and other fiscally troubled countries. She argues for supporting the poor and unemployed, fiscal restraint and micro-loan investments, in a blend of disciplined economics and merciful opportunity.
- **Bono, Lead Singer, U2:** He has traveled the world to enlist major companies, kings, presidents, popes and millions of people to fight HIV/AIDS, poverty and preventable diseases through his ONE and (RED) campaigns.
- **Oprah Winfrey, Media Mogul, Philanthropist, Actress, Health and Educational Advocate.** In 2005, *Business Week* named her the greatest African American philanthropist in American history. Oprah's Angel Network has raised more than $50 million for charitable programs, including girls' education in South Africa and relief to the victims of Hurricane Katrina. Among numerous awards, Winfrey was named the first recipient of the Academy of Television Arts & Sciences' *Bob Hope Humanitarian Award.*
- **Warren Buffett, Investor, CEO Berkshire Hathaway, Philanthropist:** The "Oracle of Omaha," and founder of the world's fifth most valuable company with followers who use his values-based, hands-off style that gives managers wide leeway and incentivizes them like owners. His influence and support in giving a helping hand to big and small causes is known the world over.
- **Angela Merkel, Chancellor of Germany:** For many years she has been viewed by the political class as the leader of the European Union, which is the world's largest economy. She has played a leading role in managing Europe's debt crisis and immigration policies. While controversial, her commitment to families fueled policies to support the immigrant community.

Many of those listed above create the conditions to provide a better, richer future for differing communities. Respect, honor, truth, fairness, and giving back are all common traits in these *globalists.* With their expanded, attuned conceptual and emotive capacity they bring vision, insight, intellect, empathy and care to their days. Some of these qualities are also most salient in the following *globalist* interviews with David Gergen (b. 1942), and Leslie H. Wexner (b.1937). They both speak of their early days, influences and opportunities as well as later phases of their life in terms of key learnings, principles and values that make a difference, particularly in high-demand, high challenge environments. Both, as *globalists*, they speak of ways to develop civic, commercial and public communities for strength, wealth of many kinds and opportunity for the greatest good.

Gergen shares key highlights of his childhood; a frightening experience with the Klu Klux Klan; days at Yale University during the Eisenhower administration; reminisces of his mentor, former North Carolina Governor Terry Sanford; the Navy, aboard ship as a war-time damage control officer; and later his work in the White House, particularly during the Watergate scandal. He tells what he learned, and conveys what he has passed on to the next generation. As a *globalist* he continues to build communities of thought that are respectful, inclusive, challenging of the status quo; and occasionally, moments of bravery, nudging or revealing unspeakable truths in ways that can be heard and considered for the larger audience.

****

Dr. David Gergen Interview

Growing up in a cramped house that sat on a dirt road in Durham, NC, David Gergen had no way of knowing that his career would take him to the White House, where he served as advisor to Presidents Nixon, Ford, Reagan and Clinton.

Although he has had many profound influences and experiences in his lifetime, Gergen credits his family as having the biggest impact on who he is today. "My mother gave me the grassroots, my dad helped me to fly," Gergen said. "They were very strict disciplinarians. It was a happy house-hold, though — we felt very secure. It was an optimistic environment and a lot of love and security was there."

Even though Gergen was raised in the white, segregated south of North Carolina, he said he recalled less race consciousness in those days. He was interested in sports but had a big growth spurt one year and lost some coordination. He became a bat boy during baseball games and started delivering scores to Durham's local newspaper, for which he began reporting on high school sports. "I was paid 10 cents an inch and was making $2.50 per month," Gergen said.

In high school, he covered local sports and obituaries. When the football games ended around 10 p.m., he had until midnight to file his story. His father would wait for him at the newspaper offices to drive him home and during that time the two bonded particularly deeply.

He started school at Yale in 1959, where he broadened his interest in journalism by beginning to write about politics during the time that Dwight Eisenhower and Nikita Khrushchev were center-stage and the civil rights movement was gathering steam. He interned for one of his role models, North Carolina Governor Terry Sanford, from 1960 to 1964.

"The crucible of those times was the civil rights movement and [Sanford] was very committed to both civil rights and education," Gergen said. "He had something called 'the good neighborhood council' and I really looked up to him. He was my mentor. I think role models and heroes really are important, they're huge, they're big. It's a way of being inspired."

Gergen said his passion for journalism and for understanding the world around him led him to attend a Ku Klux Klan rally in North Carolina as an observer. "I remember, since I grew up in the South, I wanted to understand the KKK which was very much alive and all around us," Gergen said. "Three of my friends and I went to a KKK rally to really just try to understand what was that all about. That may not have been the best thing to do, but we wanted to get some kind of under-standing of who these people were and what they were about. Everyone was behind masks and it looked like there was a lot of anger and hatred. They looked down on certain classes of people."

Several hundred KKK members chased Gergen and his friends after they were spotted driving too near the rally in their car. "They completely surrounded us in their hoods and gowns," Gergen said. "It looked pretty scary. This was the summer three young men were killed in Mississippi. It was a time the South was inflamed with racial anger and hostility of all kinds. To have 300 Klansmen literally circling our car while we were inside, was not a great thing. Basically, they were giving us a message: 'Don't go where you're not supposed to be.' We weren't sure what they were going to do as they started to rock the car. We had both panic and fear."

The incident came to Gergen's mind when he read a book by Vice Admiral James B. Stockdale, Ross Perot's third-party vice-presidential nominee, who wrote about his experiences as a fighter pilot facing extreme danger. "I'll tell you, you don't really want to trust anyone who hasn't seen suffering or hasn't been in the heat of the fire," said Gergen. "That is where character shows up. That's where leadership shows up. When we have to start taking responsibility for others." Gergen and his friends drove slowly away from the rally so as not to antagonize the KKK, but a whole caravan of Klansmen followed them out of town for miles. "I think about that night and it still is with me many years later," Gergen said. "I thought about the importance of sticking together and being a help to each other. Someone I've studied a lot is Robert E. Lee. His favorite word was "duty—duty to others."

After graduation from Yale, Gergen joined the U.S. Navy and served on a ship in Vietnam as a damage control officer, which is where he said he learned the importance of listening to others and trying to undo damage. "Learning how to unpack damage and bad things was very helpful for later on when I worked in the White House—particularly in the Nixon White House where I took responsibility for some 50 speech writers," Gergen said. "That was a really tough and trying time for all of us, not just the 50 speech writers and myself, but for the whole country." Gergen said he and his team struggled with the ethics of serving as President Nixon's speechwriters. Some felt like they should leave, to which Gergen replied: "You're free to leave. What's important is that you go by your conscience."

Gergen did not always agree with his leaders, or feel they were doing the right thing. However, he decided his presence was necessary, and that he was responsible for serving the American public as well as the White House. "Some of the leaders above us, my boss, President Nixon and others around me were very hard to understand at points," Gergen said. "Some of what they were saying really required serious questioning as to whether it was believable. I felt like the leadership had betrayed us. It was abusive and really was putting people in harm's way. It was really asking for the country to forgive them, particularly after Nixon had resigned."

"I had decided that it was important for me to stay," Gergen explained, "because I was really the one responsible overseeing all of my charges and if I left, I felt that it would just not be the responsible thing to do for those that decided to stay. So, I did. I ended up actually writing Nixon's letter of resignation, but it was not an easy time and I really felt, bottom line, that there was real betrayal which is a lesson in itself in terms of what not to do but, also what *to* do. That is why I go back to heroes and the importance of having standards and principles."

One of Gergen's other role models is Peter Gomes, a Harvard Divinity School professor and a minister at Harvard's nondenominational Memorial Church, who wrote a book called *Strength for the Journey*. Gomes was a very popular and respected black, gay Republican who offered prayer at the presidential inaugurations of Ronald Reagan and George H. W. Bush.

"He spoke about the importance of having strength, to keep grounded, and that you needed to care for others in the midst of adversity," Gergen said. "You need to be there to care for others, to support them in their weakness as well as their strength building. Part of that strength is to have an inner fire and have ambitions. Ambition for self and others is what really lights your passion. You need to have passion. You need to also have a caring way to be about community building, to be about what's best for others in total. Usually, as one gets a bit older, that becomes more of a natural way. A leader, wherever they are, should keep all of that in their mind—the greatest good, that is."

From Gergen's perspective, everyone has two stages of their career. The first stage is the building stage: You begin your own journey of growth and success and build yourself into the best you can possibly be at whatever you have decided to do. The second stage is to use the leadership you have created for yourself to give back by empowering and teaching others.

"I think that millennials are particularly very open to rejecting the poison of today's politics," Gergen said. "I think they are willing to actually embrace Teddy Roosevelt's idea of wanting to get into the arena and strive for moving forward. He also pointed to insights from Bill Moyers, a former presidential press secretary and speechwriter for Lyndon Baines Johnson (1965-1967). "The fact that this path through adversity and strength building is in part about keeping your space, your camp site clean," said Gergen. "Bill Moyers has referenced tribes in South Africa—how in their community and culture it is important for everyone to bring a log to the fire to keep it going. It is really a powerful metaphor in life that we must bring a log to our daily camp fires to keep it going to help feed, and develop, and grow not just ourselves and our passions, but that of the community as well."

Although he has met many insightful and valuable leaders during his life, Gergen still reflects on the mentorship he found in Sanford during his internship at the beginning of his professional career. "Terry Sanford was often considered by many as being one of the standout leaders of the last half of the century," Gergen said.

"He was in World War II as a paratrooper," Gergen continued, "and he talked about the Battle of the Bulge and D-Day and referenced his cherished Boy Scouts and how important some of those principles helped him during an incredible battle. He said that honor and duty, doing the right thing, being prepared, and helping others were thematic through what good leadership is about and what he stood for. He died when he was 80 years old. At his funeral, he was eulogized by a childhood friend, who said: 'Sanford took the Boy Scout oath when he was 12 years old and kept it. It started out: On my honor, I will do my best to do my duty, to God my country, and it included such things as helping other people at all times. He believed it. He was the eternal Boy Scout.'"

****

Similar to David Gergen, Les Wexner described his early days growing up, key influences particularly with his family and later with premier executive business leaders like John G. McCoy, Banc One Chairman; John Galbreath, commercial real estate developer; and Max Fisher, gasoline retailer. As a *globalist*, Wexner grew into a broader world view committed to developing major institutions like *The Ohio State University*, the people and institutions of his home state of Ohio, including the Jewish community; and broader philanthropic and organizational support for such organizations as the *Center for Public Leadership at Harvard's Kennedy School of Government*, where he is the Co-Chair. His efforts to make a difference were often born out of life's crucibles which he says is the platform for cultivating personal leadership. Beyond Wexner's outsized success in the commercial world, this is a story of a *globalist* who continues to seek a better world and a better future through hard work and service to his fellow man on many levels.

Leslie Wexner Interview

Leslie H. Wexner is the founder and chairman of global retailer L Brands, the parent company of Victoria's Secret, Pink, Bath & Body Works, with more than 3,000 stores and annual sales of $13 billion.

Wexner grew up in Columbus, Ohio where his Russian immigrant father and U.S born mother ran a store called Leslie's. He graduated from The Ohio State University and in 1963 opened his own shop, The Limited, in a Columbus shopping center. His aunt gave him $5,000 as "show money" to get the store started. Wexner never spent the money. "If you had $5,000 in the bank, the bank would loan you money," she said. "So, I never touched my aunt's $5,000. And with that $5000, I was able to get a $10,000 loan."

After six years The Limited had grown to six stores with annual sales of $2 million. At 30, Wexner was earning $200,000 a year. "My lifetime ambition before starting the store was some time in my life to be able to make $15,000 a year," he said. "My dad made maybe $8,000. So, $15,000 income was a vast sum of money."

Wexner compared himself, at that point, to a high school quarterback who never lost a game, then went on to play in college and never lost there either. But in the 1970s profits slumped. "The notion of profitability at zero, or slightly above zero—a low level of profitability—I never even considered it. To me it was catastrophe," Wexner recalled. "Friends, people who were close to me, never knew how crushed I felt," he said. "It would be like you were a singer and suddenly you couldn't sing. I had lost my voice."

Then Wexner's banker, John G. McCoy, chairman of Banc One, called and Wexner grew even more concerned. "When your banker wants to come to your office, you know there's something really bad." When the two met, McCoy put Wexner at ease. "Of all the things you have to worry about don't worry about me," Wexner recalled the banker said. "You've led the business to this point, you'll figure it out."

At home that night Wexner sat in the dark. At first all he felt was enormous relief. Then he realized he had come through a crucible. "I think the lesson of all that was just say, 'O.K. If there's a problem, I created the problem. Come to grips with it.'" McCoy's confidence in him allowed Wexner to see the situation clearly and move forward instead of seeking blame. "Where I would say look, the weather was bad or whatever, the government had created a recession, external things were giving me all this aggravation. I wasn't standing up to it. I think for me it was that challenge. It comes together with that person, and saying you made the mess, or you made this success. This is a little mess. Just fix it. I have confidence in you."

"I hadn't had a reversal," Wexner explained, "and it was like I was just crushed—instead of facing it." Wexner said McCoy's confidence gave him some perspective. "It was 'Hey, figure it out. God didn't do this to you. This is a man-made made problem.'" Wexner's father had a similar message. "If I were you I would do something, because worry is not going to solve the problem."

The incident changed Wexner. "It gave me perspective," he said. "I didn't have any confidence in myself, because if you always succeed, or you are only succeeding, without visiting or living the reversal, it's a very difficult thing. People that knew me very well didn't know the agony I was going through," he said. Perspective, Wexner stressed, allows a leader to look at a situation from the outside, a view, a perspective that can provide breakthrough insights and solutions. "There's a lesson about that in seeing yourself and maybe the situation in perspective," he said.

Wexner, who is co-chair of the Center for Public Leadership at Harvard University's Kennedy School, said he believes that "leaders are made, not born, and what makes them is how they learn from adversity. "Leadership is about you. Leaders lead themselves differently than normal people. They really can lead themselves."

Wexner said he was a late bloomer and went through high school and college without much coaching or academic striving. He said he was more focused on how to make a living and help support his family. Wexner recalled attending a school conference with his mother who was told her son had a high IQ and should be doing better in school. "The point of it was why don't you do better? And I said I don't know, I'm a kid. My mom would say you should do better and I'd say you're right. And we go home, and she'd say why don't you read, and I'd say why don't you? She'd say, well, I'm too busy." When he moved to a more competitive high school as a sophomore, Wexner said he was "completely lost" as his schoolmates began to discuss going away to college. "I couldn't understand why they would leave home, why would you go away, don't you like your parents? I had no idea what was going on."

Wexner said he was always self-employed. When he was around 11 he worked as a babysitter. "I figured if I earn 25 cents an hour babysitting, if I took 10 kids to the park on Saturday I could make $2.50 an hour. So, if I took them for two hours I could make five bucks, instead of babysitting one kid for three hours and making 75 cents. At a very early age I understood leverage."

In high school Wexner did well on an English reading test even though he had not read a book since sixth grade. His teacher asked, "Could you explain how you had such extraordinary reading abilities?" Wexner told the teacher he read magazines, including *Time, Newsweek* and *Reader's Digest*. When he was then asked why, Wexner replied: "Because I want to know what's going on," and added, "I don't read books, I don't have time."

When he was in his 30s, Wexner became a reader. He said he had come to a point where he realized what he didn't know. "I'm self-employed, and I'm running a business, how do I learn?" Wexner asked himself. "You could talk to people, which I did, and I could learn by other people's experience. I would never self-describe myself as curious until maybe I was 40."

Wexner started reading books on leadership "because I wanted to know what one was and that kind of opened up the whole subject." He said, "People would say, 'You're a leader' and I'd say, 'I'm not a leader, I'm just a lucky guy, I just got here first.' People would say, 'You're capable, and I'd say, 'No. No. I'm just lucky. I'm a lucky donkey! I just happened to be here, and I have this savant skill to pick sizes and colors.'"

He learned one lesson from a Columbus real estate developer, John Galbreath, who raced two Kentucky Derby winners and owned the Pittsburgh Pirates and Penguins. When Wexner only had a few stores, he called Galbreath and asked if they could talk. "I said I need some personal advice—not money—just advice about life." So Wexner went to his office and Galbreath told how his career evolved. Growing up on a farm he played baseball and had a horse. Later, Wexner said, Galbreath bought a horse for $75 and sold it for $200. After that sale, he got involved in horse racing. Then, through racing, he met an investor in professional baseball who, in turn, brought Galbreath in to that business.

Galbreath told Wexner to remain open-minded. "How that path then unfolds is unpredictable. He said if you're trying to say why would I do this or why would I go there, you'll shut yourself down. Basically, he was talking about curiosity," said Wexner. "I think that helped me because I was so narrowly focused." Wexner said most people become successful as they know more about less. "You become so narrow that pretty soon you're the doctor that knows about thumbnails on the right hand, and you're the world's expert. I saw that in myself, that I had no exposure."

In the second half of his life Wexner began to devote more time and money to philanthropy, supporting The Ohio State University, community causes in Columbus and Jewish religious retailing. Fisher asked Wexner if he could retire. "Yeah, I could," Wexner replied, "But why would I?" Fisher said he retired in his 40s to start a second career in public service. "It's really an interesting thing to have a second career," Fisher told Wexner.

The meeting with Fisher was a turning point for Wexner. "Max made me think about maybe being more purposed in community. It was more of an avocation. I thought if I'm creative, or if I have organizational skills and leadership skills, I can apply it to the university, Columbus, Jewish community, where those skills are transferable." Wexner said he looks at life as a three-legged stool. "Part of it is personal, your career, your own relationships; part of it is friends and family; and part of it is community."

Wexner's father questioned his son's involvement in philanthropy because he didn't want him to be disappointed if he was unable to make major change. Wexner said he remembers his father once told him, "You can't change the world, my Dad knew I was beginning to think things through. I thought about it. My dad was right about a lot of things. I decided even if you can change the world a little bit it's worth trying. And if you're successful without some kind of broader purpose, the way I thought about it is you're like Silas Marner, you're just racking up the score. So, you're thinking if I was the richest person in Columbus, or the richest person in Ohio, would that matter? And I thought no, for what purpose? If that's so, then God has got a funny sense of humor."

Legacy, he said, is "just nonsense." "No one will ever remember who sold the most togas in Rome, or in 2016 or 17 who sold the most underpants in the US, which is what I do. It's irrelevant. People remember the despots in history, maybe a few heroes. I think doing things to be remembered is really a fool's errand. I think people in a selfish way should feel good about what they're doing."

Wexner said his non-business interests keep him engaged. "When I look in the mirror I don't see a leader. I think for me, I try to challenge myself, and to me it feels like I don't get much done. My wife and kids laugh, I go home and say I didn't do anything today, I wish I had been more productive," he said. "It never feels like I get anything done. It's kind of like I have got this devil inside, I wish I could go home and say I had a good day. No, there's just restlessness. And I'm really happy. The notion of running out of work will be terrible for me."

His second career in philanthropy also provides perspective to lead the company, said Wexner. "I have insights because I am away from the business," said Wexner.

Leadership, he said, should be the most important course in high school and universities, to encourage students to think about perspective, or time managements and other personal traits. "Leadership is about yourself primarily. Secondarily it's about others," he said.

Wexner concluded that leadership is both an art and a science. "I think that leaders are made. You may be born with the aptitudes but if you don't go through these crucibles, whether it was mine or Lincoln's or Washington's or yours," he said, successful leadership will be difficult to achieve. "You could put different people through the same circumstance, and people have their aptitude to get through them and learn. That's really important," he continued. "If leadership begins with leading yourself and you have no instinct to want to influence others, to get them to a better place, I can't arbitrarily tell you that you should. But if you just lead yourself thoughtfully that's a good thing."

****

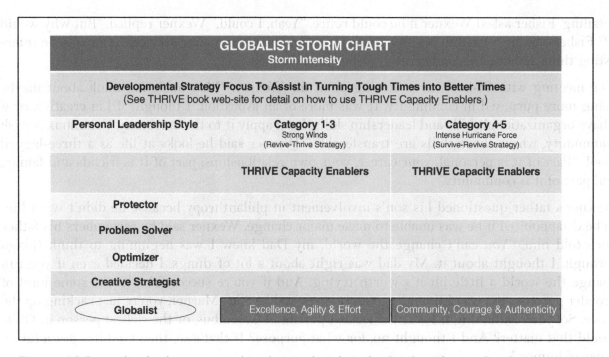

GLOBALIST STORM CHART		
Storm Intensity		
Developmental Strategy Focus To Assist in Turning Tough Times into Better Times (See THRIVE book web-site for detail on how to use THRIVE Capacity Enablers)		
Personal Leadership Style	**Category 1-3** Strong Winds (Revive-Thrive Strategy)	**Category 4-5** Intense Hurricane Force (Survive-Revive Strategy)
	THRIVE Capacity Enablers	THRIVE Capacity Enablers
Protector		
Problem Solver		
Optimizer		
Creative Strategist		
Globalist	Excellence, Agility & Effort	Community, Courage & Authenticity

Figure 10.2 can be further reviewed and considered in the book web–site for developmental exercises.

The Promise of Life-Long Potential – The Evolving Self

The Challenge and Opportunity of Transformation

"Huxley suggested rock climbing as an ideal basic training for citizenship. This sport teaches young people that survival depends on developing skills and on preparing oneself to face risks and unexpected contingencies. They discover that every move they make has real consequences involving life and death. In addition, a rock climber learns to take responsibility for another person's life, and learns to trust his life in the hands of the companion who holds the other end of the rope to which he is attached. What could be a more concrete way of shaping a complex self?"

Mihaly Csilkszentmihalyi, The Evolving Self

"Successfully functioning in a society with diverse values, traditions and lifestyles requires us to have a relationship to our own reactions rather than be captive of them. To resist our tendencies to make right or true, that which is nearly familiar, and wrong or false, that which is only strange."

Robert Kegan, Immunity to Change

Examples of Expanding Capacity – Featuring

Ms. Jane Grote Abell: Chairwomen – *Donatos Pizza*: 150 locations in 9 states; featured in Emmy-winning TV reality series, "Undercover Boss."

Photo © Donato's Pizza

© Scott Olson/Getty Images News/ Getty Images

Dr. Delos (Toby) Cosgrove: Retired President and CEO of the Cleveland Clinic, the no. 1 hospital for cardiology and heart surgery 23 years in a row, as ranked by *U.S. News.*

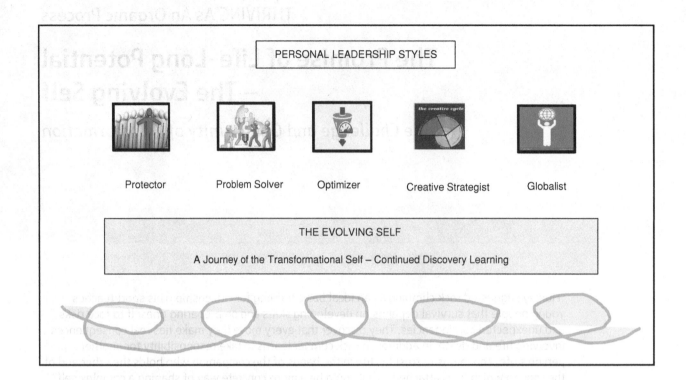

One More Time: What is *Personal* Leadership?

Most of us have a working description of what leadership is about and why it is important. It is in fact one of the most frequently searched topics on the Google[1] platform. Amazon sells more than 60,000 different leadership book titles per year through all of its many mediums.[2] Most of the time, leadership is described in some manner as being able to lead, manage or influence others. But regardless how you define its scope of purpose, leadership begins with oneself.[3]

Literature on leadership focuses on how the individual relates or interacts with others externally.[4] Leadership is often framed as a list of adjectives, personal traits or behaviors joined in some particular way to deliver desired outcomes. Prescriptions for good leadership generally include words like honest, accountable, goal-directed, pro-active, inclusive, collaborative and communicative. From a thinking perspective, leadership is described as a set attitudes or state of mind to position intent with effect. From a doing point of view, the definition may add superlatives such as results-focused, outcome-based, value-add, difference-maker, and so on.

---

1   Googles frequency count on the topic of "Leadership" led a veteran engineer, Chade-Meng Tan in 2007 to create an internal course at Google collecting experts in mindfulness, neuroscience and emotional intelligence. The course quickly became so popular at Google that eventually in 2012 it evolved into a program Google referred to as: *"Search Inside Yourself Leadership Institute"* (SIYLI). It has now become a global non-profit and has tools to help teach compassion, empathy and wisdom.

2   Amazon leadership topics are refreshed daily with the count listed on any leadership search.

3   Neck, Christopher P., Manz, Charles C. and Houghton, Jeffery D. (2017). Thousand Oaks, CA: Sage Publications. P2.

4   *Sage Publications, Harvard Business Review* (HBR), *Association for Talent Development* (ATD, formerly ASTD), *Society for Human Resource Management* (SHRM), The *National Conference Board* are a small number of the many available sources to find a rich collection of leadership focused on influencing, collaborating and managing others, teams and products. In some cases, there are select topics and training opportunities in these sources that also focus on personal leadership as well.

However, these perspectives often fail to recognize the role of readiness and maturation of adult capacity across a life-long developmental continuum. How we address the same challenge or issue in high school, college, mid-career or later-in-life is often very different. And how we respond to the usual leadership prescriptions may also be equally different, opportunistic or futile. We may in fact be trying intentionally to be honest, accountable, goal-directed, pro-active, inclusive and communicative at each stage in our life journey, but our effectiveness, outcome and satisfaction, and our way of engaging, may vary widely.

Intuitively we know that our inside influences the outside. Our interior world[5] influences what we see, sense, feel and do, as described in Chapter 4 regarding the *Path Toward Meaning and Value*. What happens at this deeper level begins to influence our perceptions, thoughts, feelings and actions. We essentially become a different person as we evolve. Constructive, timely feedback, lived-experience, and other situational factors add to the mix of meaning. This influences who we are and the way we embrace the world. Our personal leadership, whether engaged in intentional, unconscious or non-directive expression of self, shapes our way of leading our self and the environment in which we live. These factors co-mingle in a dynamic fashion that evolves and unfolds as postulated in the personal leadership continuum.

Notice below in Figure 11.1 how key questions that shape meaning vary based on personal leadership style or stage of development. At the earlier stages of the adult developmental continuum, the focus is more concrete and self-oriented (i.e. protector and problem solver) in high-demand environments. These styles are suited to situations that demand immediate and clear direction for some actionable result in the moment. In a crisis context, such as an airplane going down as described in Chapter 4, protectors and problem solvers are needed to right the aircraft, maintain order on board and communicate with the control tower. What would not be wanted in a compromised glide path is a creative strategist or globalist crew facilitating an inclusive, collaborative brainstorming session with passengers on varied ditching protocols to survive the plane crash. If at all possible, the protector would save your life. Thankfully we have them in all walks of life. They bring control, order, speed, decisiveness and a win-at-all-costs attitude. At the same time, they can be disruptive and manic if threatened, or find themselves in an environment that is not responsive to them. Fit and alignment of interests, intentions, perceptions and actions is consequential.

On the other end of the personal leadership style continuum (see figure 11.1) notice the questions are more conceptual, big picture, and community-oriented. Following the same plane analogy, it would helpful and timely to have creative strategists and the globalists shape the future direction of airline safety, assessing and visioning as-is and to-be conditions, principles and policy. Optimizers would be useful in developing operating steps and new regulatory practices. Problem solvers and protectors would be helpful in implementing and maintaining the new rules and regulations. A mix of styles and skills would be best in aligning a multi-faceted situational demand.

---

5 Our interior world reflects the unconscious, subconscious and conscious images, feelings and ideas perceived in varied forms within our cognitive, affective and psychomotor domains. Clinical, developmental, behavioral and social psychology offers a range of practitioner tools and insights for both providers and subscribers to harvest and apply insight in some meaningful manner. Some of this work is based on an intrapsychic level (i.e. within the mind) as reflected in such tools as mindfulness, meditation and therapy; while other work is more on an interpersonal level (i.e. between self and others) and involves coaching, counseling and training in teams, retreats and training workshops.

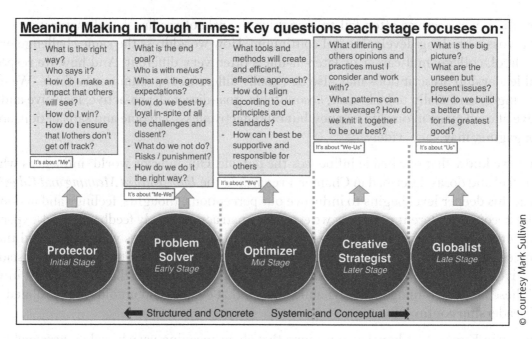

Figure 11.1:

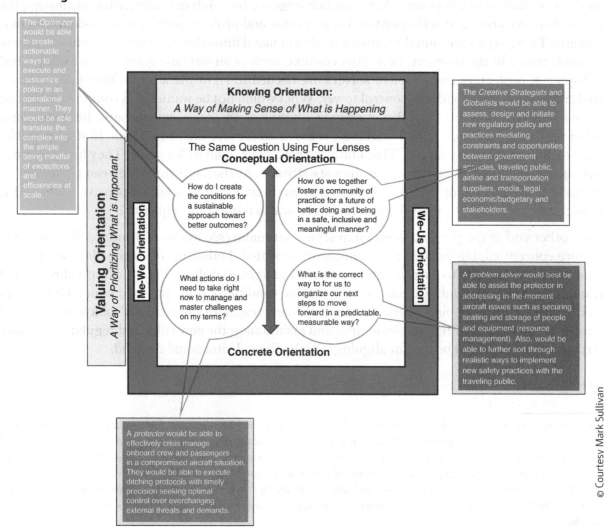

Figure 11.2:

Personal Leadership Styles: A Way of Knowing and Valuing

The above observations may lead to the natural conclusion that no one style is best for all situations. Different styles bring different strengths. At the same time, earlier stage styles will be both devoid of some significant conceptual leaning capacity, but at the same time also uniquely qualified in execution, speed and mobilizing of resources. Later stages bring big picture, original thinking as opposed to iterative suggestions or conversational builds on to other individuals' original ideas or observations. Later stages can draw on the assets and insights of earlier stages but not the reverse. Earlier stage styles cannot leverage what they do not have from later stages (see Chapter 4 and 5 for further detailed explanation). Other key concepts to keep in mind about knowing and valuing within each of the personal leadership styles include the following:

- Growth occurs in a sequential order from protector to globalist. Generally, the opposite is not true. One does not usually regress from a later stage to an earlier stage unless there is significant, sustained trauma or conditions that reconfigures one's knowing and valuing at a core level.[6]

- Each style regardless of where they fall in the continuum can reflect as much or more success and satisfaction as any other style. A *protector*, based on their criteria, may experience more satisfaction than a *globalist*, even with less overall capacity.

- While structured and linear from a staged continuum perspective, varied developmental platforms of knowing and valuing (as embedded in thinking, being and doing) may reflect a dynamic and interactive dimension within each style. These embedded style interactions may shape earlier stage behavioral response conditions,[7] and at later stages, may generate conceptually-organized insights leading to transformative movement of some kind.

- Transformative growth may lead to moving from an earlier stage to a later stage through a transition phase. This phase is a temporary holding environment that often requires expanding perspective-taking capacity. For example, moving from a first-person to a second-person perspective. This broadening of perspective-taking expands awareness through external feedback or self-initiated insight from experience and observations as briefly referenced earlier in Chapter 3 regarding the *Johari Window*.

- Each later stage is simultaneously more differentiated and integrated than preceding stages. They grow more flexible and durable, and complex but efficient in addressing challenging goals, decisions, issues, feelings, and actions in what is often in a more dynamic and ambiguous environment. Earlier stage functions often reflect deeper, more concrete versus broader conceptual ways of engaging. By holding on, as opposed to adjusting and adapting, they orient to what is proven and secure.

---

6 Susanne Cooke Greuter in some of her pioneer ego development stage theory work, as a successor to Jane Leovinger, provides some similar thinking in a broader stage model that includes child and adolescents as part of her developmental continuum.

7 This is based on conducting 63 one-on-one interviews within the first of multiple samples.

Style Envy

Naturally, some of us tend to stand in judgment and make quick assessments of each style based on our own preferences and aspirations. The first question many of us will ask of course is, *"what is my style and is that good* (according to some criteria one holds)?" *Am I where I want to be? Does this make sense?* (see figure 11.3 and 11.4 for further style descriptions). However, it is suggested to also suspend judgement in the process, if that is possible. Take a moment in a non-critical manner to reflect on who you really are in an everyday way. Judgement-free reflection is a practiced art that has a big pay back when we have the courage to solicit, support and affirm our inner voice with new emerging insights. It is easy for many of us to say we want to be at a place that is different than where we are at the moment, if in fact it doesn't line up with our image of our best self. However, Stephen Covey,[8] of the *Seven Habits* series, often reminded us that we need to start with where we are, rather than where we would like to be. Therefore, the cautionary note here is that we do not want to create false-truths or artificially manufactured feel good places that claim to be what we are not.

Yes, it is helpful to have a targeted destination point for growth and impact. However, it is not helpful to distort our reality to make it fit some conflated image or identity not real for us now or later. The challenge is to have a healthy balance between the promise and potential of what we aspirationally desire; with what we are willing to recognize and appreciate as our current strengths and weaknesses. For some of us, it may be easy to have an instinctive defensive reaction about being a certain way. It may be hard to unplug some of our defensive routines but one of a number of antidotes is to genuinely appreciate what are our unique skills and strengths as reflected by our true style. This appreciative stance in the moment is a good place to start and to finish. For some, this requires both a reduction of our *"inner critic"* and an increase of our *"inner angel."* (See the book web-site, under *Role Navigator*, for descriptions and exercises related to this area.)

Those of us, including me, who frequently use judgment and an embedded status hierarchy of what is better and worse for big and small occurrences, may struggle a bit with letting go of such judgment, even if it is for but a moment. Suspending judgment is referred to as being in a non-normative or as mentioned, in a judgement-free space. Ironically, suspending judgments about our habits and practices can create new awareness and insights into what we are experiencing. It requires us to adjust our filters or perceptual screens. Arriving at a judgement-free space in an intentional manner can not only change our perspective, but it can help us to facilitate new ways of seeing, sensing, feeling and doing in a repeatable and more effective manner in the future. For some, this may sound a bit out there, or a trek into pscho-babble.

Yet coaches of elite athletes and executive coaches of talented high impact players on the corporate playing field know that getting in the zone and being able to execute (or re-shape energy with new thoughts and skills) in new ways, in difficult times, involves reflection, awareness and action in an interdependent and practiced manner. Changing habits to improve outcomes involves intentional and focused awareness in a systemic manner in an effort to break through the resistance. Resistance, ironically serves to protect us from adopting scary, threatening new behaviors with unknown outcomes. We may want to do something new or better particularly in trying times but never seem to step up to what is required, on our end, due to

---

8   "we need to start with where we are…" and related principles of good living can be found in this *New York Times Best Seller* classic: Stephen R. Covey. (1989). *The 7 Habits of Highly Effective People*. Salt Lake City, UT: Franklin Covey.

our own resistance to the novel change required from within. Resistance promises safety and predictability. However, new awareness of options that concretely tie new benefits with attractive results, offering actionable baby steps forward, reduces the personal risk and improves the incentives to initiate and innovate. This awareness or insight into options helps to reconfigure the energy around resistance and alter the subtle but powerful *affirming messages that reinforce the new, sometimes scary experimental baby steps of improvement; instead of staying or retreating to safety and doing more of the same.*

Enriching awareness and insight into a new way of doing may be facilitated through a variety of exercises including meditation, guided imagery and deliberate practice regimens. These self and other-directed activities can alter how we see and be. In shifting attention and what we are attuned to in-the-moment, also requires us to move from an active to a reflective stance, which for some is an effort into itself. Our culture rewards action, less so reflection. However, we can make the job easier by soliciting outside assistance by a skilled coach or counselor. If the effort is first to create heightened awareness around new truths, and initially less around follow-on actions and experimental (transitional) behaviors, than additional sources of input may be timely and more effective than simply depending on one's own biases and filters. These outside sources may include a good and trusted friend or family member, a special and skilled boss or peer, or even sometimes a stranger who has nothing to lose in sharing the unvarnished truth. Accepting and appreciating truths about ourselves often involves finding a safe space within, where we first are valued by our self and valued by others for who we are. With that, we can explore the new, the disruptive, the provocative and the affirming all in respectful and treasured way.

I remember many years back on a summer Saturday afternoon in Manhattan, when I was riding a NYC subway from 81st street near the Natural History Museum. It was mid-afternoon. There were a dozen or so passengers on the train sitting near me. In the mix were three very busy, active, "playful" children who were jumping off the empty seats and swinging back and forth, dangerously close to other passengers, while hanging on the empty ceiling straps (i.e. meant for standing passengers to maintain their balance while the train is moving). The train was moving and shaking side-to-side as it was circumnavigating a twisted track in the intermittent squeaky, dark space. Somewhat nearby was a middle-aged man that appeared to be their father. He was hunched over, and only occasionally looking at the children. At this point the kids were singing and screaming, excitedly talking and yelling while even jumping on top of each other at certain intervals. The rest of us were looking at each other with grave concern as the hunched man continued to look more dazed and indifferent than ever. We were upset. It seemed the rest of us were looking at each other and then at the man with angst. The children's safety was at risk and he was doing nothing. How could he not bother to look after his own children in the midst of the mayhem? It seemed more than a few of us were looking at this shameful man with disgust.

Then, coming from another train cab, was a women who walked in between the jumping children directly over to the hunched man. She leaned over, while gently placing a hand on the man's back, and quietly, ever so tenderly spoke. "John, I know this has to be a hard day with the funeral and all; and after burying your beautiful wife that you were so in love with. Let me take the children back with me and give you a moment of peace and quiet." The women and the children left. We were stunned. I am sure every one of us on the train was instantly shocked. This was not a lazy, uncaring hunched over man doing a despicable job as a father. This was a husband painfully grieving the loss of his love.

This was a humbling moment for me, and probably for a few others on the train. In the process, I couldn't help but realize how judgment and attribution[9] had gotten the better of me and perhaps others. Perception and reality seemed the same until truth showed up. It is easy to talk about suspending judgment after the fact. Much harder to intentionally create moments of reflection that bracket activity with our reaction to it. Yet the opportunity to see things differently and perhaps more clearly may sometimes sit on that other side of such reflective pauses.

Deep(er) awareness of our exterior world often requires a shift in what we do in our interior world. Holding-on and letting-go of positions and perceptions is a dance that requires us to quiet the mind; to allow new voices and images to emerge within, on its own time; and to soften and strengthen our present moment with acceptance of the new and even the startling. The more startling or threatening the idea or insight is, the more we must also affirm and support ourselves and others in what often is a sacred, tender space of doubt and fear mixed with hope and need. This is often a place of vulnerability which requires both a push and a pull: a lot of real time caring support with a defined actionable challenge to concretely step out of the comfort of the known. To some this may take the form of tough love. (*Note: More of this is discussed with exercises in the book web-site.*)

Linking Awareness and Action to Our Personal Leadership Styles

As you look at the figures below, reflect on which *personal leadership style* resonates with you. Be attentive to what you appreciate about yourself and how that is resonant with one of the five styles. Suspend judgment if that is possible and take in what appears to make sense as the working, every day you.

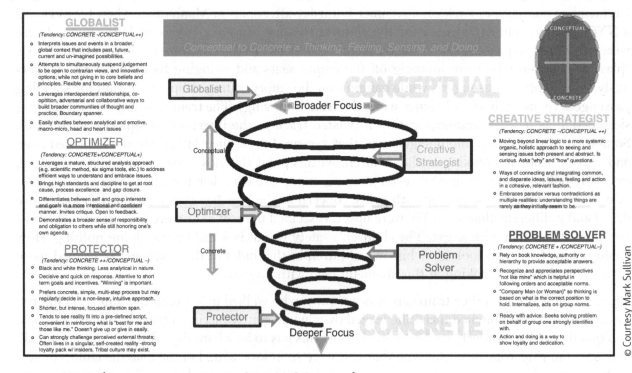

Figure 11.3: (*Concrete-to-Conceptual* Ways of Knowing)

---

9 Attribution, or the act of inappropriately assigning a cause or reason when facts are missing, is considered by the *American Management Association* (AMA) as one of the biggest challenges in North American management today, based on Gallop Poll surveys on management behavior.

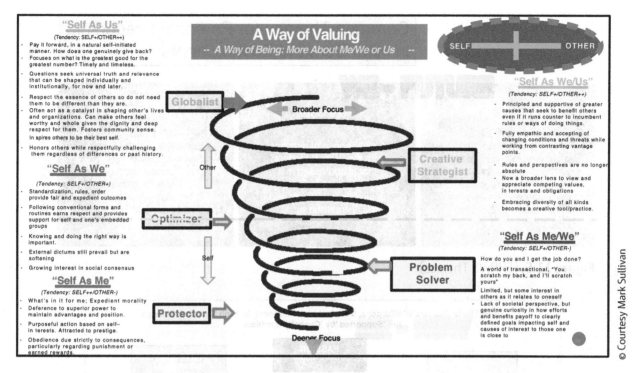

Figure 11.4: (*Self as ME-to-Self as Us* As Ways of Valuing)

Both figures 11.3 and 11.4 spirals in a deeper more compact manner in the southern part of the spiral; and a more broad and loose fashion in the northern area of the spiral. Each have the five styles, but figure 11.3 (i.e. immediately below) focuses on our ways of knowing from a concrete to conceptual perspective. Figure 11.4 focuses on our ways of valuing from a *me-we* in the south to a *we-us* in the north. Remember, each style has value and can leverage our success and satisfaction in unique but meaningful ways for us.

The Different Ways THRIVING As Capacity Enablers Shows Up

Thriving during tough times requires fuel for the journey. Current research I have conducted involves one-on-one interviews with dozens of notable high achievers who have turned difficult times into better times. The thematic qualitative analysis indicates that thriving in high demand environments is supported by an appreciative level of purpose, passion and presence. Further, twelve capacity enablers support the purpose, passion and presence themes. These capacity enablers (**Purpose:** *Competence, Curiosity, Care, Courage and Community*; **Passion:** Enjoyment, Excellence and Effort; **Presence:** *Agility, Awareness, Authenticity and Affirmation*) are represented in Figure 11.6.

The above capacity enablers support the thrive themes, I referred to as P3, or *purpose, passion and presence*. These thrive themes and capacity enablers are interdependent and can look different in each of the five personal leadership styles. They all do not necessarily need to be present in all high-demand environments for all styles. Yet while they play differing roles in assisting personal leadership styles to thrive, they are valuable and supportive in their own way. Different configurations of these capabilities will provide utility and expression influencing the look and feel of each personal leadership style. Below is an illustrative mapping of the capacity enablers to the P3 in Figure 11.7. Notice the THRIVE Map has a different configuration in the earlier stages

Common Themes for Personal Leadership in High Demand Environments

PRESENCE:	PURPOSE:	PASSION
An ability to focus and to connect under-the-skin in an agile and meaningful manner, with differing others and situations; Creates sustained attention, interest and (consequential) outcomes	A clear sense of direction with the "Why It Matters" that is addressed in a compelling fashion; aspirational, relevant and realistic	Cultivates energy that resonates with a key part of who you are that helps to guide engagement in a sustainable fashion particularly as it gets difficult

© Courtesy Mark Sullivan

Figure 11.5: (THRIVE Themes)

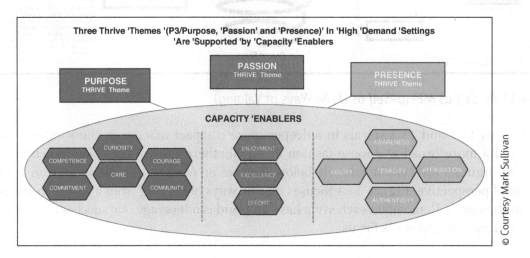

© Courtesy Mark Sullivan

Figure 11.6: (12 Capacity Enablers That Support the 3 THRIVE Themes)

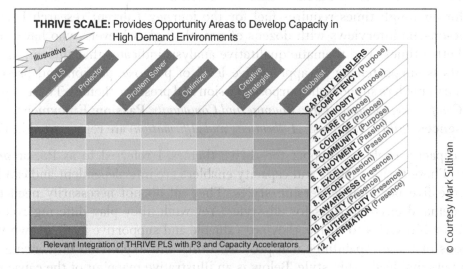

© Courtesy Mark Sullivan

Figure 11.7: THRIVE Map Summarizing Illustrative THRIVE Scale Results (See book website for more detail) (i.e. protector and problem solver) then in later PLS stages (i.e. creative strategist and globalist) in the THRIVE map. Again, this reflects a multi-faceted dynamic but is only illustrative in nature as one's own Thrive Map may be different.

Evolving Self as An Inside Job

I remember many years back, when I was starting a new assignment, in the early days of my career as a sales trainer at United Airlines Executive Sales Institute in Chicago. I had the good fortune of learning under two seasoned executive trainers. Technically they were my peers but in reality, for the first year, they were my teachers. They both had more than 30 years of experience as sales executives, negotiators, organizational consultants, managers, motivational speakers and change agents. They had managed a book of business, raised a family, and talked regularly to our senior executives. They were grey hairs – I was a kid just four years out of college. It was a privilege to be around them. They were bright, funny, very sharp and skilled. I didn't realize how much I was learning at first. Also, initially, I didn't realize just how much I didn't know.

I spent hours watching them give workshops, hotel-ballroom motivational talks to travel agents, and coaching and consulting sessions. They were often flown in to talk to high level United Airline executive customers having issues with our sales force. I had the good fortune of watching them up close. I also saw them teach more than ten three-day negotiating skills workshops before I taught just one. They made it look easy to both handle big customers and teach advanced negotiating skills to seasoned sales reps hardened by real world deal-making. I had a sales background myself after a few years as a door-to-door Prudential insurance sales rep. However, this was a different league.

I started conducting my own negotiating workshops and while I eventually became pretty good at it, after teaching over 500 negotiating workshops around the world, those first few were rocky. I barely got through each of the three-day sessions. I would finish at six and then prep until midnight for the next morning. My executive training peers made it all look so easy. They would stop and start the video role plays of sales students calling on customers. They would freeze the video capture of sales reps attempting to handle customer objections and debrief with ease. They knew which questions to ask when, and more importantly, the follow-on questions that explored more deeply on intent and underlying beliefs and assumptions of the customer.

It took a while from a knowing perspective to figure out–to conceptualize—what questions I was missing. From a valuing perspective I also had to leverage more of the *we* and *us* views drawing on second-and third person-perspectives. What made a difference in my learning[10] was the nature of the help that I got. I ended up getting regular coaching from my peers. On good days I tried to be open to their painful feedback that I needed to hear. I also had to be willing to experiment with very different ways of leaning into the student learning space. I was coached to strategically self-disclose parts of the more intimate me, and my own sales performance gaps, that were relevant to sales students. This helped to build trust and safety between me and my sales reps in the learning environment. At times, this was difficult for me, at other times it was exciting. I was told that I was a natural and even gifted but I really didn't feel it for a very long time. However, being affirmed and supported was far more important to

> The truth that makes men free is for the most part the truth which men prefer not to hear.
>
> *Herbert Agar*

---

10 "made a difference in my learning," is a reference to discovery learning processes as robustly covered in the following source: Robert E. Quinn. (1996). *Deep Change Discovering the Leader Within*. NYC: Jossey-Bass.

me and my sales students than I ever could have originally imagined. This process is also described as deliberate practice.[11] Briefly, it works like this: (1) *initiate behavior*, (2) *get feedback from a skilled colleague*, (3) *initiate with more intensity at a continually higher level of difficulty*, (4) *practice, assess and reflect*, (5) *revel in affirmation and support*, (6) *get more skilled feedback*, (7) *and do it again*. It was both exhausting and exciting.

A Perspective on Learning and Development

Growth. It is not always pretty, nor predictable. More often than not, one cannot control experiential learning and growth. In many regards it is like trouble – it can visit us when we least expect it; and then other times when we schedule the learning, it may take on a different form or none at all. Many times, learning and development may be organic, sporadic, and improvisational. We can hope for insight-on-demand, or enhanced skill or value by a set deadline. However, intent doesn't always align with results.

As a dynamic, creative learning machine influenced by time, insight and experience, we often seek to learn by ideally creating the right conditions, approach and effort. Sometimes we may be fortunate enough to suitably calibrate within and between ourselves and others as we observe, reflect and analyze the progress. This happens when we are trying to learn how to run a meeting, give feedback to someone, or practice how to complement or critique with care and candor. Learning about ourselves and our world, unfortunately, cannot be manufactured, bottled or packaged. It takes deliberate practice: effort, feedback, increased demand, assessment, reflection, affirmation, and practice again. And again. This deliberate practice method is used everywhere from Olympic coaches and elite athletes; to award-winning teachers and students, to high-performing managers and their employees. Each step is important and part of what helps to get through the knowing, not knowing new knowing and optimal knowing as displayed in Figure 11.8.

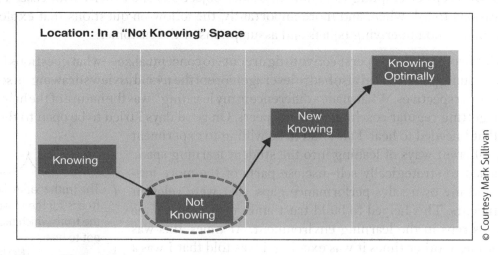

Figure 11.8:

---

11 Deliberate practice is further discussed as a systematic performance improvement method in a number of sources including: David Epstein. (2014). The Sports Gene: Inside the Science of Extraordinary Athletic Performance. Chicago: Penguin Random House.

The journey along the personal learning and leadership continuum is never the same for any two individuals. Personal circumstances, aptitude, filters, capacity enablers all help in facilitating the backdrop for moving from a state of *knowing*, to *not knowing*, to *new knowing* to *optimal knowing*. For the following are stories of two very successful individuals who like many of us have traversed this same knowing journey.

****

Jane Grote Abell grew up in a family business where in the early days, Donatos pizza and customers were literally served and entertained in her dining room. She came from a strong family where love, kindness, service and care ruled the day. This not only became the essence of who she was as a mother, business retailer and customer advocate; but it was what was infused into the Donatos culture for the thousands of employees, suppliers and customers to appreciate and acknowledge in an everyday way.

Abell did not have it easy growing up, but she also had parents that gave her a special upbringing with values she took with her in the midst of fighting and winning her family business back from the world's largest fast-food retailer. Abell, like most of the rest of us, had her fair share of ups-and-down. Yet on the corporate front, in the midst of the battle of her life, she eventually found her voice, and in the process, the courage to stand up and claw back Donatos from a corporate giant that was suffocating her and those who were a part of her life. She successfully re-negotiated better terms, and in the process a better way of life for her, her family and her business. This is a story of a very successful business woman and family matriarch coming into her own and finding ways to live her values while supporting others to do the same.

Ms. Jane Grote Abell Interview

Jane Grote Abell, grew up in a family business, Donatos, a pizza company with presently over 150 locations in 9 states. The company, at an earlier stage, was acquired by McDonald's, but Abell later led a fight to buy the company back from the global fast-food giant and went on to serve as its chairwoman.

Starting as a child, Abell learned from the example her parents set. "I've been very blessed to have grown up in a home, while not perfect by any means, we were transparent, and authentic, and genuine, but also faced really hard times," said Abell. "I grew up behind the very first Donatos restaurant and I remember lots of people coming back to the house because my dad didn't have a dining room in his first restaurant, and entertaining people." Her mother, Abell said, always opened the door for guests. "My mom taught me all about how to open your home to strangers who become your friends and family."

"My dad worked really hard all the time, most birthdays or holidays. His restaurant was right in front of our house, literally 25 feet. We would go to the restaurant to see him," she continued. Her father's childhood experience working in a pizza place for an unscrupulous boss formed his own attitudes about running a business. "He wanted to provide an environment where people could treat others the way they wanted to be treated with trust, respect, dignity, caring, and basically the Golden Rule," said Abell.

While he continued his education at The Ohio State University, Abell's father continued to work in the pizza business. When he had an opportunity to buy the business, he dropped out of school, borrowed money from his dad and his wife's father to start Donatos. "So, that's the restaurant I grew up behind. I say that I'm blessed because I really didn't know any other way."

'I can share this now, but my mom, on all of those evenings, also began to drink a lot," said Abell. "My mom has been sober for almost 40 years. It's day-by-day obviously, if you know anything about recovery and addiction. She taught us about addiction and disease and she was open and honest about the struggles with it. While my memories of those evenings were awesome, the memories of the mornings were not. In the mornings, we were cleaning up beer bottles when we were getting ready for school and taking care of things." This part of her childhood helped to teach Abell the importance of balance in life, and the fact that not everything is perfect for anyone. "It may look like they have it all together but, everybody has a story."

Abell was focused on competency even while growing up. "I became that middle child in the role of responsibility. During that time, I thought it was difficult because I didn't know it wasn't normal. To me, that was just what we did. We had to get up and clean up and go to school, then start all over again," she said. Abell's mom became an inspiration for taking control of addiction and helping other people in the same situation. "She just knew alcohol was getting in the way of her life. She decided to go to AA meetings and then decided to stop because she felt like it was something she didn't need in her life. Then, she started a non-profit for a drug and alcohol rehabilitation center just for women."

From both her parents, Abell learned about the importance of persistence and passion. "No matter what we face in life as a family or as a business, the quote in our family is, 'Love your way through it.' That resonates with me every time. I've applied that to my business life, to my personal life. No matter what anyone's spiritual belief is, love is that golden thread that weaves its way through every religion. Every spirituality is love," she said.

Abell's parents helped her to understand that sometimes the people who need the most love are those who seem the least needy, depending on the situation. Abell recalled a day she received a call at 10 a.m. about a driver who never made it back from a delivery the night before. "I got a call in the morning that they had found him and on his last delivery, two gentlemen had met him in the street and beat him up and left him to die for 20 bucks. He was an older gentleman who had been with us for five years in Cincinnati." Abell dropped everything and decided to go to Cincinnati, even without really knowing what she was going to do there. "I was just packing my bags when my dad came in my office, very teary eyed and sad. He said, 'Now remember when you get there, not only to love your way through it with the people in the store, but I need you to send love to the two people that left him on the street to die'."

"I had a good two hours driving to Cincinnati to be able to pray and meditate," Abell said. "Loving your way through it doesn't mean you don't have consequences for human behavior, but you do it with love," said Abell. Her father was a guiding light to help her see the other side of a tragic situation. "I was not going out that door thinking, 'I'm going to love those two guys.' I'm going to love on the store and love on the managers and the gentleman's family. I didn't even pause long enough to think about how I would feel about those two guys, that's why it was so powerful." Being able to think of this situation from another perspective was a powerful moment for Abell. "Sometimes, you need people like that in your life to make you pause and think."

Even though Abell was raised with a family that continuously taught her the importance of keeping her heart open, she understood that not everyone grew up with the same kind of childhood experiences. "I also think people in our world have experienced trauma. When people experience trauma, they don't always know how to take care of themselves. When people don't love themselves, they can't possibly learn to love others."

The family business grew around the central concepts of treating people with love, compassion and integrity, said Abell. "It was truly a family business. We started franchising. We had growing pains, but really it was based on the Golden Rule." Abell saw her dad make customers the priority of the business and keeping the business focused on the core values it was built on. As the business grew, her dad talked about expansion and the future of where the company was going. "He would talk about our future, and our growth at Donatos, and how we were going to grow the business and be around the world. He's very philosophical and would always talk about, 'Why?' The why was always because we were going to make a difference on every block that we did business and we were going to treat our customers with respect and our associates with respect."

Abell's father emphasized consistency in the kitchen. His other company, Grote Manufacturing Company, focused on food processing so that the products were the same for all the customers at Donatos. McDonald's also emphasizes consistency and was in the market for new product lines to reduce its reliance on burgers. "They decided they wanted to buy us," said Abell. "Through our three months of trying to decide whether we wanted to do this as a family, for my brothers and my sister everybody was feeling all the pros and the cons. The biggest con was how do you sell your family business and keep your soul. I was in charge to do that. That was going to be my role and figure out by studying the companies that grew big and their culture, and spirit, and who they were."

Abell got in contact with the HR representative of Chick-fil-A, and they spent two days talking about how to keep love in a business and grow it. Following her conversation, the family made a decision. "We sold. Shortly after that, my mom left the business and my youngest brother never came back. My oldest brother who was our COO, stayed for about a year and a half. The culture changed so drastically and so quickly," said Abell.

Immediately there was a difference in tone and attitude from the new CEO. Abell felt as though her ability to voice her opinion was going away. "Not very long after, my brother left, my dad became a chairman and the person who was our CEO began making decisions that were inconsistent with who we were and what we were about. We were building way faster than we could develop our people, changing the concept, not the product. Going through that process, I slowly lost myself."

The new CEO brought a lot of changes. One time, Abell said, during a conference, the CEO asked 26 of 28 vice presidents to get up and stand at one corner of the room, while telling them 'you have a future here' as they walked. Slowly the numbers of people sitting decreased, until it was just Abell and a franchise partner of 40 years. The CEO looked at them both and said, "The people standing at the end of the room have a good future here, the people left sitting at the table need to think about their careers, put their resumes together, and think about their next career opportunity."

This was the time that Abell found herself approaching her job as if it were a game to be played, rather than something she did out of passion. "I wasn't afraid I was going to lose my job because I had an employment contract. I knew I could still speak my mind, but I lost my courage to do it."

Abell said she had lost out on what she had held as the important parts to her life. "I remember not seeing my kids and not balancing my time at the office. I also had stopped spending time in prayer and meditation and being grounded in my faith because I was working too hard." One late night in the office, Abell became highly aware of what was happening. "I had one of those moments in life where I was like, wait a minute, what am I doing, and who am I? It was as if the Holy Spirit had washed over me and woke me up, like the lights came on."

Four years later, it was rumored that McDonald's was going to close Donatos. Abell felt as though the company had a destiny and that it was up to her and her father to buy it back. From there, she set up a team and presented her plan to McDonald's, and it agreed to sell. Looking back at this time, Abell said it was when she realized what was important in life. "It became about the four Cs for me. Character, courage, conviction and compassion." Abell said she understood the ideas of "courage to fail, and courage to take risks, but the courage to keep your voice in really hard times is really important." She added another C. "I think being curious is really important for growth."

Throughout her career, Abell recognized that there have been times she wished she kept a better balance with her own family. "Because my dad worked so hard, the one thing I said when I was young, was 'I'm not going to do that.' I wanted to make sure that I learned how to balance my life and I didn't. The hardest thing was a personal one. You only get one chance with your kids and I didn't want to mess that up," she said. Abell changed her role from CEO to chairwoman. She understood that in the beginning she was too caught up in her own agenda, and the work to buy the company back. As she continued to accomplish goals, she kept trying to motivate herself to focus on balance next. But she came to understand, "You're never going to have an 'after this' until you stop long enough to change what you're doing because there's always an objective. You're a hard worker and you're passionate about what you do. You just have to learn to prioritize." As she started to see her life from this alternate perspective, she realized she wanted to make room in her life, first and foremost for her faith and family, and then the family business.

This change in her priorities came following Abell's divorce. She realized that she needed to make a lot of life changes. It also helped bring her to the conclusion that she did not have to have a leading role in the company to be able to give back. "I'm honestly not the best person to take our company to the next level. It's recognizing that and where I was in my life to make a change to make it better and make room for my kids."

From this personal experience, Abell knew that she missed some of the important moments in her kids' lives. She made sure that when her son grew up, became the owner of a business and started a family that she stressed the value of that time spent focused on family. "He's working too much, and I keep telling him, 'You're doing too much, you're following my same path,' He's like, 'Yeah, but I admire you, you worked hard, and I appreciated what you did.' But, you just don't get those moments back. It's not worth it."

****

Dr. Delos (Toby) Cosgrove, a world renowned cardiac surgeon and former health care executive can teach us much about persistence when the odds are long and the resources are limited. As a dyslexic who struggled through school, to continue to expand the expertise and reputation of the Cleveland Clinic as one of the best hospitals in the world, he has many lessons on how to leverage the best you have when at times it may not be good enough.

His 'never-say-die' spirit, discipline, creativity, competence and quality-consciousness was thematic throughout his days at the Cleveland Clinic and beyond. Interestingly, on the day I met Cosgrove, I had a brief hallway conversation with a security guard while en-route to the CEO's office for an 8:30 am appointment. "Do you ever run into the man?" I asked the guard. "All the time," the guard said. "How is that" I asked. "Well for example today he has his doctor's rounds with his patients from early morning until his first meetings with his day job as the CEO. He always passes this corner to-and-from his patients."

I walked away thinking what drives this man? I am sure as CEO he doesn't have to see patients. Fast-forward two hours and I realized post-conversation, this is someone committed to always getting better, and doing better, even at 76 years of age, and helping others to do the same. Here is a story about life-long learning and the dividends it pays in leveraging attitude and effort into excellence in an everyday way.

Dr. Delos (Toby) Cosgrove Interview

In his 13 years as President and CEO of Cleveland Clinic, Toby Cosgrove oversaw local, national, and international growth. The Clinic has grown to be an international force in healthcare. Cosgrove, the architect of this expansion, was once a risky hire who struggled with dyslexia and poor self-perception.

Cosgrove grew up in a small town in New York and struggled with schoolwork. Small town life has its benefits for a kid, though. Cosgrove said of his hometown, "You had the sense of accomplishment, then you shoveled walks and raked leaves, and collected newspapers. You know, it was perfectly safe to do it. And people were supportive. You became entrepreneurial at a young age."

That sense of accomplishment was marred, however, by his scholastic struggles. Cosgrove was dyslexic, but said he had never heard the word until I was 34. "I was dating a teacher and I was trying to read the *New York Times* out loud to her as we were going someplace in the car and she said, 'You're dyslexic.' And I said, 'What's that?'"

Dyslexia has caused struggles throughout his life, but never more than his college and medical school years, Cosgrove said. "I have to laugh when I went to college and I was a terrible student. Highlighted by the fact that I thought that somehow, they had a language requirement, and somehow, I decided to take French. God knows why I did that. I got in remedial French, meaning five days a week at eight o'clock in the morning. I got three D-minuses and a D. And, of course, the reading requirements for dyslexics in college at a liberal arts school were challenging to say the least. So, I got into one of thirteen medical schools that I applied to. Scholastic life didn't get a lot better until I got into clinical medicine." It was then that Cosgrove said his world changed.

Cosgrove does not see his dyslexia as a curse. "I think it's been a real gift because two things. First of all, if you survive scholastically as a dyslexic it teaches you perseverance. Secondly, I think you think differently about problems than other people do, you seem to be more creative in your thinking. I think the third thing is that you're not afraid to fail, because you've already failed, a lot of times."

So, when he was rejected from twelve medical schools, it didn't deter him. One school accepted him, and he ran with it. "I went to medical school not to become a medical doctor, but to be a surgeon," said Cosgrove. "I was just hell bent on it." Getting a residency was difficult, though. "I didn't get my first choice in residency," said Cosgrove. "When I got to Mass General they told me that I was the thirteenth man in my group and I ought to be damn glad to be there."

Cosgrove's perception of himself began to change when he got the chance to sail with an elite group on an America's Cup boat. After growing up sailing on Lake Ontario, he valued this experience.

"I had a friend who had a bunch of money and he got me a chance to try out for the boat, which was sailing out of Boston. And I was going to be a substitute, is the best way of looking at it. One day we were sailing off of Marblehead, out of Boston, and they had a position on the boat called the ship's husband and that was the guy who did all the work below decks." Cosgrove remembered that the man who had that job was breathing hard and generally struggling with duties below deck. He was feeling sick with the boat's bouncing and water coming in on his head. Cosgrove jumped on the opportunity to be the substitute ship's husband. "I said, 'That's my spot.' I became known as the sewer man. Every boat subsequently, that was a named position, the sewer man. I worked my ass off. I did all the work below and I did all the work at the top of the mast. I worked my way up so the second year I became a relief helmsman. Just a matter of working it to death. It was fun. It was a privilege."

"Persistence is the thing. The main event," he said. Cosgrove never lost his need to persist but being part of the sailing team taught him something else that is not always emphasized in medical school—the need for teamwork. "You have to have an appreciation for other people's talent and allow other people to shine to be a good member of a team," he said. Cosgrove is the first to admit that he isn't a star, but he is a great team member because of his upbringing and later experiences. "I loved the America Cup's team aspect of things, people and so on. I loved cardiac surgery because it was a huge team event. I like being in this environment because it emphasizes team play. This Cleveland Clinic is all built around team. And I frankly think teams accomplish a lot more than individuals do."

Even with his continuing persistence and team focus, Cosgrove faced yet another challenge. He struggled to find a job after his residency. "I thought I had a job in San Francisco, but they withdrew their offer. And then I found a job that I thought I'd like to have in Albany, N.Y. and they didn't hire me. So, I didn't have a job." He found other ways to be productive and improve his resume, though. He explained, "During those six months, I wrote a book about care of congenital heart surgical patients."

Then he got a letter from Cleveland Clinic. "It was an opportunity no different than being the sewer man on the boat," said Cosgrove. "So, the first year I'm here, there's a shooting murder at the front door. The bank in the basement was robbed. The CEO left town in the middle of the night having bribed a councilman and didn't come back for 20 years. I thought this was the Wild West. I mean what on earth was going on? There were prostitutes working up and down Euclid Avenue. There was a big sign out there that said, 'Cleveland Clinic Unfair to Blacks' and had a picture of Nazi swastikas on it. You couldn't walk from the hotel to the front of the hospital because it wasn't safe, so there was a bus that went back and forth all day long. The CEO's offices, had bulletproof glass. The Hough riots happened about three blocks from here. This was a really rough area."

Despite the environment, the hospital provided a tremendous opportunity for cardiac surgery. "They had just done the first coronary bypass surgery in 1967. The place was just cranking, because people came from all over the world to have their heart surgery. There were five of us doing 3,000 heart operations. Within a year, I was one of the busiest heart surgeons in the country. Which as a young person, it was unbelievable? Just to be part of the team, cranking, doing, and thinking—put me on the international stage in about, late thirties, which is just because I fell into this place. At least I recognized the opportunity. I had an offer to go to Harvard at that time. And I decided to stay here."

The opportunity was alluring. "The first year I was here I did 500 heart operations and got paid $60,000. A year later, I was offered to go into private practice for a million," said Cosgrove. He thought the opportunity cost was too high, though. At Cleveland Clinic, he "saw an opportunity to make a difference." Cleveland Clinic would also encourage him to work harder and learn more than at any other hospital. So, he stayed.

"People said, 'Why did you go to that clinic place instead of the nice university hospital?' But the thing that happened there, is they're allowing me to learn my craft and get damn good at it. I did it three times a day, every day of the week, over and over and over and over and over and over again," Cosgrove explained.

Beyond his drive to learn, Cosgrove's entrepreneurial spirit was beginning to show once more. "I started to think, what else could I do? Well, I could improve the care in the intensive care unit and teach the residents, and then I eventually got to the point where I was writing articles and speaking places and that just fueled it."

When he moved into his role as president and CEO, he continued to face his failures head on. The hiring process has always been hard for Cosgrove, because "there's a resume, there's an interview, there is recommendations, but I would never hire anybody in cardiac surgery until they've been here for a year. I say, 'If you want a job here, you need to come here for a year. Spend some time here. Technically they may not have it, emotionally they may not have it, interpersonally they may not have it, intellectually they may not have it, and you can't tell." He admitted that he has made mistakes at even the highest levels of hiring. "It took me four times to get the right COO. And he's a peach. And three times before I got the right HR person, she's fabulous."

Now, at 76, he isn't sure of his next move. He's interested in "everything from Wall Street to teaching." He plans on figuring that out as part of the next phase of his life and career. He devoted his early life to becoming the best cardiac surgeon he could be, then his career to improving all aspects of the hospital that allowed him to grow as a surgeon. But he doesn't believe he made Cleveland Clinic what it is now. Instead, he explained, "I've poured everything into this institution. I've always said this place made me, I didn't make it."

****

Chapter 12

The Summary – A Few Thoughts About Us, the Situation, and Our Future

Looking Back – Looking Forward: Packing for the Journey

"How we spend our days is of course, how we spend our lives."

Annie Dillard

"Feeling lost, crazy and desperate belongs to a good life as much as optimism, certainty and reason."

Alain de Botton

"There are better people in the world, do not let the worst do the worst to you, you deserve the best in life."

Michael Bassey Johnson

PERSONAL LEADERSHIP STYLES

| **Protector** | **Problem Solver** | **Optimizer** | **Creative Strategist** | **Globalist** |
| Advocate/Enforcer | Go-To-Professional | Excellence | Systemic Thinker | Institution-Builder |

Looking Back – Looking Forward
Continuing the Transformational Journey–Agile and Reflective Learning

Examples of Transformational Journeymen – Featuring

Dr. Scott Cowen: 14th President of Tulane University; named by Time Magazine as One of America's Ten Best College Presidents

Photo © Jeffery S. Johnston

Photo © Molly McGinn

Dr. Molly McGinn: Founder, Tree-House, a nationally recognized Arizona-based, collegiate residential addiction recovery institution

Agility in Our Personal Life

What's new or different can be incremental or transformative. Part of embracing the new or disruptive is being able to appreciate both an agile and a reflective stance in busy, demanding, high-density contexts. Agility is not simply about doing more or less, moving faster or slower, appearing in louder more visible manner or softer, stealth like fashion. It's about awareness and attunement with ourselves and others, as change continues all around us. It is about functioning in a 180-and 360-degree way.

That means how are we functioning within and between self and others at multiple levels (i.e. on a point to point basis, between you and me–180 degrees)? Or how do we function in a big picture, self and the whole operating environment between a variety of stakeholders both in and outside our varied organizations, now and in the future (i.e. in a more organic, 360-degree outreach perspective)? Being well-practiced at seeing things as differing others do; being able to see what is felt but not articulated; being able to read a mix of relational (i.e. people-to people) signals to help preemptively position for a range of potential threats and risks; and being able to craft ways to provide support and appropriate actions for self and the community is what often translates capacity into impact. This all requires being agile and reflective to read and respond to incoming signals and requisite action in a timely manner.

This reading and responding to signals involves our perceptions, or how we see and experience things. Interestingly, research on perception indicates that the general population miss or distort about 70 percent of what is in our environment.[1] This is why key highway road signs are often posted in triplets. It appears we often do not see or process two of the three signs we are driving by as determined by many state highway departments.[2] If we have missed it (i.e. for example road signs), we are not aware of it so we would define the experience differently than those that have picked up on the stimuli or signals—in this case, road signs. In fact those that miss the signals might complain of the environment not being favorable or helpful for them. This is where emotional intelligence, or the capacity to identify and engage others' perspectives and experiences from their point of view, on their terms, and not ours, can be such a difference-maker, for both self and other.

---

1 A primary source on perceptual error research can be found on www.open.lib.umn.edu

2 "posted in triplets " . . . this was confirmed with a Columbus, OH Department of Public Works manager indicating the posting of duplicate highway signs is a long standing tradition given the public misses up to two-thirds of all signs and will complain about lack of signage in high density areas if there are not duplicates.

Further, brain performance research indicates that when we are in high emotional states or stressed due to demanding situations, our awareness and attunement is further compromised.[3] All of this influences our capacity to be agile, to be responsive and appropriately aligned, and engaged

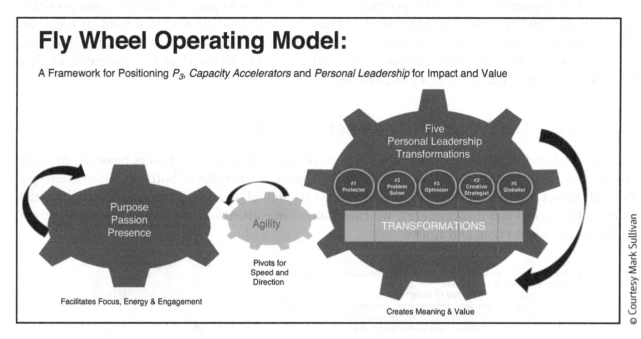

Figure 12.2

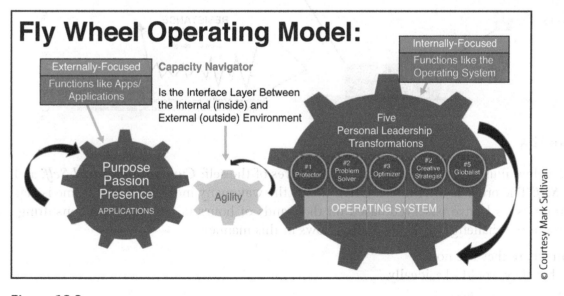

Figure 12.3

---

3   Brain research on cognitive functioning and awareness under stress can be found in multiple sources with this one being focused on a more psychological perspective: Junichi Chikazoe, Daniel H Lee, Nikolaus Kriegeskorte, Adam K Anderson. *Population coding of affect across stimuli, modalities and individuals. Nature Neuroscience*, 2014.

in-the-moment. We know situations can unwittingly be made worse due to a lack of awareness and agility in responding to changing conditions.

Finally, regarding Figure 12.2 below, based on conversations with the book contributors, agility is critical in appropriately aligning personal leadership styles to purpose, passion, and presence thrive themes and also its embedded capacity enablers. Agility is the glue that holds it together. The illustration shows the personal styles as the operating system; the P3 thrive themes (purpose, passion and presence) as a set of applications; and the agility flywheel as the navigator, or that which helps to align and pivot in a timely manner.

Challenging the Better You For a Better Future

As discussed earlier, growth within and between personal leadership styles is possible. Moving out of the 'not-knowing' space, as illustrated in Figure 12.4, reflects both intentional energy, through direct (or tacit) awareness and indirect, sub-liminal awareness. Staying focused on the former, intentional and direct energy, we can channel our attention and awareness leveraging a combination of reflection, and agility.

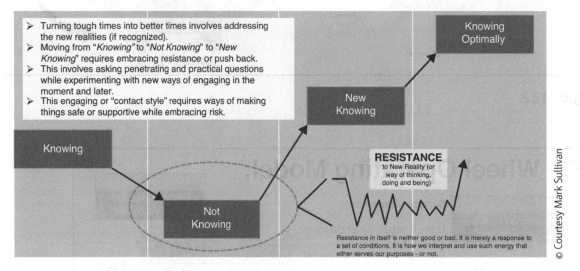

Figure 12.4

Figure 12.5 below, illustrates three different perspectives of the self: ***Current Self, Ideal Self,*** and the ***Better Self.*** The order is intentional. Often this is the way many individuals will frame issues and opportunities, as I have observed based on thousands of hours of coaching and consulting. This framing of the challenge or demand often flows in this manner:

- from where they are now
- to what they would like, ideally
- to what they will accept

This process can be applied to yourself or others, or even both simultaneously, if you are in a group or team setting with multiple issues happening all at once. For illustrative purposes I will refer to the process from a peer coaching perspective, but this can be applied with yourself only, or between you and others that may positionally be above or below you, if you are in a hierarchy.

On a conversational big picture or meta-level it is best to start by following the other person's path of how meaning making (or making sense of things) is unfolding. It can be disruptive to follow your path (i.e. what you are thinking in the moment) versus their path (i.e. what they are thinking in the moment), a potentially competing path of inquiry and reflection. This misalignment, on not being on the same page of how one or both are thinking may actually confuse or constrain the exercise. This means one must simultaneously be aware and agile in attending to both the *content*, or what is being said, and also the *process*, how it is being said.

Initially, this dual dynamic may have an out-of-body quality to it as you try to pay attention to both content and process at the same time. However it is a skill that can be developed with rich dividends in harvesting new shared meaning, solutions or agreements that stick and sustain in a high change, high demand environment.

Successful executives, negotiators, influence brokers, counselors, great orators, comedians, and others charged with connecting and engaging in-the-moment (i.e. presence) with one-on-one or large groups, will do this kind of conversational and meaning making alignment with agility and precision. A good comedian that tells a joke in a monologue and it falls flat will often be aware and act in several ways:

1. They don't miss the fact that the joke fell flat. They read the signals right.
2. They accept the reality as it is. The joke fell flat. It is a fact, not an opinion.
3. They own it. "I did it. I need to change in some way if I want a better outcome."
4. They acknowledge the fact with the audience/clients, often with endearing laughter or acceptance from others (e.g. "boy that was really funny – NOT!"). Builds more trust and credibility)
5. They pivot with a re-start, a new or different joke, often more attuned to the moment. They watch for goodness-of-fit or alignment with the audience.

In the process, the comedian was paying attention to what was being said, how it was being said, and how it was being received.

In terms of this simultaneous content-process dual track, think metaphorically of an example of how an airplane lands from a flight-in-process. Two things are happening. The pilots in the cockpit are focusing on the pitch, pace, altitude, and operating mechanics with the yoke and control panel. The control tower is looking more broadly at "the grid" or map of other nearby flights; overall operating conditions in the grid; and the status or cue of the many planes "in the stack," approaching the glide path to a given tarmac on the landing strip (or destination point). Both significantly different data streams of simultaneous observation and activity from the cockpit and control tower is essential and interdependent for the mutual goal of safely landing the plane. Conversely, with humans versus airplanes, conversational gridlock happens when no one is watching both content and process. Moving beyond the words of what we are hearing to what we are actually understanding of other's intentions behind the words is the more challenging and often more salient part of the conversation.

Specifically, from my work in developing or advising executives, clients, and MBA students, I have found it useful to focus on the following path when supporting others in their efforts of moving from insight to action, or from recognizing the visible and invisible in high-demand or high-challenge environments:

COACHING IN HIGH-DEMAND ENVIRONMENTS

- **Observations**
  - ➤ What is happening that is stated?
  - ➤ What is not-stated but present?
  - ➤ Check your assumptions of what you are observing in others (often in question form).
  - ➤ Leave judgment at the door. State factually but tentatively what you are observing.
  - ➤ Be open to changing your assumptions or gently challenging contraditctions of others while still being supportive of them (and sharing your support as well. Intent matters.)
  - ➤ Refrain from seeking solutions at this point. You are gathering facts and opinions. Do not be tempted to jump to conclusions with missing facts or a messy conversational pool.
- **Aspirations**
  - ➤ Ask what matters?
  - ➤ Ask what do they want?
  - ➤ Why?
  - ➤ Explore the why-why. Why is the why so important?
- **Pain points**
  - ➤ Explore the nature of the presenting issue or concern/s: causes, operating dynamics?
  - ➤ Are there different characteristics with different implications? Are they related to each other or not?
  - ➤ Be curious about the way the issue or demand is being framed? Are there alternatives?
- **Behavioral choice points and actions**
  - ➤ Begin to organize an emerging framework of how things are operating for other.
  - ➤ Explore options jointly, implications and consequences.
  - ➤ Test the scope of what is in and what is out?
  - ➤ Craft a working hypothesis and an operating model of what to do going forward.
  - ➤ Is it actionable? Does it makes sense? Is there commitment?
  - ➤ Explore details of ways to initiate new behavior as part of the operating model
  - ➤ Brainstorm areas of resistance or roadblocks for now and later.
  - ➤ Flesh out ways to engage potential roadblocks preemptively with concrete actions (contingencies and risk mitigation).
  - ➤ Identify ways to build muscle with new habits or to personally support and sustain self during moments of temptation or fatigue.
  - ➤ Continue to appreciate legitimate progress. Provide constructive, timely, supportive feedback to share ways to ensure success and satisfaction.

(Note: This *'High-Demand Coaching Tool'* is further explained with examples and exercises on the book web-site.)

Triple Loop Learning: Linking and Leveraging Capacity for Impact

As we consider improving our effectiveness in high demand environments, note figure 12.5, as earlier mentioned. While often there is much initial attention on the 'ideal' state. However, I am proposing that we focus less on the 'ideal self' and more on being our 'better self.' In many cases, this not only becomes more realistic but also more hopeful because the line of sight is more attainable. However, that is still easier said than done. There is a dynamic relationship between the *current self, ideal self and better self.* It is dynamic because each have a push-and-pull, force-field that offers resisentance and incentives to change, or to maintain the status quo.

On an organization level this is further described by noted organizational psychologist Chris Argyris in his 'Double loop Learning' concept (1964).[4] He refers to the double bind that organizations and there different layers of management and employees get into as they attempt to reconcile errors in organizational operating systems. Do they recognize and communicate errors that challenge boundaries of what is tolerated or acceptable and potentially get punished for doing so; or do they continue to live with the errors and adjust or game the system so as to comply with norms and maintain the status quo at the expense of costly inefficiencies?

Somewhat similar but distinctly different, I have coined a term referred to as *Triple Loop Learning, as* it is applied on an individual level (as opposed to organizational) to personal leadership styles in high-demand environments. Triple Loop Learning, in this context, focuses more on how *protectors, problem solvers, optimizers, creative strategists and globalists* respond very differently to threat and risk while in an unknowing state (see related figure, 12.7). Their way of knowing and valuing within each style pulls for a different way of negotiating between one's current self and one's better self. The way one supports oneself in the face of resistance is different and therefore strategies on how best to accelerate and leverage capacity for impact will vary. The triple loop aspect relates to the pattern between where, how and why more energy is initially on current self versus our better self and how that changes by style. This has a significant implication on how best to get stronger in the face of blind spots and developmental gaps. More on this is mapped out in the web-site with practical exercises on addressing triple loop learning in high-demand environments, delienated by style.

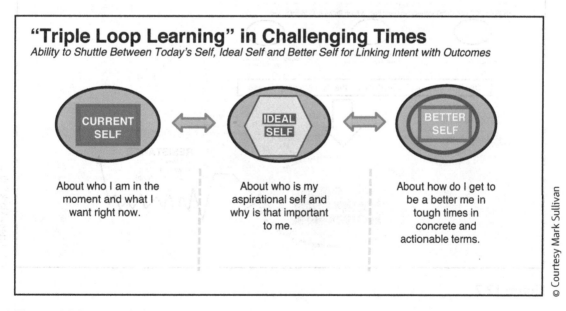

"Triple Loop Learning" in Challenging Times
Ability to Shuttle Between Today's Self, Ideal Self and Better Self for Linking Intent with Outcomes

CURRENT SELF ⟷ IDEAL SELF ⟷ BETTER SELF

About who I am in the moment and what I want right now.

About who is my aspirational self and why is that important to me.

About how do I get to be a better me in tough times in concrete and actionable terms.

© Courtesy Mark Sullivan

Figure 12.5

---

4 Chris Argyris is the James Bryant Conant Professor Emeritus of Education and Organizational Behavior at Harvard University in Cambridge, Massachusetts. He is the author of "Good Communication That Blocks Learning" (HBR July–August 1994), a McKinsey Award winner. He is also a director at Monitor Company in Cambridge. Other related sources on Argyris's 'Douple Loop Learning' include: 1. Argyris, Chris. (1974). *Behind the Front Page.* San Francisco: Jossey-Bass. 2. Argyris, Chris; Schon, Donald. (1976) *Organizational Learning* (Reading, Mass.: Addison-Wesley, to be published). 3. Argyris, Chris. (1976). *Increasing Leadership Effectiveness.* New York: Wiley-Interscience.

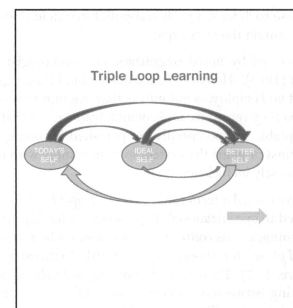

Triple Loop Learning

Triple Loop Learning (Thinking, doing, being):

A series of observations, questions, thoughts, feelings and actions within and between different sides of self:

Today's Self, Ideal Self, and Better Self. All are interdependent and necessary for optimal growth; Later stages of development embrace interactions in a concrete, conceptual, active and reflective manner in a different manner than earlier stages of development. Earlier stages tend to leverage concrete or 'hands-on' ways of knowing; and later stages tend to use more conceptual or thinking ways of knowing. Both can be effective based on the situation.

© Courtesy Mark Sullivan

Figure 12.6

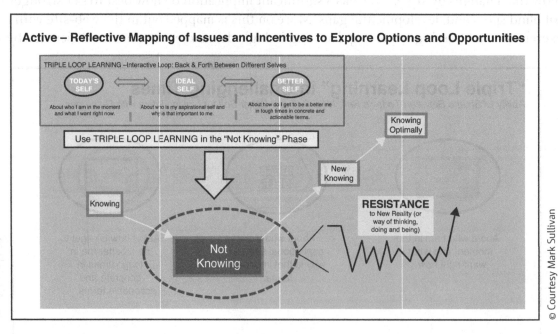

© Courtesy Mark Sullivan

Figure 12.7

Remembering the Context: Recognizing the Severity of the Demand

Ever get metaphorically blown over because you either didn't see or didn't adjust to changing conditions coming from within or coming at you? Figures 12.8, 12.9 and 12.10 describe the storm conditions using hurricane language: Categories 1-5. This is descriptive of hurricane-force weather that may reflect a mounting or current storm within you or between you and your external environment. Figure 12.11 further describes differences during or after the storm from a surviving, reviving and thriving perspective. Each figure provides greater detail about either the nature of the storm category or the way we embrace the storm at a survive, revive and thrive level.

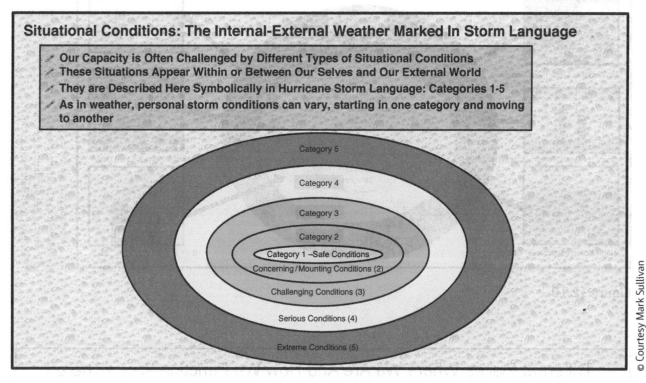

Figure 12.8

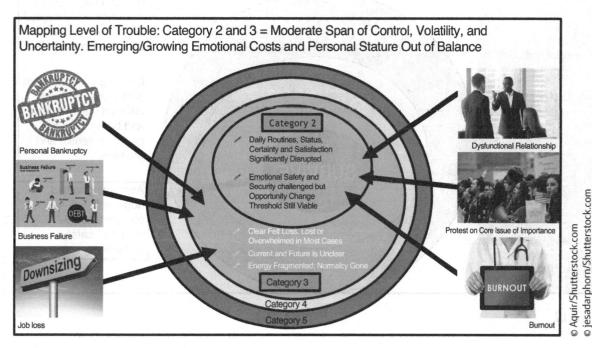

Figure 12.9

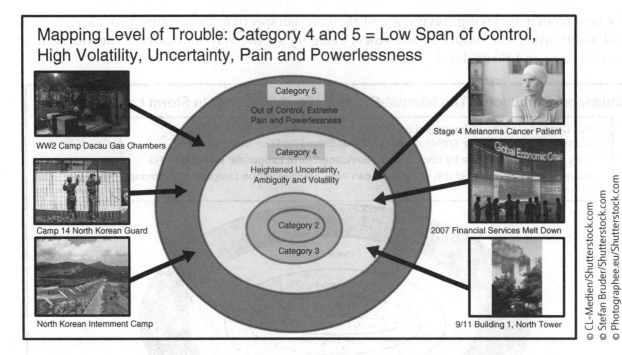

Figure 12.10

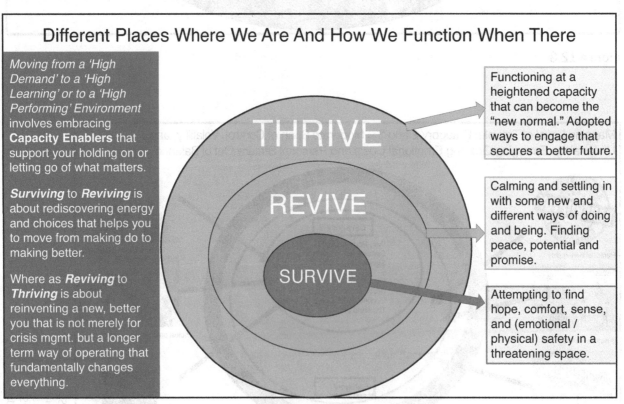

Figure 12.11

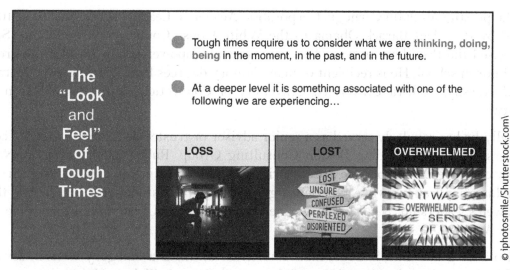

Figure 12.12

The Future

Inevitably trouble arrives. Maybe not now, but at some point. It may not sound encouraging but it is helpful to be ready and perhaps in some constructive way, actually appreciate part of the ride.

We know trouble comes in all sizes and all forms. Some of it is predictable, some of it is a surprise. Some may be a bit of both. Whether it is a form of loss, being lost or being overwhelmed as in figure 12.12, it is our 12 capacity enablers in our embedded P3 (i.e. Purpose, Passion and Presence) thrive themes, and how they unfold within our personal leadership, that may make an outsized difference in our way of leveraging crucibles for our long term advantage.[5]

Our challenge is to harness our gifts and our personal leadership to live life as we hope and expect it to be in spite of surprises or challenges. If we can survive, revive and thrive through our crucibles we can leverage the wisdom of our lived experience as discussed in the many stories in this book. The following final stories from Dr. Scott Cowen and Dr. Molly McGinn offer timely insights into two similar but different ways of embracing and transforming crisis into a better future. Both are inspiring as they draw on lived experience, struggles, and tremendous accomplishments in trying times.

****

Final Stories: On A Life Worth Living – Embracing the Heat of the Fire Close-Up

Dr. Scott Cowen, is Tulane University's President Emeritus and Distinguished University Professor at the Freeman School of Business. He was named by *Time* magazine as one of the nation's *Top 10 Best College Presidents*. He was only one of four university leaders nationwide to

---

5   Research is in progress to test the relationship and supporting nature within and between the 12 capacity enablers, three thriving themes and five personal leadership styles. Multiple samples and methods are being used to develop outcomes which will be reported in v2.0 of THRIVE.

receive the prestigious 2009 Carnegie Corporation Academic Leadership Award. In 2010, he was appointed by President Barack Obama to the White House Council for Community Solutions, which advised the President on ways to reconnect and empower young people who are neither employed nor in school. He is recipient of many honory degrees from University of Notre Dame, Brown University, Yeshiva University, University of Connecticut, and Case Western Reserve University.[6]

Additionally, he has regularly served as a senior advisor or trustee on a large variety of corporate and university boards including Boston Consulting Group, Rubbermaid, Barnes & Noble and University of Notre Dame, to name a few. During his 16-year tenure at Tulane, he quadrupled the undergraduate applications while experiencing all-time highs in student quality. During that time, under Cowen's leadership, *Newsweek* magazine declared Tulane University as one of the "Hottest Schools in America."[7]

It was also during this time, in 2005, that Hurricane Katrina as a Category 5 storm devasted the Gulf of Mexico region, the city of New Orleans and Cowen's Tulane University campus. As a tropical cyclone, there was up to 175 mph winds and $125 billion dollar damage in the region[8]. Over 1,245 people died making it one of the deadliest US hurricanes. Katrina flooded 70 percent of Tulane's uptown campus and all of the buildings in its downtown health science campus. While the university was required to shutdown due to safety considerations, a record 87 percent of its undergraduates returned after temporarily being dispersed to other schools across the country that 'adopted' the Tulane students, during the campus shutdown. As recognized by many awards and media coverage, Cowen was lauded by Congress, state legislatures, government agencies and universities across the country who interfaced with him day and night non-stop during and after the crisis, as clearly being instrumental in bringing New Orleans and Tulane University back to becoming an even better place, post Katrina.

His humble yet confident insights and wisdom about living in the midst of a physical and metaphorical storm are timely today as it was in the days of Katrina. Cowen begins with his early days of growing up, challenges then and later, and shares perspectives of best ways to position oneself for success going forward.

Dr. Scott Cowen Interview

Scott Cowen was president of Tulane University in New Orleans when Hurricane Katrina struck. He became a national champion for rebuilding the city following the death and dislocation caused by the storm.

Cowen, a New Jersey native, is an accomplished academic even though he struggled as a student early on. Neither of his parents graduated from college which was typical living in the 1950s and 1960s. Despite growing up in a traditional family, he said, "I wasn't able to read or write when I went to school. It turned out, at the age of 21, I was diagnosed with dyslexia. I mentioned this because it turns out it explains a lot of what happened to me over time."

6 Vanacore, Andrew; Maggi, Laura. (2013). *"Cowen to retire as Tulane's president,"* Advocate. Baton Rouge, Louisiana. P. 5a.

7 Cowen Institute web site.

8 Blake, Eric S; Landsea, Christopher W; Gibney, Ethan J. (August 2011). *The Deadliest, Costliest and Most Intense United States Tropical Cyclones from 1851 to 2010.* National Hurricane Center.

Dyslexia left an impression on him. "I grew up with lack of confidence, feeling inadequate--I wasn't very smart. I was lazy. Most people interpret it that way, because of my poor performance at school. During that time period, as a little background, I developed some coping mechanisms, which over-time proved to be very important."

Cowen continued, "I struggled, but I was elected president of the class. That give me the confidence I didn't have before. So by the time I graduated from a good high school, I had a good record. At that time, I was still immature; still wouldn't stay on my feet. I will tell you because some of this shaped what happens later on in my life."

After graduating from high school, Cowen was recruited to play football for the University of Connecticut. When he had finished college, he said, was accepted to the graduate school in the University of Hawaii to get an MBA. But in 1968 he was drafted and spent three years in the military rather than going to graduate school. He served with the army, part of the time in the Middle East and also worked security. When he left the service his first wife was living in Washington, D.C. so he attended George Washington University, earning a MBA and doctorate.

He did not know what to do after school, and ended up teaching finance and accounting Bucknell University in Pennsylvania. Then he went to Case Western Reserve where he worked for 23 years, starting as an assistant professor and rising to become dean of the management school. He was in the running to become president of the university but eventually chose not to pursue the job.

Eventually Cowen's career took him to Tulane University in New Orleans, where as president he was instrumental in rebuilding the university and the city after Hurricane Katrina. "The most defining moments in my career are from Katrina. Together, they are the forces that shape my life. I will tell you a little bit about Katrina. Eighty percent of the land was massively damaged. It had been flooding for 57 days. The university had to be closed for the entire semester. It was the first time since the Civil War that a university had to be closed. We had $650 million of damage."

Cowen explained how the hurricane affected him. "Days and years after Katrina, without a gap, were the most difficult in my entire life. The first three years after we needed to get out of the woods. First, we needed to physically rebuild the university. It takes 10 years to do that. Around 2014, there were still challenges that were brought up."

He was quick to acknowledge the peers he worked with. "I get a lot of kudos for what we've accomplished, but I would tell you we had a terrific and unbelievable team. Without them, that couldn't have happened. Whatever skills I have, it all came together when the moment is hard. Fortunately, we worked it out." Cowen also said he wasn't afraid to ask for help. "I always tell myself, I'm not the smartest person in the room. I will be with the brilliant and find the talent and say, 'Could you help me with this?'"

Cowen leveraged his communication skills and relationships to ensure that all Tulane students were able to attend other universities while Tulane was closed for a semester. Despite sending students away, more than 85 percent returned the next semester. "You want to bring hope to people, but also be realistic. You don't want to be naïve that everything's going to be fine. I used to quote it all the time: Hope is not a plan. Hope is not a strategy. Hope is something we have. Hope is something based on fact, is something we thought through about what place could we go."

He spoke about importance of finding the root cause of any problem. "It's hard to get the truth. It's really understanding the reality, the situation," explained Cowen. "I find a lot of people don't really understand what they are confronting, what the situation is. If you never diagnose the situation, there's no way you can put a plan in short-term and long-term to grab it. I always try to figure out what's really going on here. What we need to do?"

"I believe very strongly in evidence in making decisions, seeking the truth about the situation," said Cowen. "To seek truth, I talk to a lot of people. I think it's being knowledgeable. Find people who are constantly asking questions. And see if you could get the answers consistently. I think the secret is being curious. Always trying to seek what's considered to be the truth."

With so much at risk, Cowen said, there was no room to fail. "We knew the survival of our institution was at stake. It wasn't the physical survival, it was a reputational survival. We couldn't come back, just the way it was before. We knew it was going to take a lot of work."

Cowen knew that he couldn't manage this crisis alone. "I realized I wasn't capable of doing that. So I gathered two groups together. One was five senior people in the country, the ones that helped me to plan the future of the institution. This group was amazing and helpful. There were people like Malcolm Gillis, the president of Rice School of Business. James Duderstadt, who was the former president of University of Michigan. I gathered these four or five and said, 'Here's what I am faced with.' I knew I was not going to come back in the same way, so I had to find a way to rebuild the academics very quickly."

His team crafted the strategy that restructured Tulane. "At the same time, I had to save a lot of money, because we'd lost a lot of money. They were basically helping me craft the plan. They closed departments and schools. It turned out, on the bright side, it worked. I give them total credit for that. Without them, I wouldn't be able to do that."

Cowen argued that whatever the challenge, it is important to believe in yourself. "Consciously or unconsciously, give yourself some confidence that you will do well," he said. "Start developing the things you are good at, that give you confidence and make you try different things. I was not the guy most likely to conquer in academia, right? Let's face it. But part of it was I got over confident. I got out the army and set myself apart.

He also acknowledged his support system. "Have somebody believe in you. They believe in you and then you work a little harder," he said. "If one thinks he is the smartest he will be in trouble. Always think about what's right and you will always do what's right. Be with those smartest."

Relationships, and humor, were critical to Cowen after Katrina when he and key members of his team relocated to Texas for six months. "We became very close," he said. "I always use humor and fun. It's part of my social type. I started to do something stupid. People will relax. We did several kinds of things."

Looking back, Cowen had no idea how much he would be changed by Katrina. "When this happened, I was 59. I wouldn't have thought at 59-years-old, that somehow this would have changed me as much as it did. It does give you confidence and a sense of pride, that you live with. That you say to yourself, 'Whatever demons I have in the past, I think I can deal with those demons.' So you will always have the kind of background, the burden of gifts or whatever, you always have this kind of notion, 'Could I do this?' I really was standing. I went through that. I feel pretty good about myself. Nobody is perfect. But there's no question that it does change you."

Even now, he questions his success. "You always wonder if you are a fraud. You just had a lot of good luck. You've been at the place the right time, the people. And it's all not right, but you really have to test it. One of the lessons I learned in Case Western University was I had a wonderful career there, and I was told I was going to be the top candidate to be the president. And I kept thinking to myself, could I survive outside of Case Western? Maybe I was only good here, because I started as a young kid, everybody knows me, and I know them. I wondered if I left, will I be any good? And that was part of the reason why I left to go to Tulane. It was to say, 'If I am ever going to test this hypothesis, I need to start doing this now.'"

Cowen said he knows that the challenges Katrina presented led him to reach his full potential as president of Tulane. "I was working well before Katrina. I'd been president for seven years. But I will tell you this, if Katrina hadn't happened, I don't think I would have accomplished what was accomplished. The crisis there transformed me in a way mentally about my own capabilities, that otherwise without it, I would not have."

"I say this to students: 'We are byproducts of the defining moments in our life. And how we respond in those defining moments ultimately shapes who we are. My view is making mistakes can be defining moments. You learn from them," he said.

Cowen who is now president emeritus said he has no plans to slow down. "If you are still having a curious mind, you are constantly adding new things to your storehouse, wisdom and knowledge, which keeps you professionally learning and feeling good about it. I can't imagine if I retired for a long time. I just can't imagine. I don't know how people do it. People say, 'Why don't you retire? Getting the phone calls you get.' I said, 'Each one is different, is a new challenge, and the ones that keep you alive.'"

****

Our final story features Dr. Molly McGinn, PhD., cultural anthropologist from the University of California at Los Angeles. She has spent four decades creating and cultivating healing and thriving communities in the Pacific Rim, US and other regions of the world. She speaks Mandarin, Japanese, Spanish and English. As a noted thought leader, teacher and consultant in adult learning, recovery from addiction and design of transformational processes she is regularly asked by governments and companies to provide insights and guidance on collaborative strategies and change initiatives.

McGinn is also co-founder of TreeHouse Learning Community, a nationally recognized college addiction and recovery program headquartered in Arizona with an informal network of approximately 100 professionals in the fields of treatment, education, government, business, leadership and medicine.[9] Her vision is to foster communities of support in Higher Education for young adults who have struggled with addiction. Her own recovery path from addiction informed the insights of the recovery process sparked to her efforts to change the lives of many young adults at a most fundamental level.

---

9   "TreeHouse is a nationally recognized addiction and recovery program " as referenced in varied sites on www. treehouselearningcommunity.com; and from personal discussion with McGinn over a multi-year period, 2010-2018.

The eight guiding principles[10] at TreeHouse reflect her team's values and the ingredients of good living include:

1. *BELONGING:*
   feeling at home—the state of being accepted and comfortable in a place or group

   > "Positive feelings come from being honest about yourself and accepting your personality, and physical characteristics, warts and all; and, from belonging to a family that accepts you without question."
   >
   > *Willard Scott*

2. *INTEGRITY:*
   possession of firm principles—the quality of possessing and steadfastly adhering to high moral principles or professional standards

   > "Try not to become a man of success but rather a man of value."
   >
   > *Albert Einstein*

3. *DISCIPLINE:*
   conscious control over lifestyle—mental self-control used in directing or changing behavior, learning something, or training for something

   > "I am indeed, a king, because I know how to rule myself."
   >
   > *Pietro Aretino*

4. *PASSION:*
   intense enthusiasm—a strong liking or enthusiasm for a subject or activity

   > "If there is no passion in your life, then have you really lived? Find your passion, whatever it may be. Become it and let it become you and you will find great things happen FOR you, TO you, and BECAUSE of you."
   >
   > *T. Alan Armstrong*

5. *CONTRIBUTION:*
   donation—something such as money or time that is given, especially to a common fund or a specific purpose

   > "If you have anything really valuable to contribute to the world, it will come through the expression of your own personality, that single spark of divinity that sets you off and makes you different from every other living creature."
   >
   > *Bruce Barton*

6. *HUMILITY:*
   modesty or respectfulness—the quality of being modest or respectful

   > "Humility is the only true wisdom by which we prepare our minds for all the possible changes of life."
   >
   > *George Ailiss*

7. *SUSTAINABILITY:*
   maintaining ecological balance—exploiting natural resources without destroying the ecological balance of an area

   > "No house should ever be on a hill or on anything. It should be of the hill. Belonging to it. Hill and house should live together each the happier for the other."
   >
   > *Frank Lloyd Wright*

---

10 The TreeHouse *Eight Guiding Principles,* a guide for better living offered to all students, faculty and the broader global community can be found in the TreeHouse web site: www.treehouselearningcommunity.com. It is championed by co-founders and Managing Partner Dr. Molly McGinn and Managing Partner Susan Adams along with their faculty.

8. *KNOWLEDGE*:
information in mind—general awareness or possession of information, facts, ideas, truths or principles

"Your visionwill become clear only when you look into your heart. Who looks outside, dreams. Who looks inside, awakens."

Carl C. Jung

Dr. Molly McGinn Interview

In the mid 1970s, in her early 20s, Dr. Molly McGinn moved to Kyoto Japan to pursue her study of Zen Buddhism; and lived in a Buddhist monastery for three years. Later, as China opened to the West, she and her husband, Gary Wintz, entered Tibet to document the treatment of Tibetan monks who had been imprisoned by the Chinese.

Her early days as a global adventurer and seeker of freedom and Enlightnment in far away lands were equally relevant for building a better future for youth men and women in her own backyard in Prescott, Arizona. Also, aside from directing TreeHouse, a nationally recognized addiction recovery program, she is regularly called on as thought leader, learning specialist, and consultant to governments, consulting houses and a variety of non-profits and NGOs. McGinn facilitates group meetings for companies and institutions that bring together people with different expertise and personalities. She draws on her background as a cultural anthropologist and a life-long study of human psychology stemming, in part, from her own experience with addiction.

McGinn said she is influenced by the myth-based hero's journey, popularized by Joseph Campbell[11] and based on analysis developed be Carl Jung. The myth holds that those with the courage to set out and leave the comfort of their current life are transformed by the experience and return with new understanding and strengths.

In addition to the hero's journey, McGinn said she was profoundly influenced by Marion Woodman, a Jungian analyst[12]. She wrote books on the the guidance we get from myth, addiction to perfection, symbolic language of dreams, and feminine psychology. "She had a powerful capacity to tell the great myths at the headwaters of our Western culture and relate them to our personal, cultural and political lives. Marion was invaluable," said McGinin. "She brought the Jungian archetypes to life."

"There are many of us who dream of an adventure, but after we hear that call, we freeze and get cold feet," she said. "So we never escape our ordinary world. The hero's journey is getting out of the ordinary world and then there is the challenge, the crisis." McGinn explained. "It is always scary. Fear is the first step of the journey. Some of us don't have any interior resources beyond being scared and imagining how bad it could be and decide not to go. We stay in the loop and get back to the ordinary world. And things really don't change. We don't get to grow much."

In 1982 McGinn and her husband Gary Wintz started on there own adventure. They were among a six-member group of teachers who were invited to come China as "foreign experts" to help

---

11 Campbell, Joseph. (1949). *The Hero with a Thousand Faces* (1st ed.) Princeton, NJ: Princeton University Press. (2nd ed. 1968, 3rd ed. 2008).

12 Marion Woodman (1928-2018), was a Canadian poetic author in myth (i.e. mythopoetic author), analytical psychologist and women's movement figure. She has written and spoken extensively about the dream theories of Carl Jung. The source to her popular book on addiction as referred by McGinn is the following: Woodman, M. (1982). *Addiction to Perfection: The Still Unravished Bride.* Inner City Books.

Chinese research scientists translate their work into English. At the time, China was just emerging from the Cultural Revolution and 10 years of isolation from the West from universities and from scientific work. "We ran a course for Chinese scientists who had finally returned to their research. Their specialites spanned from hydrolic engineering to microbiology and nuclear energy," said McGinn. "Our graduating class was the first Masters and PhD level group graduating from Chengdu University of Science and Technology in 10 years because all universities in China had been shut down from 1966 to 1976. The Cultural Revolution ended in 1977. Only in 1978, for the first time in 10 years, the graduate students were admitted. They were all 10 years older than most of the college students because they had been in work and "education" camps doing labor in the countryside."

Our students were among the best and brightest in China. They were recepients of Fullbright scholarships and woud be headed to the US or Australia or the UK as soon as they passed their TESOL (test of English as a second language). "Our role," she said, "was to teach technical English and to help translate their scientific work into English and to give our students practice speaking about their research in English. It was primarily an academic role of helping them articulate their research and understand other people's research," McGinn said. "We also taught social skils. The basics of greetings, handshakes, appropriate ice breaker questions and social norms. It was strange for them to not ask a persons age and marital status in the first five mintues of a conversation. They had never been to the West, or seen western media so they didn't know much about it."

McGinn and Wintz used their invitation to teach in Sichuan to ultimately find their way into Tibet. Closed to outsiders, Tibet was off limits to foreigners anxious to learn the fate of the Tibetan monks and the once 6000 monasteries in Tibet. We loved teaching in China and our teaching eventually helped us find a passage way to Tibet. "We got the University to give us a big lecture hall for open lectures every Monday night. We called it the Monday Night Class and it was open to the public. We taught so-called "Special English" using easy to follow speech and vocabulary. We had about 400 people every Monday night that would bicycle in from the factories to the town to learn English from native speakers. We gave vocabulary handouts every week and our passionate students grabbed up the pages and studied diligently to be ready for the following week's lecture. In one lecture we mentioned that we thought that Tibet was a very interesting culture and not just a backward minority as the Chinese students tended to think.

We let it be known that we were interested in going to Tibet," McGinn remembered. "Then one night one of our students who was an attendant at the local hotel in Chengdu came to our flat at the university at 10pm and said, 'There's a foreign woman, who's probably German or European. She just checked-in to the hotel, and she has just come from Tibet.' She said it was the first time they had seen foreigners come from Tibet, and she thought we'd like to know."

McGinn and Wintz immediately went to meet the traveler that night. "This foreigner had in fact found a loophole in the system and it was that there is one police station in Inner Mongolia where the guy working on Saturday didn't know that foreigners were not supposed to be going into Tibet. They were giving out permits," McGinn said. "That was our way in. Over spring break we got to Inner Mongolia and as soon as our term was over we were on a flight to Lhasa.

McGinn made it into Tibet and found work easily. "We went to the local teacher's college and offered our services," said McGinn. The local officials did not know they did not have permission to be there. "We managed to get a couple of jobs in a department on the teachers' college campus. We were working on the language program. We were teaching at the police station. We just went to work teaching. In the meantime we started to go over to some monasteries to find out what was going on in the prisons. Most of the monks were still in prisons but some were starting to get out. We began to understand the situation and to be as supportive as possible for positive outcomes."

Soon, however, Tibetan officials noticed. "The school came to us and said they were not sure if what we were doing was a good idea. Well, they didn't say it quite like that. But, we had to stop teaching and stop working. We said, 'Okay' and started to travel a little bit. We travelled all over Tibet," she said. They caught rides from local truckers, and stayed on in the region for four months.

Also in her early 20s. McGinn lived for three years in a Zen Buddhist monastery in Japan. "I was trying to see what I could experience if I stopped thinking and doing. What was left in the pure field of perception. That environment, the transformational environment of the intentional community was another calling for me," said McGinn. "Where you create the conditions for transformation to occur, you sort of design it so that you can have a different outcome: the you that is experiencing the world is not the same you because you dropped off the filters."

Journeys through trauma were not new to McGinn. "I came from a family that had alcoholism. My own parents were not alcoholics, but I had very close family members who died from alcoholism. The women in my generation my female cousins are all dead from drugs or alcoholism.. And for me, I struggled with an eating disorder," McGinn admitted. "In college, I used study-drugs to fuel intense work and study, managed the eating disorder and drove myself to exhaustion. Fortunately I knew enough to avoid alcohol it was just too scary. Since I was afraid of alcohol. I didn't drink a lot, but when I did drink, it never went well."

Her own journey of recovery was filled with obstacles both external and internal. "It took me a little while, but I realized I had been trying to wake up, become conscious and be on a path of waking up, but I still couldn't stop. When I was using varied crutches, it felt like such a departure from the things I was shooting for. I really didn't like not being able to be transparent, open, and connected with people because of it, so I eventually went to an AA program. That was exciting to me because I finally got the monkey off my back. For me, I was hoping to get up, be freed and get more active in my interior world. I eventually got there."

McGinn needed a lot of internal motivation and strength to get through a difficult recovery, but she was able to take away valuable skills. "I looked at the possibility of freedom and formed a ritual of getting up every morning and doing meditation, journaling, or working out which helped the recovery process. This created more productive days when compared to the days not following the pattern. Meditation creates the capacity for a much greater engagement in the outside world," McGinn explained. "You feel less fear. You have to do hard work and examine it to find the ways that work best for you. Then what happens, the outside world begins to shift. It's kind of humbling. You deal with your interior demons, your fear, your resentment, all that first. Going back to the notion of addiction, people that have a history of addiction have now transferred, leaving those patterns and gaining these patterns, knowing they have a big impact on bringing your greatest self to life. You learn a lot from dealing with addiction. There are transferable skills."

How does a person successfully complete a journey of recovery? McGinn said she believes, "You need to step back from your own perspective and be willing to listen to what people say," she explained. "It's truly getting all the perspectives about yourself and about the world. People who are willing to continue, to step outside their expertise, to cross over to other fields, and reach out when they need help, are the successful ones. We need to be able to really be willing to see what other people are seeing and be open to other people's opinion."

"What matters is always what's next," McGinn concluded. "On a personal level, most people can't get out and move from bad to better. If they get stuck in how messed up they are they get stuck in 'it's never going to be different'. I've been there, and I was ashamed. I think the key to being able to go forward a little bit is to not get stuck in the pattern. It's being able to know that you actually just need to stop making things worse for a while. Make a different phone call, hang out with different people. And that's the defining thing – you need to be with people that are supportive and helpful, or you are going back to the comfort zone and will get isolated. It's your job to want to be truthful and put yourself in a different situation whenever necessary.

"It's a series of very small steps," McGinn continued. "Just today. What's the one thing I can do today, to know or not do, to not create suffering for myself and others for the next couple of hours?" Finally, she said, "Be a servant for somebody else for a while. And that is the best antidote to the poisonous self-judgment. Go and help somebody else. That changes the chemistry and it change the day. And if you can change the day you get a different tomorrow and a future life worth living."

****

A Few Final Thoughts

As a concluding thought, one of my favorite poems summarizes a few points for consideration moving forward:

Leading the Band

He was going to be the President
Of the U.S. of A.
She was going to become an actress
In a Broadway play.

As younsters—these were their dreams;
The visions they aspired to.
They truly thought these aspirations,
Eventually, would one day come true.

But he did not become President.
The reason is the ultimate sin.
He never ran for office.
He feared he would not win.

She didn't make it to New York City.
In fact she never set foot on the stage.
She thought she'd forget her lines.
In other words—she was afraid.

The lesson in these stories
Is that you must get up and try.
If you let your fears control you,
Your dreams will quickly die.

Because if you want to hit a home run,
You have to go up to the plate.
If you want to meet that special person,
You have to ask them for a date.

The biggest crime in life
Is to forget what you have dreamt.
It's not the act of losing
But to have never made the attempt.

So as you battle with your fears in life,
Remember this brief command:
"If you're not afraid to face the music,
You may one day lead the band.[13]

So some of us though may not be leading the band. We don't always have the answers. We don't always know what to do next. We may in fact be afraid, tired, bored, confused, disinterested or angry at the world, at our self or someone out there. We've all been there, sometimes more than a few times. Our less then optimal self does not need to block us from seeking a better day or a better way. Yes, life is not always simple or easy and we don't always get answers or results on our terms or timetable. Solutions and satisfaction don't usually come conveniently in pill form, if we want it to be lasting. Solutions and satisfaction may often be hard and well earned; and not always pretty in effort and execution.

However, our capacity to care enough to do something is a start. Also, for some of us, being able to both be gentle on ourself while maintaining effort and concrete expectations to create a way forward can be helpful. For example, even a few timely questions such as this may be a starting point:

- what would a good day look like?
- What would I get excited about—what is my passion?
- What would be meaningful if it was a good day—what is my purpose?
- How would I connect in a deeper, more memorable way with myself and others that matter to me today, that's different than what I usually do—How does my presence present itself?
- What can I do to support myself to be more purposeful, passionate and present with the moments and memories I am making today and in to the future?

We don't have to be waiting for better days as if it will be delivered to us. Many of the stories in this book involved people who didn't know what was going to happen but they just kept putting one foot in front of the other. They kept trying. Some asked for help. Some were humble and hungry enough to ask for a lot of it, needed a lot of it, and were willing stay with the pain or frustration until they moved from the "not knowing" to the "new knowing."

Whether trouble is about loss, being lost, or living in crisis we all have our way of enduring and embracing the journey. The stories in the book and on the website reflected people who often either crawled back or bounced back. Neither way was necessarily better than the other. Ironically, some who crawled were full of busyness and even hyper-activity often doing more of the same,

---

13 The author and source of the poem *Leading the Band* is: Neck, Christopher P. (2012). *Medicine for the Mind: Healing Words to Help You Soar*, 4th ed. New York: John Wiley Publishers.

over-and-over hoping to get over it, out of it, or through it with speed--and found they needed to slow down to discover a new way. Others who crawled barely moved for a long period. They may have been frozen with fear, in denial or not conscious of what would be helpful in that moment. Some got through this not knowing-to-knowing with the help of a friend or colleague, self reflection, practice, or changing conditions external to them.

Those who bounced back did not necessarily have a pain-free trip either. Their bouncing back may have appeared on the outside as being relatively smooth and drama-free. But for some, from the inside, there was intensity or speed that shaped the experience like a roller coaster ride—a lot happening, moving forward but feeling like it was herky-jerky, little control and a lot of action, and sometimes a sense of recklessness at the core or on the edges. For some, it actually was a smoother ride in the bounce as there may have been some familiarity in the nature of the trouble. Or one was able to read the signals of incoming demands while processing the immediate with a level of agility that continued to align effort, intent and outcome.

All continued to say that while trouble was not something they were out looking for, it was often consequential in discovering or deepening an awareness of new or different resources they could leverage within. This process was often transformative in many ways. However, sometimes, trouble was debilitating, damaging and disruptive. And it ended there. Yet most often it was instructive particularly for those that used a learning stance to inventory the present, reflect on the past and to take stock on future options, approaches and support to carry forth. Also, the 14 capacity enablers (i.e. Purpose: **competence, commitment, curiosity, care, courage** and **community**; Passion: **enjoyment, excellence** and **effort**; Presence: **agility, awareness, tenacity, authenticity,** and **affirmation**) that supported the three thrive themes: *purpose, passion and presence*, were influential in sustaining or accelerating efforts for impact and value.

Some individuals appeared to have less of a portfolio of trouble than others. This did not necessarily mean they had a charmed life, were lucky, brilliant or better than the rest. Interestingly one person's nightmare was sometimes another person's opportunity. How one perceived and felt the experience was often part of the phenomenon. More than that, their history played a part. A few said what made a difference was not simply being able to duck and dodge the trouble as if it was something out there beyond themselves. Rather it was an ability to leverage previous experiences and craft a pre-emptive stance that reflected an integration and re-purposing of learning from the past.

In other cases, some also described a risk tolerance that was higher than others. So regardless of other factors, the experience whether it was new or not, looked different. It looked less scary or troublesome. One could negotiate the landscape with a certain appreciation for unpredictability or the unknown, being somewhat immune or desensitized to the danger. This is while they were still encountering the trouble, but reporting it more at a hurricane, designated as a Category 1 or 2; while others were reporting it as a Category 3, 4, or even 5.

Finally, and most significantly, the personal leadership styles (i.e. *protector, problem solver, optimizer, creative strategist* and *globalist*) provided a dramatic range of capacity from early to later stage in the developmental continuum in embracing and addressing trouble. Again, success and satisfaction could be found at all styles and stages but generally the style was consequential in being able to "frame, fix and fit" the trouble ecosystem in a way that was more or less helpful, for success and satisfaction.

The challenge is to work toward our better self at whatever our age and life situation may be. We are never too old, too young, too perfect, too helpless, too healthy, too ill to begin now in the moment. It is for a good cause—for you. In the process, your efforts benefit your loved ones, your friends, your bosses, your peers and the communities of practice and geography in which you live. A better you is a better place for the world around you and consequently for the world-at-large. Beginning with you to create the change you desire will also create the rippling effect that enriches all those around you and all those around them.

Yes, you are more powerful and influential than you may ever imagine. May your journey forward be full of the many gifts, grace and gratitude that you so richly deserve and reflect as a member of the human race. Journey forward. May it be full of discovery, new learning, humble victories, well-earned insights and love and kindness from those that matter to you. Best wishes in continuing to fully embrace the peaks and valley's with an open, spirited, caring and courageous way. Finally, always remember, you are not alone in this journey. You have a support team in those who know and care about you. Know also, I am rooting for you.

Best,
Mark Sullivan

Contributors Appendix: Profile

Included are a broad mix of notable contributors who have uniquely addressed a significant range of adversities and opportunities, with constrained resources in demanding environments. Their struggles, pain, determination, and optimism in the face of hardship, at times unrelenting, are inspirational and thematic throughout. These individuals include the following:

Government

- **Governor Steven Beshear**, Struggled to unify a divided state government, while building a coalition to secure healthcare for half a million Kentuckians.
- **Governor Mike DeWine**, Ohio AG and former U.S. Senator and Lt. Governor and current candidate for governor. Noted efforts to successfully shut down a state-wide pill mill—illicitly distributing oxycodone and other prescription drugs to addicts and dealers. Personally challenged after his 22-year-old daughter was killed in a car accident while he was running for U.S. Senate.
- **Dr. David Gergen**, Advisor to four U.S. presidents: Nixon, Ford, Reagan, and Clinton; CNN Senior Political Analyst; and Harvard Kennedy School Professor of Public Service and director of the Center for Public Leadership. Perspectives on tough choices at the top and reflections on day's working for President Nixon during Watergate.
- **Dr. Elaine Kamarck, PhD**, Former Clinton White House Senior Staff and Senior Policy Advisor to Al Gore. Currently, senior fellow in governance studies at the Brookings Institution, and lecturer at the Harvard Kennedy School of Government. Reflections on challenges in running a presidential campaign.
- **Dr. Story Musgrave, MD**, Surgeon and astronaut credited with flying on all five space shuttles. Creatively solves death-defying challenges in constrained environments. With advanced degrees in medicine, business, sciences, and literature, he works as a consultant to Disney's Imagineering group.
- **Ms. Valerie Plame**, Former covert CIA ops officer and wife of Ambassador Joseph Wilson outed by senior Bush White House administration officials in retaliation for her husband

questioning the central rationale for invading Iraq, that is, that Saddam Hussein posed an imminent nuclear threat to the United States. Her memoir, *Fair Game*, was made into a 2010 movie starring Naomi Watts and Sean Penn.

■ **Astronaut Al Worden**, USAF/NASA, test pilot, U.S. astronaut and command module pilot of Apollo 15 lunar mission in 1971. Noted by *Guinness Book of World Records* as being "the most isolated human being" while singularly traversing the other side of the moon in the first lunar roving vehicle, subjected to overwhelming risk, fatigue, and isolation.

Business

■ **Ms. Jane Grote Abell**, Chairwoman, Donatos Pizza. Fought to buy back family business from McDonald's and featured in Emmy-winning TV reality series, *Undercover Boss*. Cofounder of the Reeb Avenue Center that champions support of the urban poor with housing, education, healthcare, and jobs collaborative.

■ **Ms. Jeni Britton Bauer**, Founder and CEO of Jeni's Splendid Ice Cream, a fast-growing purveyor of premium ice cream in storefronts and national distribution to grocers. Efforts to balance home-spun quality in the midst of exponential growth.

■ **Mr. Bill Diffenderffer**, Former CEO of Eastern Airlines System One and SkyBus Airlines. Founder of startups: travel reservation technology; Silvercar, high-end auto rentals; and ReHava, botanic healthcare products. Entrepreneurial zeal and fighting fear while placing it all on the line.

■ **Mr. Jordan Hansell**, President of Rockbridge Capital Partners, and formerly president of NetJets Airlines. Living with heartfelt memories of an early death of a beloved brother while moving on with life.

■ **Mr. Chris Kowalski**, Owner of popular Jack's Diner in Columbus. Marathoner and widower who reopened his restaurant after customers, running community, and even competitors challenged him to start a new life after the painful death of his wife.

■ **Mr. Steven Lindseth**, Sr. Advisor (Aspen)—Triple Tree Capital Partners. Founder of technology firms and venture capitalist who manages risk in business and family upheaval.

■ **Mr. Cameron Mitchell**, Founder and CEO of Cameron Mitchell Restaurants *(CMR)*, 32 restaurants, 13 different concepts, within 12 states. The company also oversees the Rusty Bucket Restaurant and Tavern, which operates in 23 locations in six different states. From a renegade dishwasher and troublemaker to a celebrity chef and national restauranteur.

■ **Mr. Jim Roth**, Co-founder and CEO, Chicago-based, Huron Consulting, a global, publicly traded healthcare consulting business. Highlighted the importance of collaborative learning and collective leadership for clients and his own firm.

■ **Mr. Joshua Siegal**, Principal, 66 Design Studios. Millennial entrepreneur delivering innovative, on-demand design services with Asian importing-exporting supply chain. Managing risk in managing cash flow with his own personal net worth at stake.

■ **Weston Smith**, Former CFO of HealthSouth Corp. and whistleblower. Reduced Federal prison time after exposing massive fraud estimated at $3 billion at once fast-growing health company. Dedicated to teaching lessons on ethics to American MBA classes.

- **Mr. Yaromir Steiner**, Founder and CEO of Steiner + Associates. Born in Istanbul, attended college in France, and creatively grew a global, retail development and leasing company based on mix-use American malls and office space. A story of taking what you have and creating something special out of it.
- **Ms. Emilia Kovacevic Vogue-Tipping**, Founder and CEO of Hummingbird Real Estate Group, Inc. and 360 Tech Labs, Inc. A Croatian war refugee subject to danger and disruption of many kinds, determined to have a better life and education, built a career as a commercial realtor and developer in the United States and Europe.
- **Mr. Les Wexner**, Founder and CEO of L Brands, which include Victoria's Secret, Bath & Body Works, and Pink. At one point, he was on the edge of losing it all but climbed back to dominate in a highly competitive environment with current corporate sales of over $13 billion.

Health and Science

- **Dr. Delos (Toby) Cosgrove**, Retired president and CEO of the Cleveland Clinic: Overcame early childhood learning disability to become a prominent surgeon and global healthcare executive.
- **Mr. Peter Geier**, Former president, Huntington Bank, and later CEO/CFO of The Ohio State University Wexner Medical Health System (Ret): With the advent of a new bank CEO, squeezed out of the top as a rock-star financier and 38-year-old bank president (Deceased).
- **Dr. Jonathan Heavey**, Emergency services physician at Cleveland Clinic, Iraq War combat physician who helped to keep his company alive and fit under fire.
- **Jo-Anne Lema**, Founder and CEO of AfterFiftyLiving.com (AFL) and long-term survivor of deadly stage IV melanoma. After career in higher education, she created North Carolina-based lifestyle social media business focused on Baby Boomers.
- **Ms. Helene Neville**, Nurse, public speaker, and author. Cancer-survivor turned marathoner and coast-to-coast runner to raise cancer research funds and awareness.
- **Ms. Barbara Lopez Kunz**, CEO of Washington, DC-based, DIA/Drug Information Association, former president of Battelle Memorial Institute, Health and Life Sciences business. Manages a powerful, advocacy enterprise in the midst of high stakes, competing interests from global governments and pharmaceutical and related drug industries.
- **Dr. Ehud Mendel**, Clinical director and chair, neurological surgery, professor of internal medicine, emergency room physician, The Ohio State University Wexner Medical Health System. Former Israeli soldier and immigrant to United States, he provides counsel to families in life and death decisions.
- **Ms. Lindsey Moeller**, Founder of Concur. After her mother's painful death from mesothelioma, she quit her career in digital marketing to develop a natural lifestyle, organic health, and wellness product company.
- **Dr. Ryan Nash, MD**, Clinical director and chair, The Ohio State University Center for Bioethics. An on-going intense career tug-a-war between medicine and music, a not so pleasant dilemma with high stakes impacting family and future.

Sports, Media, and Entertainment

- **Dr. Raphael Pollock**, Director of the Comprehensive Cancer Center at The Ohio State University Wexner Medical Health System; he has chronic leukemia. Hospital staff is sometimes uncertain if he is there as a patient or as a doctor.
- **Ms. Jansi Straveler**, Nurse, Ohio Health HomeCare and Hospice. Indian immigrant who has struggled with U.S. culture and customs and a failed, mixed marriage.
- **Miss Molly Upton**, Aspiring neuroscientist. Honor roll and Advanced Placement student in high school; pregnant at the age of 16, she lived 3 years on the streets. After serving prison time and dealing with her addiction, she returned to college.
- **Miss Emma Baranski**, Three-time gold medalist, collegiate synchronized swimming champion. Now Wynn—Las Vegas Casino swim show performer who confronted body image issues to continue with her sport.
- **Ms. Karen Hough**, CEO of ImprovEdge, and former member of Chicago's legendary Second City comedy troupe. Uses improvisation skills in business training company.
- **Mr. Dolph Lundgren**, Starred in more than 40 Hollywood movie roles including Rocky IV as Ivan Drago, boxing opponent of Rocky Balboa played by Sylvester Stallone. Grew up with a physically abusive father, yet transformed his life through meditation, therapy, and service to others.
- **Mr. Jim Morris**, Proved it is never too late with dreams deferred as a rookie walk-on MLB pitcher for Tampa Bay Devil Rays at age 36. His story from high school science teacher to the big leagues was the basis for Disney movie, *The Rookie*.
- **Mr. Tom Meagher**, U.S. Olympic Trials starter, and director, Boston Marathon Finish Line. Managed the 2013 race ending and rescue and care of athletes and fans injured in the marathon bomb explosions by the radicalized Kyrgyz-American Tsarnaev brothers.
- **Mr. Vince Papale**, former teacher and professional football player. Basis for Mark Wahlberg's character in the film *Invincible* about Papale's improbable career with the NFL Philadelphia Eagles. Now an inspirational speaker who addresses his health struggles and faith.
- **Mr. Irlan Silva**, Brazilian ballet dancer and Soloist for the Boston Ballet. Featured in the *NYC Tribeca Film Festival* documentary *Only When I Dance*, a true-life story of being raised in a violent favela of Rio de Janeiro to become a world-leading performing artist-athlete in a premier ballet company.

Education

- **Miss Sara Abou Rashed**, Syrian refugee and poet. She went from non-English speaking immigrant to United States, to nationally acclaimed poet in 3 years. She is a Ted Talk presenter on war, death, and deprivation through moving and poetic prose.
- **Dr. Joseph Alutto**, two-term interim President of The Ohio State University and formerly the Dean of the university's Fisher College of Business. Held together a Big 10 University through controversy, change, and challenging times.
- **Dr. Scott Cowen**, Former president, Tulane University. Championed the rebuilding of New Orleans and restructured Tulane after Hurricane Katrina.

- **Dr. Michael Drake**, President of The Ohio State University, physician, and distinguished professor of ophthalmology. Battled controversial faculty and staff firings in the support of a united, inclusive culture of opportunity.
- **Mr. David Freel**, Ethicist and attorney, former executive director of the Ohio Ethics Commission, and business professor at The Ohio State University. Discernment and action with politics in play between the Ohio state executive and legislative branches.
- **Mr. Batmandah Mangalam**, Business honors students at The Ohio State University. Raised in Mongolia, infused with Buddhist rituals and principles as a context for building a new life in the West.
- **Mr. Jim Tressel**, President, Youngstown State University, former OSU Head Football Coach. Embracing a hands-on approach to education and shaping young lives while under the microscope of public scrutiny and scandal.

Faith and Community

- **Miss Isatu Barry**, Sierra Leone immigrant to United States and activist. Subjected to culturally mandated genital mutilation, she is now a health and community advocate and educator.
- **Ms. Ann Bischoff**, CEO, Star House, a nationally recognized model for serving homeless youth. Provides effective, 24/7 youth development, care and community drop-in center for young people living on society's edge with no money, home, or family.
- **Ms. Cheryl Cromwell**, Mashpee Wampanaug Tribal Council leader, People of the First Light, New England; Overseer of Health, Human Services, and Education and representative to U.S. government agencies: Deeply involved in addressing native American opiate crisis while dealing with her own personal addiction.
- **Shin Dong-hyuk**, Survived dramatic escape from North Korean prison camp after 24 years of torture and starvation. Now, a human rights advocate and critic of North Korea's Kim regime.
- **Mr. Rick Hahn**, Owner of Columbus-based Nancy's Diner, a favorite of local and out-of-town visitors and featured on Food Network's *Diners, Driven-Ins and Dives*. Raised by a community-minded mother with a drive to meld business with family and a larger purpose.
- **Ms. Mary Jo Hudson**, Former director of the Ohio State Insurance Commission, current member of Columbus School Board, and lead insurance counsel at Squire, Patton, and Boggs law firm. A spokesperson for the LGBT community providing leadership to collaboratively engage in controversy with intense, diverse stakeholders, and interests.
- **Mr. Ben Lesser,** The last survivor of the notorious Death Train which traveled from Buchenwald to Dachau with 3,000 inmates without food or water for weeks before arriving in Dachau, one of Hitler's WWII prison camps for exterminating Jews. Only 18 of the 3,000 got out alive from Dachau. He is the last remaining survivor left alive.
- **Mr. Jorge Mendoza**, Owner of Boston's North End four-star Vinoteca di Monica restaurant and community leader. From a wealthy South American family that left it all behind under death threats and political repression to become a U.S. citizen. Years following immigration, he climbed out of abject poverty to become a noted successful entrepreneur and community advocate for at-risk urban public school children trapped in their own generational poverty.

- **Dr. Molly McGinn**, Cultural anthropologist, learning consultant, and founder of TreeHouse Learning Community, addiction recovery institution for college-aged residents in Arizona: Worked with monasteries in Japan and Tibet during the Chinese Cultural Revolution, and now helps young adults in life transformation.
- **Reverend Dr. Otis Moss Jr.**, U.S. theologian, Southern Baptist Minister, and prominent national activist in the Civil Rights movement. Worked closely with Martin Luther King Jr. to seek justice for African Americans through non-violence.
- **Mr. William Raff**, Former Fuji Bank vice-president and the only survivor of 9/11 among 23 colleagues on the 82nd floor of the World Trade Center's South Tower. He now volunteers as a docent at the National September 11 Memorial and Museum in tribute to his colleagues and others who lost their lives that day.

Military and Law Enforcement

- **Colonel Charles Buchanan**, Army Ranger with combat command responsibilities in Afghanistan. Battled intense crisis of war-time casualties and personal loss.
- **Sargent Adam Carr**, Executive Director, Save-A-Warrior at Warrior Village Compound; Former Army Special Forces Green Beret (Airborne). Based on personal postcombat reentry experiences, he helps to lead military soldiers to transition to civilian life from near suicide to purpose-led lives.
- **Master Sargent Daniel Dixon**, Green Beret Special Forces sniper. During multiple combat tours, challenged to bring focused energy, skill, and purpose to changing conditions.
- **Detective John Foley**, Crisis in an explosive form with former FBI Asst. Special Agent in Charge (ASAC): Field Commander and Investigative Lead in the 2013 Boston Marathon Explosions. Featured in the movie, "Patriots Day," and featured in the National Geographic documentary "Inside The Hunt for the Boston Bombers."
- **Major Francis Leahy**, Massachusetts State Police, executive officer, Intelligence, and Investigative Services (Ret). Reflections on doggedness and respect of human nature and human kind in the underworld and gang culture.
- **General Stanley McChrystal**, Retired four-star general and former Commander of Joint Special Operations Command (JSOC), including U.S. Forces in Afghanistan. Engaging trauma and disruption at the personal, military-combat, and national-state level with strategies to bounce back from loss, failure, or disappointment.
- **Major Michael Thesing**, Marine naval aviator, professor at Marine Officer Candidate School, and pilot instructor: How to engage physically and mentally with in-the-moment, high-risk activity.
- **FBI Deputy Director James Trainer**, Retired senior executive and FBI special agent with operational and investigative experience in cyber, counterintelligence, counterterrorism, intelligence, and criminal matters. Reflections on strategically shaping safer ways of functioning in an environment with invisible, but present danger.

About the Author: Mark J. Sullivan

Mark Sullivan, an organizational psychologist, is an Ohio State University Fisher College of Business MBA, Executive MBA and Executive Education faculty member. Additionally, he coaches and consults executives and government leaders and is a noted motivational speaker on resilience and performance in high-demand, high-challenge environments.

Over the last 25 plus years, Sullivan has served in leadership and operating roles in four Global 1,000 and Dow 30 companies. For Honeywell International, he cofounded and managed a Corporate Business Accelerator that grew into a $1 billion product portfolio. Additionally, he assisted in creating a mid-market business in developing organizational capacity as an APEX Managing Partner, McKinsey & Company Alliance Partner; and an Accenture P&L executive, coleading the North American Human Capital Practice in the telecom industry. More recently, he was Chief Talent Officer for Battelle, a $5 billion government contractor of classified and commercial technology for the three-letter community (i.e., CIA, FBI, DOD, etc.).

Earlier in his career, Sullivan was based in Tokyo, Singapore, and Chicago for United Airlines (UAL). He was UAL's lead negotiator in the Pacific Rim for vendor contracts, trade, and government agreements. Simultaneously, he oversaw UAL's Executive Sales Institute world-wide, and was on the flight school faculty; he is FAA certified for hostage negotiating and emergency services. He was recognized for coleading the emergency response for UA Flight #232, that crash-landed in Sioux City, Iowa (with no hydraulics or control).

He was also briefly on special assignment with the U.S. State Department to support Prime Minister Gorbachev's political reform efforts in the latter stages of Perestroika. Moscow- and Leningrad-based, he worked with a select team of Soviet generals in developing practices in negotiating peace agreements with their regional neighbors.

Sullivan earned his PhD in Organizational Behavior at Case Western Reserve University's Weatherhead Management School, and his MA from Harvard University. He is a Kauffman Foundation Scholar; a Weatherhead Horvitz Family Business Fellow; a post-doctoral clinical resident at the Gestalt Institute of Cleveland; and visiting faculty at the Roman Catholic Pontifical College.

A former British Outward Bound Survival School Instructor and Eagle Scout, he enjoys outdoor pursuits: running, sailing, and camping. He is married and has three sons.

About the Author Mark L. Sullivan

Mark Sullivan, an organizational psychologist, is Ohio State University Fisher College of Business A/BA, Executive MBA and Executive Education faculty member. Additionally, he coaches and consults executives and government leaders and is a noted motivational speaker on resilience and performance in high-demand, high-challenge environments.

Over the last 20-plus years, Sullivan has served in leadership and operating roles in four Global 1,000 and Dow 30 companies. For Honeywell International he cofounded and managed a Corporate Ventures Accelerator that grew into a $1 billion product portfolio. Additionally he assisted in creating a billion-dollar business in developing a generational capacity as an APEX Managing Partner, McKinsey & Company Alliance Partner, and an Accenture P&L executive, releading the North American Human Capital Practice in the telecom industry. More recently, he was Chief Talent Officer for BearingPoint, a billion government contractor of classified and commercial technology for the three-letter community (i.e., CIA, FBI, DOD, etc.).

Earlier in his career, Sullivan was based in Tokyo, Singapore, and Chicago for United Airlines (UAL). He was UAL's lead negotiator in the Pacific Rim for vendor contracts, trade, and government agreements. Simultaneously he oversaw UAL's Executive Sales Institute worldwide, and was on the flight school faculty, he is FAA-certified for hostage negotiating and emergency egress. He was recognized for reloading the emergency response for UAL Flight 232, that crash-landed in Sioux City, Iowa (with an International Control).

He was also here on special assignment with the US State Department to support Prime Minister Gorbachev's political reform efforts in the latter stages of Perestroika, Moscow, and Leningrad. Based he instructed a select team of Soviet generals in developing practices in negotiating peace agreements with their regional neighbors.

Sullivan earned his PhD in Organizational Behavior at Case Western Reserve University's Weatherhead Management School, and his MA from Harvard University. He is a Baldrige Examiner under the Weatherhead Diversity Faculty Business Fellow; a post-doctoral fellowship student in culture of Christianity and History of Bioethy at the Roman Catholic Pontifical College.

A former British Citizen, Mark is a naturalized United States citizen. He enjoys outdoor pursuits including sailing, woodworking. He is married and has three sons.

Bibliography

AP Archives. (1984). Harold Donahue dies; was member of house. *New York Times*.

Argyris, C. (1974). *Behind the front page*. San Francisco, CA: Jossey-Bass.

Argyris, C. (1976). *Increasing leadership effectiveness*. New York, NY: Wiley-Interscience.

Argyris, C. (1990). *Overcoming organizational defenses: Facilitating organizational learning*. Cambridge, MA: Harvard Business Publishers.

Argyris, C., & Schon, D. (1976). *Organizational learning*. Reading, MA: Addison-Wesley. (To be published).

Blake, E. S., Landsea, C. W., & Gibney, E. J. (2011, August). *The deadliest, costliest and most intense United States tropical cyclones from 1851 to 2010*. National Hurricane Center.

Block, P. (2009). *Community: The structure of belonging*. San Francisco, CA: Berrett-Koehler Publishers.

Botanie Soap Blog. (2015, September 14). *From the history of liquid soap: Invention and cornering of the domestic market*. Retrieved from BotanieSoap.com

Boyatzis, R. E. (1998). *Transforming qualitative information*. Thousand Oaks, CA: SAGE Publications.

Boyatzis, R. E., & McKee, A. (2005). *Resonant leadership*. Boston, MA: Harvard Business School Publishing.

Boyd, R. (2008, February 7). Do people only use 10 percent of their brains? *Scientific American*.

Bradberry, T., & Greaves, J. (2009). *Emotional intelligence 2.0*. San Diego, CA: TalentSmart.

Bridges, W. (2003). *Managing transitions: Making the most of change* (2nd ed.). Cambridge, MA: Perseus Publishing.

Brooks, D. (2015). *The road to character*. New York, NY: Random House.

Bungay Stanier, M. (2016). *The coaching habit: Say less, ask more & change the way you lead forever*. Toronto, ON: Box of Crayons.

Campbell, J. (1949). *The hero with a thousand faces* (1st ed.). Princeton, NJ: Princeton University Press (2nd ed. 1968, 3rd ed. 2008).

Chikazoe, J., Lee, D. H., Kriegeskorte, N., & Anderson, A. K. (2014). Population coding of affect across stimuli, modalities and individuals. *Nature Neuroscience, 17*

Collins, J., & Hansen, M. T. (2011). *Great by choice*. New York, NY: Harper Collins.

Cook-Greuter, S. R. (2005). *Ego development: Nine levels of increasing embrace*. Publication review is granted by author's permission.

Cooperrider, D., Whitney, D., & Stravos, J. (2008). *The appreciative inquiry handbook: For leaders of change*. Chicago, IL: Berrett-Koehler Publishers.

Covey, S. R. (1989). *The 7 habits of highly effective people*. Salt Lake City, UT: Franklin Covey.

Csikszentmihalyi, M. (1990). *Flow*. New York, NY: HarperPerennial Modern Classics.

Cuddy, A. (2015). *Presence: Bringing your boldest self to your biggest challenges*. New York, NY: Little, Brown and Company.

David, S. (2016). *Emotional agility: Get unstuck, embrace change, and thrive in work and life*. New York, NY: Avery.

Duckworth, A. (2016). *Grit: The power of passion and perseverance*. New York, NY: Scribner.

Edwards, G. C. (1996). Frustration and folly: Bill Clinton and the public presidency. In C. Campbell & B. A. Rockman (Eds.), *The Clinton presidency: First appraisals* (p. 235). New York, NY: Chatham House.

Epstein, D. (2014). *The sports gene: Inside the science of extraordinary athletic performance*. Chicago, IL: Penguin Random House.

Eurich, T. (2017). *Insight. Why we're not as self aware as we think, and how seeing ourselves clearly helps us succeed at work and in life*. New York, NY: Crown Business, an imprint of the Crown Publishing Group.

Feder, B. (1982). *Peeling the onion: A gestalt therapy manual for clients*. Bud Feder & Ruth Ronall Publisher.

Fisher, D., & Torbert, W. R. (1995). *Personal and organizational transformation: The true challenge of continual quality improvement*. London, UK: McGraw-Hill.

Frankl, V. E. (2006). *Man's search for meaning* (I. Lasch, Trans.). Boston, MA: Beacon Press (Original work published 1959).

Gardner, H. (2008). *5 minds for the future*. Boston, MA: Harvard Business School Publishing.

Gates, R. M. (2016). *A passion for leadership: Lessons on change and reform from fifty years of public service*. New York, NY: Vintage Books.

Gergen, D. (2001). *Eyewitness to power: The essence of leadership Nixon to Clinton* (pp. 327–328). New York, NY: Touchstone, Simon & Schuster

Gilbert, M. (1983, June 27). *Finest hour: Winston S. Churchill, 1939–1941*. Heinemann.

Gladstone, J. (2016). *The common thread of overcoming adversity and living your dreams*. New York, NY: Morgan James.

Grenny, J., McMillan, R., & Switzler, A. (2002). *Crucial conversations: Tools for talking when stakes are high*. McGraw-Hill Publishers (2nd ed. 2012).

HBR's 10 must reads: On emotional intelligence. (2015). Boston, MA: Harvard Business School Publishing.

HBR's 10 must reads: On leadership. (2011). Boston, MA: Harvard Business School Publishing.

Holiday, R. (2014). *The obstacle is the way: The timeless art of turning trials into triumph*. New York, NY: Penguin Group.

Hounshell, D. A. (1984). *From the American system to mass production, 1800–1932: The development of manufacturing technology in the United States*. Baltimore, MD: Johns Hopkins University Press.

Kahneman, D. (2011). *Thinking, fast and slow*. New York, NY: Farrar, Straus and Giroux.

Kaplan, R. S. (2013). *What you're really meant to do: A road map for reaching your unique potential*. Boston, MA: Harvard Business Review Press.

Kegan, R., & Lahey, L. L. (2009). *Immunity to change: How to overcome it and unlock the potential in yourself and your organization*. Boston, MA: Harvard Business School Publishing.

Kushner, H. S. (2002). *Living a life that matters*. New York, NY: Anchor Books.

Langer, E. J. (2014). *Mindfulness* (25th Anniversary ed.). Philadelphia, PA: Da Capo Press (Original work published 1989).

Luft, J., & Ingham, H. (1955). *The Johari window, a graphic model of interpersonal awareness.* Proceedings of the Western Training Laboratory in Group Development, Los Angeles, CA: University of California.

Lynn, S. J., O'Donohue, W. T., & Lilienfeld, S. O. (Eds.). (2015). *Health, happiness, and well-being: Better living through psychological science.* Thousand Oaks, CA: SAGE Publications.

Manz, C. C., & Houghton, J. D. (2017). *Self-leadership: The definitive guide to personal excellence.* Thousand Oaks, CA: Sage Publications.

Maurer, R. (2010). *Beyond the wall of resistance* (Revised ed.). Austin, TX: Bard Press.

McCann, D. (2017, March 27). Two CFO's tell a tale of fraud at HealthSouth. *CFO.com.*

McFarland, K. (2009). *Bounce: The art of turning tough times into triumph.* New York, NY: Crown Business.

Neck, C. P. (2012). *Medicine for the mind: Healing words to help you soar* (4th ed.). New York, NY: John Wiley Publishers.

Neck, C. P., Manz, C. C., & Houghton, J. D. (2017). (p. 2). Thousand Oaks, CA: Sage Publications.

Nepo, M. (2007). *Finding inner courage.* New York, NY: MJF Books.

Norris, F. (2002, September 5). Former sunbeam chief agrees to ban and a fine of $500,000.00. *New York Times Newspaper.*

O'Reilly, B., & Reporter Associate Ann Harrington. (1999, September 6). A story of the "Billionaire Next Door, Phil Anschutz may be the richest American you've never heard of." *Fortune Magazine.* Retrieved from archive.fortune.com

Patterson, K., Grenny, J., McMillan, R., & Switzler, A. (2012). *Crucial conversations: Tools for talking when stakes are high* (2nd ed.). New York, NY: McGraw-Hill Professional Publishing.

Pencak, W. A. (2009). *Encyclopedia of the veteran of America* (p. 222). ABC-CLIO.

Perls, F. (1973). *The gestalt approach and eye witness to therapy.* Palo Alto, CA: Science and Behavior Books.

Peterson, D. B., & Hicks, M. D. (1995). *Development FIRST: Strategies for self-development.* Minneapolis, MN: Personnel Decisions International.

Quinn, R. E. (1996). *Deep change: Discovering the leader within.* San Francisco, CA: Jossey-Bass Publishers.

Rabinbach, A., & Gilman, S. (Eds.). (2013). *The Third Reich sourcebook* (p. 4). Berkeley, CA: California University Press.

Roland, C. C., Wagner, R. J., & Weigand, R. J. (1995). *Do it & and understand!: The bottom line on corporate experiential learning.* Dubuque, IA: Kendall/Hunt Publishing Company.

Rooke, D., & Torbert, W. R. (2002). *Personal and organizational transformations: Through action inquiry.* Edge\Work Press.

Rooke, D., & Torbert, W. R. (2005, April). *Seven transformations of leadership.* Cambridge, MA: Harvard Business Review.

Rosner, J. (1990). *Peeling the onion: Gestalt theory and methodology.* Toronto, Canada: Gestalt Institute of Toronto.

Sandberg, S., & Grant, A. (2017). *Option B: Facing adversity, building resilience, and finding joy.* New York, NY: Alfred A. Knopf.

Schlesinger, A. M., Jr. (1996, December 12). The ultimate approval rating. *New York Times Magazine,* p. 46.

Schwartz, J. (2013, September 11). *Robert Taylor who puts hand soap in a bottle, dies at 77.* New York, NY· New York Times Publisher.

Shapiro, M. (2000). *J. K. Rowling: The wizard behind Harry Potter.* New York, NY: St. Martin's Press.

Smith, B. (2013, February 1). Mayor Koch, self-proclaimed "Liberal with sanity" who led New York from Fiscal Crisis, is dead at 88. *New York Sun.*

Sullivan, M., & Kolb, D. (1995). *Do it ... and understand: The bottom line on corporate experiential learning: Turning experience into learning.* Concord, NH: Kendall-Hunt Publishers.

Thaler, R. H., & Sunstein, C. R. (2009). *Nudge: Improving decisions about health, wealth, and happiness* (Updated). New York, NY: Penguin Group.

Vanacore, A., & Maggi, L. (2013). *Cowen to retire as Tulane's president, advocate* (p. 5a). Baton Rouge, LA.

Webb, C. (2016). *How to have a good day* (pp. 109–110). New York, NY: Crown Publishing, a division of Penguin Random House LLC.

Wheeler, G. (1991). *Gestalt reconsidered: A new approach to contact and resistance* (chap. 5). Cleveland, OH: Gestalt Institute Cleveland Press.

White, R. C. (2002, February 10). *Lincoln's greatest speech.* New York, NY: New York Times Publishers.

Woodman, M. (1982). *Addiction to perfection: The still unravished bride.* Inner City Books.

Zinker, J. (1991). Creative process in gestalt therapy: The therapist as artist. *The Gestalt Journal, 14*(2), 71–88.